Explore Your World!

Focus on case studies to understand your world.

To learn about **Europe and Russia**, you will take a close look at specific countries. In each case study, the story of that country will be told through an important world theme—such as the relationship between people and their environment or a nation's quest for independence. After studying each country, you can apply what you've learned to understand other parts of the world.

Interact with exciting online activities.

Journey to different parts of the world by using dynamic online activities on geography, history and culture. Use the web codes listed in the Go Online boxes and in the chart below to tour this region.

Europe and Russia Activities

Web Code	Activity
	History Interactive
ldp-7702	Explore the Magna Carta
ldp-7703	Travel Along a Roman Road
ldp-7711	Visit the Roman and United States Senates
ldp-7713	Meet the Figures of Raphael's School of Athens
ldp-7714	Learn More About Education in Ancient Greece
ldp-7715	Tour a Roman Bath
ldp-7716	Explore Renaissance Art
ldp-7719	Explore the Scientific Method
	MapMaster
ldp-7701	The Empire of Alexander the Great
ldp-7704	Italian City-States
ldp-7705	Voyages of Explorations
ldp-7706	Geography of Ancient Greece
ldp-7707	Ancient Greek Religious Sites
ldp-7708	The German Invasions
ldp-7709	Geography of Rome
ldp-7710	Growth of Roman Power, 44 B.C.– A.D. 117
ldp-7712	Geography of Europe
ldp-7717	Roman Trade Routes
ldp-7718	Growth of Roman Power to 44 B.C.
ldp-7720	European Colonies about 1700
ldp-7721	Mercantilism and World Trade, about 1775
ldp-7722	The Early Christian Church
ldp-7723	Spread of Christianity
ldp-7724	The Seasons

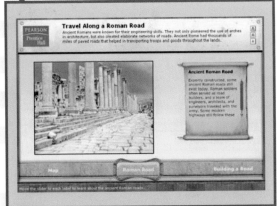

Travel Along a Roman Road

Go Online
PHSchool.com

For: An activity on Russian cultures
Visit: PHSchool.com
Web Code: ldd-7303

Get hands-on with the Geographer's Apprentice Activity Pack.

Explore the geography, history and culture of the world's regions through hands-on activities. Each activity pack includes maps, data and primary sources to make learning geography fun!

PRENTICE HALL

WORLD STUDIES
EUROPE and RUSSIA

Geography • History • Culture

In association with

BK

Discovery CHANNEL
SCHOOL

PEARSON

Prentice
Hall

Boston, Massachusetts
Upper Saddle River, New Jersey

Program Consultants

Heidi Hayes Jacobs

Heidi Hayes Jacobs, Ed.D., has served as an education consultant to more than 1,000 schools across the nation and abroad. Dr. Jacobs serves as an adjunct professor in the Department of Curriculum on Teaching at Teachers College, Columbia University. She has written two best-selling books and numerous articles on curriculum reform. She received an M.A. from the University of Massachusetts, Amherst, and completed her doctoral work at Columbia University's Teachers College in 1981. The core of Dr. Jacobs's experience comes from her years teaching high school, middle school, and elementary school students. As an educational consultant, she works with K–12 schools and districts on curriculum reform and strategic planning.

Michal L. LeVasseur

Michal LeVasseur is the Executive Director of the National Council for Geographic Education. She is an instructor in the College of Education at Jacksonville State University and works with the Alabama Geographic Alliance. Her undergraduate and graduate work were in the fields of anthropology (B.A.), geography (M.A.), and science education (Ph.D.). Dr. LeVasseur's specialization has moved increasingly into the area of geography education. Since 1996 she has served as the Director of the National Geographic Society's Summer Geography Workshops. As an educational consultant, she has worked with the National Geographic Society as well as with schools and organizations to develop programs and curricula for geography.

Senior Reading Consultants

Kate Kinsella

Kate Kinsella, Ed.D., is a faculty member in the Department of Secondary Education at San Francisco State University. A specialist in second-language acquisition and content area literacy, she consults nationally on school-wide practices that support adolescent English learners and striving readers to make academic gains. Dr. Kinsella earned her M.A. in TESOL from San Francisco State University, and her Ed.D. in Second Language Acquisition from the University of San Francisco.

Kevin Feldman

Kevin Feldman, Ed.D., is the Director of Reading and Early Intervention with the Sonoma County Office of Education (SCOE) and an independent educational consultant. At the SCOE, he develops, organizes, and monitors programs related to K–12 literacy. Dr. Feldman has an M.A. from the University of California, Riverside in Special Education, Learning Disabilities and Instructional Design. He earned his Ed.D. in Curriculum and Instruction from the University of San Francisco.

Acknowledgments appear on page 247, which constitutes an extension of this copyright page.

Prentice Hall World Studies is published in collaboration with DK Designs, Dorling Kindersley Limited, 80 Strand, London WC2R 0RL. A Penguin Company.

PEARSON
Prentice Hall

ISBN 0-13-204146-4
2345678910   11 10 09 08 07

Cartography Consultant

DK Andrew Heritage

Andrew Heritage has been publishing atlases and maps for more than 25 years. In 1991, he joined the leading illustrated nonfiction publisher Dorling Kindersley (DK) with the task of building an international atlas list from scratch. The DK atlas list now includes some 10 titles, which are constantly updated and appear in new editions either annually or every other year.

Academic Reviewers

Africa
Barbara B. Brown, Ph.D.
African Studies Center
Boston University
Boston, Massachusetts

Ancient World
Evelyn DeLong Mangie, Ph.D.
Department of History
University of South Florida
Tampa, Florida

Central Asia and the Middle East
Pamela G. Sayre
History Department,
    Social Sciences Division
Henry Ford Community College
Dearborn, Michigan

East Asia
Huping Ling, Ph.D.
History Department
Truman State University
Kirksville, Missouri

Eastern Europe
Robert M. Jenkins, Ph.D.
Center for Slavic, Eurasian and
    East European Studies
University of North Carolina
Chapel Hill, North Carolina

Latin America
Dan La Botz
Professor, History Department
Miami University
Oxford, Ohio

Medieval Times
James M. Murray
History Department
University of Cincinnati
Cincinnati, Ohio

North Africa
Barbara E. Petzen
Center for Middle Eastern Studies
Harvard University
Cambridge, Massachusetts

Religion
Charles H. Lippy, Ph.D.
Department of Philosophy
    and Religion
University of Tennessee
    at Chattanooga
Chattanooga, Tennessee

Russia
Janet Vaillant
Davis Center for Russian
    and Eurasian Studies
Harvard University
Cambridge, Massachusetts

United States and Canada
Victoria Randlett
Geography Department
University of Nevada, Reno
Reno, Nevada

Western Europe
Ruth Mitchell-Pitts
Center for European Studies
University of North Carolina
    at Chapel Hill
Chapel Hill, North Carolina

Reviewers

Sean Brennan
Brecksville-Broadview Heights
    City School District
Broadview Heights, Ohio

Stephen Bullick
Mt. Lebanon School District
Pittsburgh, Pennsylvania

Louis P. De Angelo, Ed.D.
Archdiocese of Philadelphia
Philadelphia, Pennsylvania

Paul Francis Durietz
Social Studies
    Curriculum Coordinator
Woodland District #50
Gurnee, Illinois

Gail Dwyer
Dickerson Middle School,
    Cobb County
Marietta, Georgia

Michal Howden
Social Studies Consultant
Zionsville, Indiana

Rosemary Kalloch
Springfield Public Schools
Springfield, Massachusetts

Deborah J. Miller
Office of Social Studies,
    Detroit Public Schools
Detroit, Michigan

Steven P. Missal
Plainfield Public Schools
Plainfield, New Jersey

Catherine Fish Petersen
Social Studies Consultant
Saint James, Long Island, New York

Joe Wieczorek
Social Studies Consultant
Baltimore, Maryland

Table of Contents

EUROPE and RUSSIA

Develop Skills

Use these pages to develop your reading, writing, and geography skills.

Build a Regional Background

Learn about the geography, history, and culture of the region.

v

Focus on Countries

Create an understanding of the region by focusing on specific countries.

- Learn map skills with the MapMaster Handbook.
- Practice your skills with every map in this book.
- Interact with every map online and on CD-ROM.

Maps and illustrations created by DK help build your understanding of the world. The DK World Desk Reference Online keeps you up to date.

The World Studies Video Program takes you on field trips to study countries around the world.

The *World Studies* Interactive Textbook online and on CD-ROM uses interactive maps and other activities to help you learn.

Literature

A selection by a European author brings social studies to life.

COUNTRY PROFILES

Theme-based maps and charts provide a closer look at countries, regions, and provinces.

Links

See the fascinating links between social studies and other disciplines.

Citizen Heroes

Meet people who have made a difference in their country.

Video/DVD

Explore the geography, history, and cultures of Russia and the countries of Europe.

Skills for Life

Learn skills that you will use throughout your life.

Target Reading Skills

Chapter-by-chapter reading skills help you read and understand social studies concepts.

Eyewitness Technology

Detailed drawings show how technology shapes places and societies.

Maps and Charts

MAP★MASTER™

MAP★MASTER™ Interactive

Go online to find an interactive version of every MapMaster™ map in this book. Use the Web Code provided to gain direct access to these maps.

How to Use Web Codes:

1. Go to **www.PHSchool.com**.
2. Enter the Web Code.
3. Click Go!

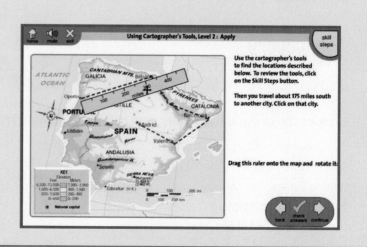

Building Geographic Literacy

Learning about a country often starts with finding it on a map. The MapMaster™ system in *World Studies* helps you develop map skills you will use throughout your life. These three steps can help you become a MapMaster!

The MAP★MASTER™ System

 Learn

You need to learn geography tools and concepts before you explore the world. Get started by using the MapMaster Skills Handbook to learn the skills you need for success.

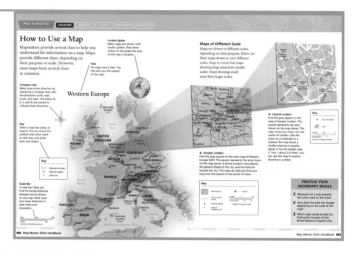

MAP★MASTER™ Skills Activity

Location The Equator runs through parts of Latin America, but it is far from other parts of the region.

Locate Find the Equator on the map. Which climates are most common in Latin America, and how far is each climate region from the Equator?

Draw Conclusions How do climates change as you move away from the Equator?

Go Online
PHSchool.com Use Web Code **lfp-1142** for step-by-step **map skills practice.**

 Practice

You need to practice and apply your geography skills frequently to be a MapMaster. The maps in *World Studies* give you the practice you need to develop geographic literacy.

Interact

Using maps is more than just finding places. Maps can teach you many things about a region, such as its climate, its vegetation, and the languages that the people who live there speak. Every MapMaster map is online at **PHSchool.com,** with interactive activities to help you learn the most from every map.

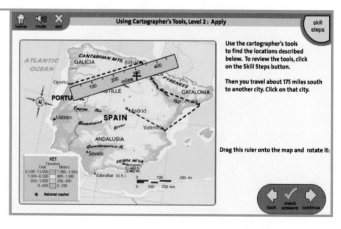

Learning With Technology

You will be making many exciting journeys across time and place in *World Studies*. Technology will help make what you learn come alive.

For: An activity on Russian cultures
Visit: PHSchool.com
Web Code: ldd-7303

For a complete list of features for this book, use Web Code **ldk-1000**.

Go Online at PHSchool.com

Use the Web Codes listed below and in each Go Online box to access exciting information or activities.

How to Use the Web Code:
1. Go to **www.PHSchool.com**.
2. Enter the Web Code.
3. Click Go!

Europe and Russia Activities

Web Code	Activity
	History Interactive
ldp-7702	Explore the Magna Carta
ldp-7703	Travel Along a Roman Road
ldp-7711	Visit the Roman and United States Senates
ldp-7713	Meet the Figures of Raphael's School of Athens
ldp-7714	Learn More About Education in Ancient Greece
ldp-7715	Tour a Roman Bath
ldp-7716	Explore Renaissance Art
ldp-7719	Explore the Scientific Method
	MapMaster
ldp-7701	The Empire of Alexander the Great
ldp-7704	Italian City-States
ldp-7705	Voyages of Explorations
ldp-7706	Geography of Ancient Greece
ldp-7707	Ancient Greek Religious Sites
ldp-7708	The German Invasions
ldp-7709	Geography of Rome
ldp-7710	Growth of Roman Power, 44 B.C.– A.D. 117
ldp-7712	Geography of Europe
ldp-7717	Roman Trade Routes
ldp-7718	Growth of Roman Power to 44 B.C.
ldp-7720	European Colonies about 1700
ldp-7721	Mercantilism and World Trade, about 1775
ldp-7722	The Early Christian Church
ldp-7723	Spread of Christianity
ldp-7724	The Seasons

DK World Desk Reference Online

There are more than 190 countries in the world. To learn about them, you need the most up-to-date information and statistics. The **DK World Desk Reference Online** gives you instant access to the information you need to explore each country.

Reading Informational Texts

Reading a magazine, an Internet page, or a textbook is not the same as reading a novel. The purpose of reading nonfiction texts is to acquire new information. On page M18 you'll read about some  Target Reading Skills that you'll have a chance to practice as you read this textbook. Here we'll focus on a few skills that will help you read nonfiction with a more critical eye.

Analyze the Author's Purpose

Different types of materials are written with different purposes in mind. For example, a textbook is written to teach students information about a subject. The purpose of a technical manual is to teach someone how to use something, such as a computer. A newspaper editorial might be written to persuade the reader to accept a particular point of view. A writer's purpose influences how the material is presented. Sometimes an author states his or her purpose directly. More often, the purpose is only suggested, and you must use clues to identify the author's purpose.

Distinguish Between Facts and Opinions

It's important when reading informational texts to read actively and to distinguish between fact and opinion. A fact can be proven or disproven. An opinion cannot—it is someone's personal viewpoint or evaluation.

For example, the editorial pages in a newspaper offer opinions on topics that are currently in the news. You need to read newspaper editorials with an eye for bias and faulty logic. For example, the newspaper editorial at the right shows factual statements in blue and opinion statements in red. The underlined words are examples of highly charged words. They reveal bias on the part of the writer.

More than 5,000 people voted last week in favor of building a new shopping center, but the opposition won out. The margin of victory is irrelevant. Those radical voters who opposed the center are obviously self-serving elitists who do not care about anyone but themselves.

This month's unemployment figure for our area is 10 percent, which represents an increase of about 5 percent over the figure for this time last year. These figures mean unemployment is getting worse. But the people who voted against the mall probably do not care about creating new jobs.

Identify Evidence

Before you accept an author's conclusion, you need to make sure that the author has based the conclusion on enough evidence and on the right kind of evidence. An author may present a series of facts to support a claim, but the facts may not tell the whole story. For example, what evidence does the author of the newspaper editorial on the previous page provide to support his claim that the new shopping center would create more jobs? Is it possible that the shopping center might have put many small local businesses out of business, thus increasing unemployment rather than decreasing it?

Evaluate Credibility

Whenever you read informational texts, you need to assess the credibility of the author. This is especially true of sites you may visit on the Internet. All Internet sources are not equally reliable. Here are some questions to ask yourself when evaluating the credibility of a Web site.

☐ Is the Web site created by a respected organization, a discussion group, or an individual?

☐ Does the Web site creator include his or her name as well as credentials and the sources he or she used to write the material?

☐ Is the information on the site balanced or biased?

☐ Can you verify the information using two other sources?

☐ Is there a date telling when the Web site was created or last updated?

Writing for Social Studies

Writing is one of the most powerful communication tools you will ever use. You will use it to share your thoughts and ideas with others. Research shows that writing about what you read actually helps you learn new information and ideas. A systematic approach to writing—including prewriting, drafting, revising, and proofing—can help you write better, whether you're writing an essay or a research report.

Narrative Essays

Writing that tells a story about a personal experience

1 Select and Narrow Your Topic

A narrative is a story. In social studies, it might be a narrative essay about how an event affected you or your family.

2 Gather Details

Brainstorm a list of details you'd like to include in your narrative.

3 Write a First Draft

Start by writing a simple opening sentence that conveys the main idea of your essay. Continue by writing a colorful story that has interesting details. Write a conclusion that sums up the significance of the event or situation described in your essay.

4 Revise and Proofread

Check to make sure you have not begun too many sentences with the word *I*. Replace general words with more colorful ones.

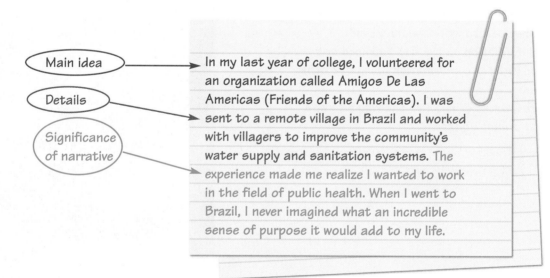

Main idea → In my last year of college, I volunteered for an organization called Amigos De Las Americas (Friends of the Americas). I was

Details → sent to a remote village in Brazil and worked with villagers to improve the community's water supply and sanitation systems. The

Significance of narrative → experience made me realize I wanted to work in the field of public health. When I went to Brazil, I never imagined what an incredible sense of purpose it would add to my life.

Persuasive Essays

Writing that supports an opinion or position

① Select and Narrow Your Topic

Choose a topic that provokes an argument and has at least two sides. Choose a side. Decide which argument will appeal most to your audience and persuade it to understand your point of view.

② Gather Evidence

Create a chart that states your position at the top and then lists the pros and cons for your position below, in two columns. Predict and address the strongest arguments against your stand.

③ Write a First Draft

Write a strong thesis statement that clearly states your position. Continue by presenting the strongest arguments in favor of your position and acknowledging and refuting opposing arguments.

④ Revise and Proofread

Check to make sure you have made a logical argument and that you have not oversimplified the argument.

Main Idea

Supporting (pro) argument

Opposing (con) argument

Transition words

It is vital to vote in elections. When people vote, they tell public officials how to run the government. Not every proposal is carried out; however, politicians do their best to listen to what the majority of people want. Therefore, every vote is important.

Expository Essays

Writing that explains a process, compares and contrasts, explains causes and effects, or explores solutions to a problem

1 Identify and Narrow Your Topic

Expository writing is writing that explains something in detail. It might explain the similarities and differences between two or more subjects (compare and contrast). It might explain how one event causes another (cause and effect). Or it might explain a problem and describe a solution.

2 Gather Evidence

Create a graphic organizer that identifies details to include in your essay.

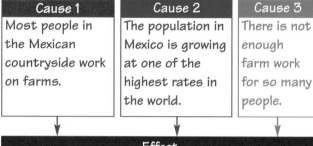

Cause 1	Cause 2	Cause 3
Most people in the Mexican countryside work on farms.	The population in Mexico is growing at one of the highest rates in the world.	There is not enough farm work for so many people.

Effect

As a result, many rural families are moving from the countryside to live in Mexico City.

3 Write Your First Draft

Write a topic sentence and then organize the essay around your similarities and differences, causes and effects, or problem and solutions. Be sure to include convincing details, facts, and examples.

4 Revise and Proofread

Research Papers

Writing that presents research about a topic

1 Narrow Your Topic

Choose a topic you're interested in and make sure that it is not too broad. For example, instead of writing a report on Panama, write about the construction of the Panama Canal.

2 Acquire Information

Locate several sources of information about the topic from the library or the Internet. For each resource, create a source index card like the one at the right. Then take notes using an index card for each detail or subtopic. On the card, note which source the information was taken from. Use quotation marks when you copy the exact words from a source.

Source #1

McCullough, David. *The Path Between the Seas: The Creation of the Panama Canal, 1870–1914.* N.Y., Simon and Schuster, 1977.

3 Make an Outline

Use an outline to decide how to organize your report. Sort your index cards into the same order.

Outline

I. Introduction
II. Why the canal was built
III. How the canal was built
    A. Physical challenges
    B. Medical challenges
IV. Conclusion

> **Introduction**
>
> **Building the Panama Canal**
>
> Ever since Christopher Columbus first explored the Isthmus of Panama, the Spanish had been looking for a water route through it. They wanted to be able to sail west from Spain to Asia without sailing around South America. However, it was not until 1914 that the dream became a reality.

> **Conclusion**
>
> It took eight years and more than 70,000 workers to build the Panama Canal. It remains one of the greatest engineering feats of modern times.

4 Write a First Draft

Write an introduction, a body, and a conclusion. Leave plenty of space between lines so you can go back and add details that you may have left out.

5 Revise and Proofread

Be sure to include transition words between sentences and paragraphs. Here are some examples:

To show a contrast—*however, although, despite.*

To point out a reason—*since, because, if.*

To signal a conclusion—*therefore, consequently, so, then.*

Evaluating Your Writing

Use this table to help you evaluate your writing.

	Excellent	Good	Acceptable	Unacceptable
Purpose	Achieves purpose—to inform, persuade, or provide historical interpretation—very well	Informs, persuades, or provides historical interpretation reasonably well	Reader cannot easily tell if the purpose is to inform, persuade, or provide historical interpretation	Purpose is not clear
Organization	Develops ideas in a very clear and logical way	Presents ideas in a reasonably well-organized way	Reader has difficulty following the organization	Lacks organization
Elaboration	Explains all ideas with facts and details	Explains most ideas with facts and details	Includes some supporting facts and details	Lacks supporting details
Use of Language	Uses excellent vocabulary and sentence structure with no errors in spelling, grammar, or punctuation	Uses good vocabulary and sentence structure with very few errors in spelling, grammar, or punctuation	Includes some errors in grammar, punctuation, and spelling	Includes many errors in grammar, punctuation, and spelling

CONTENTS

Go **O**nline
PHSchool.com
Use Web Code **lap-0000** for all of the maps in this handbook.

Five Themes of Geography

Studying the geography of the entire world is a huge task. You can make that task easier by using the five themes of geography: location, regions, place, movement, and human-environment interaction. The themes are tools you can use to organize information and to answer the where, why, and how of geography.

▲ **Location**
This museum in England has a line running through it. The line marks its location at 0° longitude.

LOCATION

1 Location answers the question, "Where is it?" You can think of the location of a continent or a country as its address. You might give an absolute location such as 40° N and 80° W. You might also use a relative address, telling where one place is by referring to another place. *Between school and the mall* and *eight miles east of Pleasant City* are examples of relative locations.

REGIONS

2 Regions are areas that share at least one common feature. Geographers divide the world into many types of regions. For example, countries, states, and cities are political regions. The people in any one of these places live under the same government. Other features, such as climate and culture, can be used to define regions. Therefore the same place can be found in more than one region. For example, the state of Hawaii is in the political region of the United States. Because it has a tropical climate, Hawaii is also part of a tropical climate region.

MOVEMENT

4 Movement answers the question, "How do people, goods, and ideas move from place to place?" Remember that what happens in one place often affects what happens in another. Use the theme of movement to help you trace the spread of goods, people, and ideas from one location to another.

PLACE

3 Place identifies the natural and human features that make one place different from every other place. You can identify a specific place by its landforms, climate, plants, animals, people, language, or culture. You might even think of place as a geographic signature. Use the signature to help you understand the natural and human features that make one place different from every other place.

INTERACTION

5 Human-environment interaction focuses on the relationship between people and the environment. As people live in an area, they often begin to make changes to it, usually to make their lives easier. For example, they might build a dam to control flooding during rainy seasons. Also, the environment can affect how people live, work, dress, travel, and communicate.

◀ **Interaction**
These Congolese women interact with their environment by gathering wood for cooking.

PRACTICE YOUR GEOGRAPHY SKILLS

1 Describe your town or city, using each of the five themes of geography.

2 Name at least one thing that comes into your town or city and one that goes out. How is each moved? Where does it come from? Where does it go?

Understanding Movements of Earth

The planet Earth is part of our solar system. Earth revolves around the sun in a nearly circular path called an orbit. A revolution, or one complete orbit around the sun, takes 365¼ days, or one year. As Earth orbits the sun, it also spins on its axis, an invisible line through the center of Earth from the North Pole to the South Pole. This movement is called a rotation.

▼ **Spring begins**
On March 20 or 21, the sun is directly overhead at the Equator. The Northern and Southern Hemispheres receive almost equal hours of sunlight and darkness.

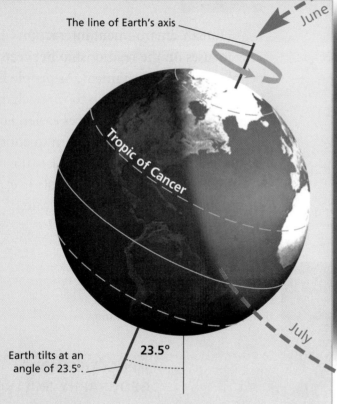

How Night Changes Into Day

The line of Earth's axis

Tropic of Cancer

Earth tilts at an angle of 23.5°.

23.5°

Earth takes about 24 hours to make one full rotation on its axis. As Earth rotates, it is daytime on the side facing the sun. It is night on the side away from the sun.

◀ **Summer begins**
On June 21 or 22, the sun is directly overhead at the Tropic of Cancer. The Northern Hemisphere receives the greatest number of sunlight hours.

The Seasons

Earth's axis is tilted at an angle. Because of this tilt, sunlight strikes different parts of Earth at different times in the year, creating seasons. The illustration below shows how the seasons are created in the Northern Hemisphere. In the Southern Hemisphere, the seasons are reversed.

PRACTICE YOUR GEOGRAPHY SKILLS

1. What causes the seasons in the Northern Hemisphere to be the opposite of those in the Southern Hemisphere?
2. During which two days of the year do the Northern Hemisphere and Southern Hemisphere have equal hours of daylight and darkness?

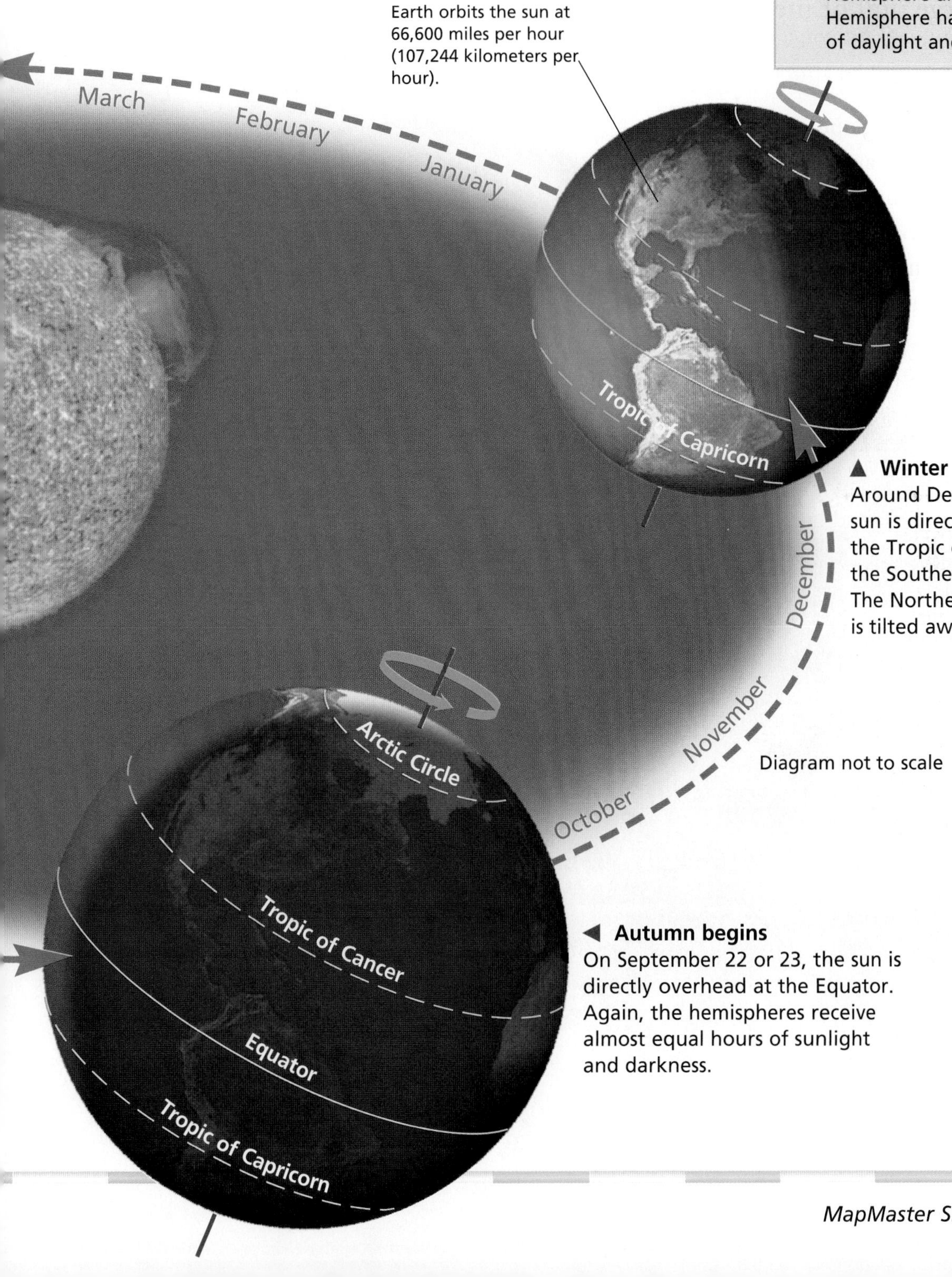
Earth orbits the sun at 66,600 miles per hour (107,244 kilometers per hour).
March
February
January
December
November
October
Tropic of Capricorn
Arctic Circle
Tropic of Cancer
Equator
Tropic of Capricorn
Diagram not to scale

▲ **Winter begins**
Around December 21, the sun is directly overhead at the Tropic of Capricorn in the Southern Hemisphere. The Northern Hemisphere is tilted away from the sun.

◀ **Autumn begins**
On September 22 or 23, the sun is directly overhead at the Equator. Again, the hemispheres receive almost equal hours of sunlight and darkness.

Understanding Globes

A globe is a scale model of Earth. It shows the actual shapes, sizes, and locations of all Earth's landmasses and bodies of water. Features on the surface of Earth are drawn to scale on a globe. This means that a small unit of measure on the globe stands for a large unit of measure on Earth.

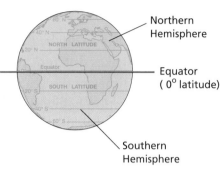

Northern Hemisphere

Equator (0° latitude)

Southern Hemisphere

Parallels of Latitude

Geographers divide the globe along imaginary horizontal lines called parallels of latitude. One of these latitude lines is the Equator, located halfway between the North and South poles. Parallels of latitude are measured in degrees (°). One degree of latitude represents a distance of about 69 miles (111 kilometers).

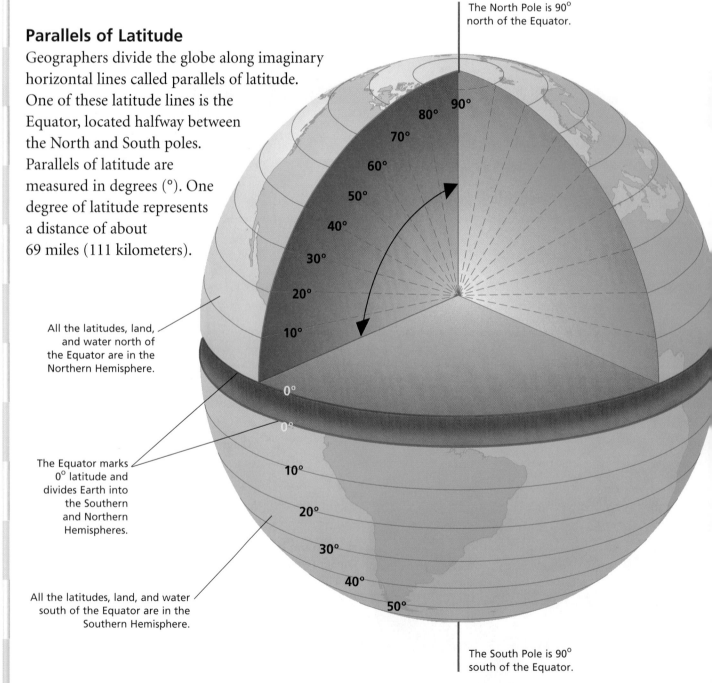

The North Pole is 90° north of the Equator.

90° 80° 70° 60° 50° 40° 30° 20° 10° 0°

All the latitudes, land, and water north of the Equator are in the Northern Hemisphere.

0°

The Equator marks 0° latitude and divides Earth into the Southern and Northern Hemispheres.

10° 20° 30° 40° 50°

All the latitudes, land, and water south of the Equator are in the Southern Hemisphere.

The South Pole is 90° south of the Equator.

Meridians of Longitude

Geographers also divide the globe along imaginary vertical lines called meridians of longitude, which are measured in degrees (°). The longitude line called the Prime Meridian runs from pole to pole through Greenwich, England. All meridians of longitude come together at the North and South Poles.

PRACTICE YOUR GEOGRAPHY SKILLS

1 Which continents lie completely in the Northern Hemisphere? In the Western Hemisphere?

2 Is there land or water at 20° S latitude and the Prime Meridian? At the Equator and 60° W longitude?

All the longitudes, land, and water west of the Prime Meridian are in the Western Hemisphere.

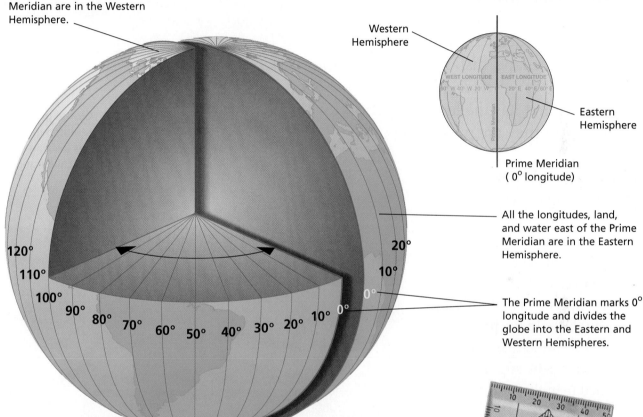

Western Hemisphere

Eastern Hemisphere

Prime Meridian (0° longitude)

All the longitudes, land, and water east of the Prime Meridian are in the Eastern Hemisphere.

The Prime Meridian marks 0° longitude and divides the globe into the Eastern and Western Hemispheres.

The Global Grid

Together, the pattern of parallels of latitude and meridians of longitude is called the global grid. Using the lines of latitude and longitude, you can locate any place on Earth. For example, the location of 30° north latitude and 90° west longitude is usually written as 30° N, 90° W. Only one place on Earth has these coordinates—the city of New Orleans, in the state of Louisiana.

▲ **Compass**
Wherever you are on Earth, a compass can be used to show direction.

Map Projections

Maps are drawings that show regions on flat surfaces. Maps are easier to use and carry than globes, but they cannot show the correct size and shape of every feature on Earth's curved surface. They must shrink some places and stretch others. To make up for this distortion, mapmakers use different map projections. No one projection can accurately show the correct area, shape, distance, and direction for all of Earth's surface. Mapmakers use the projection that has the least distortion for the information they are presenting.

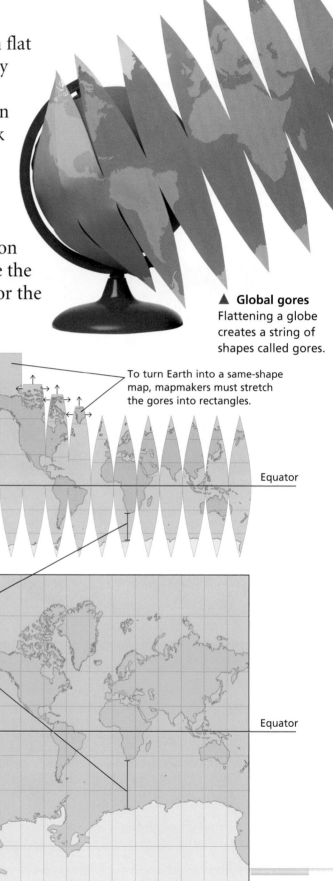

▲ **Global gores**
Flattening a globe creates a string of shapes called gores.

To turn Earth into a same-shape map, mapmakers must stretch the gores into rectangles.

Equator

Same-Shape Maps

Map projections that accurately show the shapes of landmasses are called same-shape maps. However, these projections often greatly distort, or make less accurate, the size of landmasses as well as the distance between them. In the projection below, the northern and southern areas of the globe appear more stretched than the areas near the Equator.

Stretching the gores makes parts of Earth larger. This enlargement becomes greater toward the North and South Poles.

Equator

Mercator projection ▶
One of the most common same-shape maps is the Mercator projection, named for the mapmaker who invented it. The Mercator projection accurately shows shape and direction, but it distorts distance and size. Because the projection shows true directions, ships' navigators use it to chart a straight-line course between two ports.

Equal-Area Maps

Map projections that show the correct size of landmasses are called equal-area maps. In order to show the correct size of landmasses, these maps usually distort shapes. The distortion is usually greater at the edges of the map and less at the center.

PRACTICE YOUR GEOGRAPHY SKILLS

1 What feature is distorted on an equal-area map?

2 Would you use a Mercator projection to find the exact distance between two locations? Tell why or why not.

To turn Earth's surface into an equal-area map, mapmakers have to squeeze each gore into an oval.

Equator

The tips of all the gores are then joined together. The points at which they join form the North and South Poles. The line of the Equator stays the same.

North Pole

Equator

South Pole

Robinson Maps

Many of the maps in this book use the Robinson projection, which is a compromise between the Mercator and equal-area projections. The Robinson projection gives a useful overall picture of the world. It keeps the size and shape relationships of most continents and oceans, but distorts the size of the polar regions.

The entire top edge of the map is the North Pole.

The map is least distorted at the Equator.

Equator

The entire bottom edge of the map is the South Pole.

MapMaster Skills Handbook **M7**

How to Use a Map

Mapmakers provide several clues to help you understand the information on a map. Maps provide different clues, depending on their purpose or scale. However, most maps have several clues in common.

Locator globe
Many maps are shown with locator globes. They show where on the globe the area of the map is located.

Title
All maps have a title. The title tells you the subject of the map.

Compass rose
Many maps show direction by displaying a compass rose with the directions north, east, south, and west. The letters N, E, S, and W are placed to indicate these directions.

Key
Often a map has a key, or legend. The key shows the symbols and colors used on the map, and what each one means.

Key

——	National border
⊛	National capital
•	Other city

Scale bar
A scale bar helps you find the actual distances between points shown on the map. Most scale bars show distances in both miles and kilometers.

Western Europe

SHETLAND ISLANDS (U.K.)

North Sea

Glasgow

Copenhagen

DENMARK

UNITED KINGDOM

Dublin

IRELAND

Hamburg

Berlin

NETHERLANDS
Amsterdam

London

The Hague

GERMANY

Brussels

BELGIUM

Frankfurt

Prague

CZECH REPUBLIC

English Channel

LUXEMBOURG

Luxembourg

Paris

Munich

Vienna

AUSTRIA

Bay of Biscay

FRANCE

Bern

LIECHTENSTEIN

SWITZERLAND

Lyon

Milan

SAN MARINO

Toulouse

MONACO

ITALY

Adriatic Sea

Marseille

ANDORRA

CORSICA (France)

VATICAN CITY

Rome

PORTUGAL

Madrid

Barcelona

SARDINIA (Italy)

Tyrrhenian Sea

Lisbon

SPAIN

BALEARIC ISLANDS (Spain)

Seville

Mediterranean Sea

SICILY (Italy)

0 miles   300
0 kilometers   300
Lambert Azimuthal Equal Area

60° N   0°   10° E   20° E   60° N   50° N   40° N   10° W   10° W

M8 MapMaster Skills Handbook

Maps of Different Scales

Maps are drawn to different scales, depending on their purpose. Here are three maps drawn to very different scales. Keep in mind that maps showing large areas have smaller scales. Maps showing small areas have larger scales.

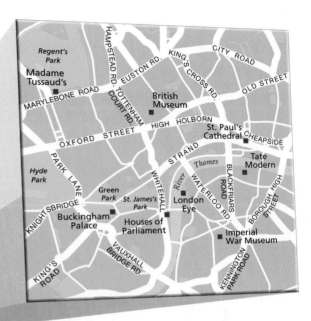

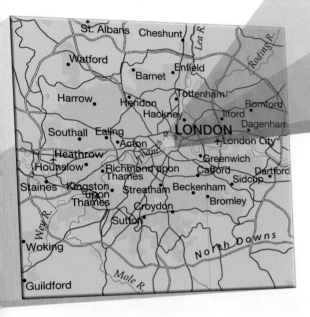

▲ **Greater London**

Find the gray square on the main map of Western Europe (left). This square represents the area shown on the map above. It shows London's boundaries, the general shape of the city, and the features around the city. This map can help you find your way from the airport to the center of town.

▲ **Central London**

Find the gray square on the map of Greater London. This square represents the area shown on the map above. This map moves you closer into the center of London. Like the zoom on a computer or a camera, this map shows a smaller area but in greater detail. It has the largest scale (1 inch represents about 0.9 mile). You can use this map to explore downtown London.

Key

- ■ Point of interest
- Park
- 0 miles   0.5   1
- 0 kilometers   1

Key

- Built-up area
- ✈ Airport
- City or county border
- ⊛ National capital
- • Town or neighborhood
- 0 miles   10   20
- 0 kilometers   20
- Lambert Conformal Conic

PRACTICE YOUR GEOGRAPHY SKILLS

1 What part of a map explains the colors used on the map?

2 How does the scale bar change depending on the scale of the map?

3 Which map would be best for finding the location of the British Museum? Explain why.

Political Maps

Political maps show political borders: continents, countries, and divisions within countries, such as states or provinces. The colors on political maps do not have any special meaning, but they make the map easier to read. Political maps also include symbols and labels for capitals, cities, and towns.

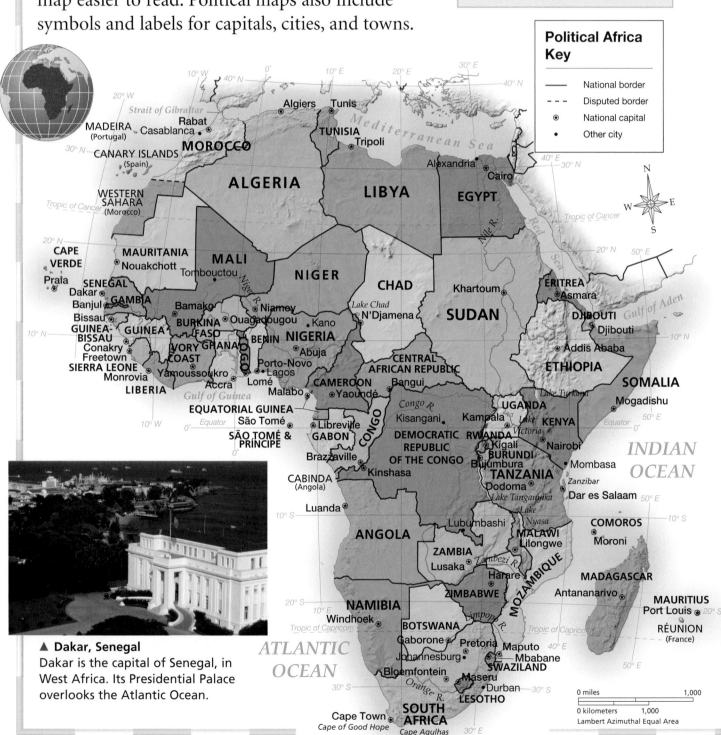

Political Africa Key

——— National border

- - - Disputed border

⊛ National capital

• Other city

▲ **Dakar, Senegal**
Dakar is the capital of Senegal, in West Africa. Its Presidential Palace overlooks the Atlantic Ocean.

0 miles 1,000
0 kilometers 1,000
Lambert Azimuthal Equal Area

Physical Maps

Physical maps represent what a region looks like by showing its major physical features, such as hills and plains. Physical maps also often show elevation and relief. Elevation, indicated by colors, is the height of the land above sea level. Relief, indicated by shading, shows how sharply the land rises or falls.

PRACTICE YOUR GEOGRAPHY SKILLS

1 Which areas of Africa have the highest elevation?

2 How can you use relief to plan a hiking trip?

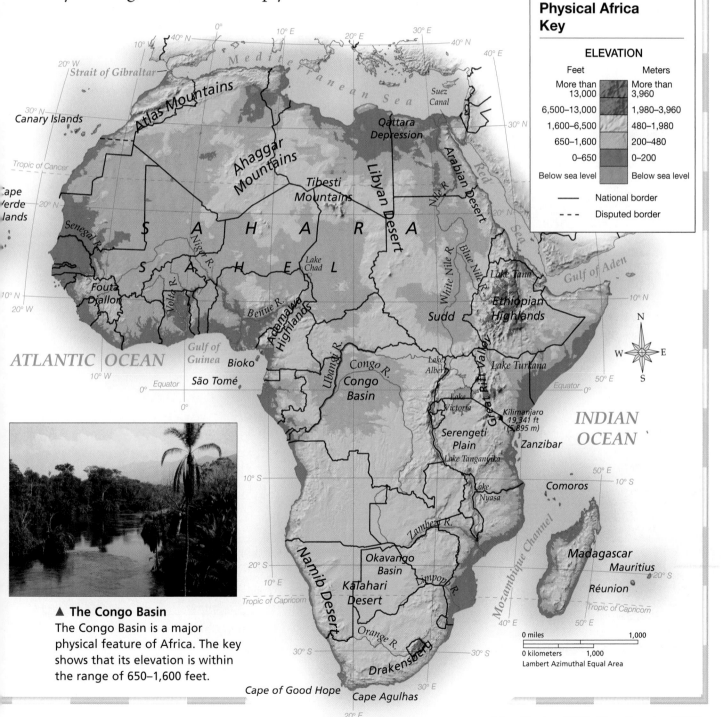

Physical Africa Key

ELEVATION

Feet	Meters
More than 13,000	More than 3,960
6,500–13,000	1,980–3,960
1,600–6,500	480–1,980
650–1,600	200–480
0–650	0–200
Below sea level	Below sea level

——— National border

- - - Disputed border

0 miles 1,000
0 kilometers 1,000
Lambert Azimuthal Equal Area

▲ **The Congo Basin**
The Congo Basin is a major physical feature of Africa. The key shows that its elevation is within the range of 650–1,600 feet.

Special-Purpose Maps: Climate

Unlike the boundary lines on a political map, the boundary lines on climate maps do not separate the land into exact divisions. For example, in this climate map of India, a tropical wet climate gradually changes to a tropical wet and dry climate.

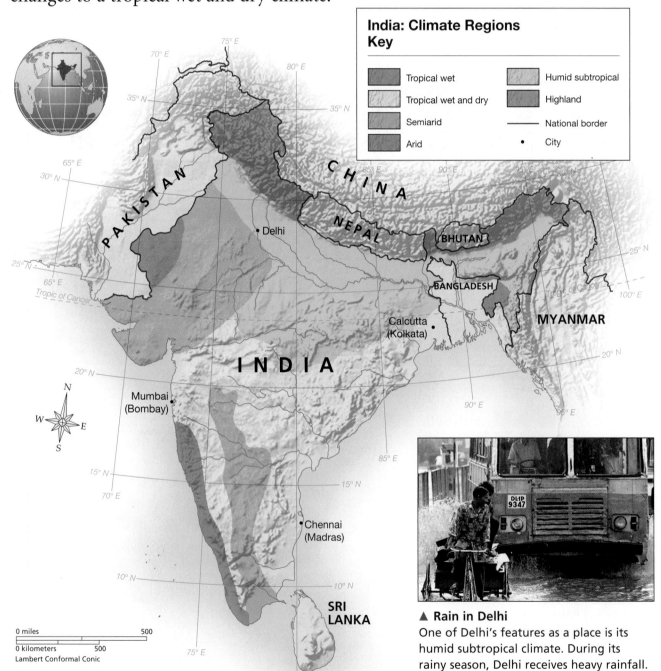

India: Climate Regions Key

- Tropical wet
- Tropical wet and dry
- Semiarid
- Arid
- Humid subtropical
- Highland
- —— National border
- • City

▲ **Rain in Delhi**
One of Delhi's features as a place is its humid subtropical climate. During its rainy season, Delhi receives heavy rainfall.

0 miles 500
0 kilometers 500
Lambert Conformal Conic

Special-Purpose Maps: Language

This map shows the official languages of India. An official language is the language used by the government. Even though a region has an official language, the people there may speak other languages as well. As in other special-purpose maps, the key explains how the different languages appear on the map.

PRACTICE YOUR GEOGRAPHY SKILLS

1 What color represents the Malayalam language on this map?

2 Where in India is Tamil the official language?

The Hindi language ▶
Hindi is the most widely spoken language in India. It is also the most popular language in Delhi.

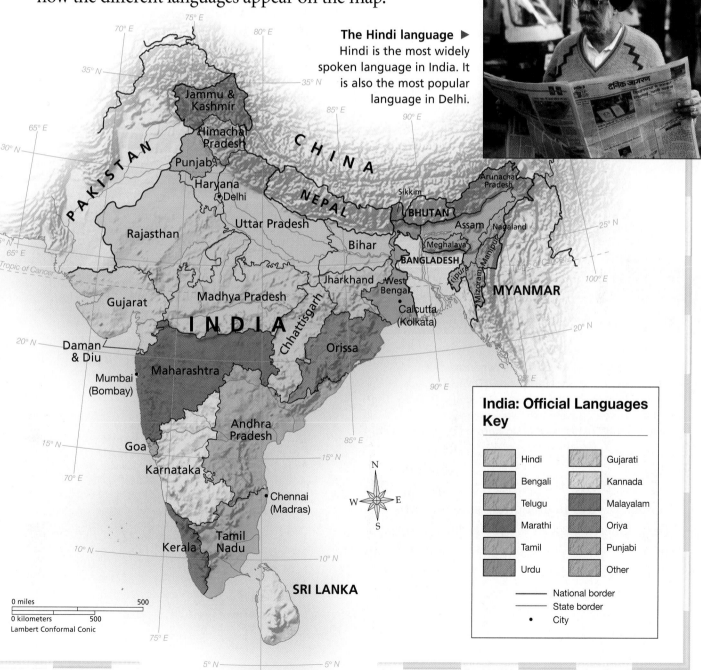

India: Official Languages Key

Hindi	Gujarati
Bengali	Kannada
Telugu	Malayalam
Marathi	Oriya
Tamil	Punjabi
Urdu	Other

— National border
— State border
• City

0 miles 500
0 kilometers 500
Lambert Conformal Conic

Human Migration

Migration is an important part of the study of geography. Since the beginning of history, people have been on the move. As people move, they both shape and are shaped by their environments. Wherever people go, the culture they bring with them mixes with the cultures of the place in which they have settled.

Explorers arrive ▼
In 1492, Christopher Columbus set sail from Spain for the Americas with three ships. The ships shown here are replicas of those ships.

▲ Native American pyramid
When Europeans arrived in the Americas, the lands they found were not empty. Diverse groups of people with distinct cultures already lived there. The temple-topped pyramid shown above was built by Mayan Indians in Mexico, long before Columbus sailed.

Migration to the Americas, 1500–1800

A huge wave of migration from the Eastern Hemisphere began in the 1500s. European explorers in the Americas paved the way for hundreds of years of European settlement there. Forced migration from Africa started soon afterward, as Europeans began to import African slaves to work in the Americas. The map to the right shows these migrations.

ATLANTIC OCEAN

NEW SPAIN
(Spain)
Mexico City

Caribbean Sea

DUTCH GUIANA
(Netherlands)

Panama City

NEW GRENADA
(Spain)

FRENCH GUIANA
(France)

Amazon R.

PERU
(Spain)
Lima
Cuzco

BRAZIL
(Portugal)

Potosí

RIO DE LA PLATA
(Spain)

Concepción

Buenos Aires

0 miles   1,000
0 kilometers   1,000
Wagner VII

SCOTLAND

IRELAND   ENGLAND

NETHERLANDS

FRANCE

EUROPE

PORTUGAL SPAIN

MOROCCO

N
W   E
S

WALO

Saint-Louis

Fort James

**AKAN
STATES**

Cacheu

AFRICA

Niger R.

BENIN

Elmina

Axim   Accra

Congo R.

*Congo
Basin*

KONGO

Luanda

Benguela

*ATLANTIC
OCEAN*

PRACTICE YOUR GEOGRAPHY SKILLS

1 Where did the Portuguese settle in the Americas?

2 Would you describe African migration at this time as a result of both push factors and pull factors? Explain why or why not.

"Push" and "Pull" Factors

Geographers describe a people's choice to migrate in terms of "push" factors and "pull" factors. Push factors are things in people's lives that push them to leave, such as poverty and political unrest. Pull factors are things in another country that pull people to move there, including better living conditions and hopes of better jobs.

▲ **Elmina, Ghana**
Elmina, in Ghana, is one of the many ports from which slaves were transported from Africa. Because slaves and gold were traded here, stretches of the western African coast were known as the Slave Coast and the Gold Coast.

Migration to Latin America, 1500–1800
Key

➤ European migration

➤ African migration

— National or colonial border

········ Traditional African border

African State

Spain and possessions

Portugal and possessions

Netherlands and possessions

France and possessions

England and possessions

World Land Use

People around the world have many different economic structures, or ways of making a living. Land-use maps are one way to learn about these structures. The ways that people use the land in each region tell us about the main ways that people in that region make a living.

World Land Use Key

	Nomadic herding
	Hunting and gathering
	Forestry
	Livestock raising
	Commercial farming
	Subsistence farming
	Manufacturing and trade
	Little or no activity
——	National border
- - - -	Disputed border

▲ **Wheat farming in the United States**
Developed countries practice commercial farming rather than subsistence farming. Commercial farming is the production of food mainly for sale, either within the country or for export to other countries. Commercial farmers like these in Oregon often use heavy equipment to farm.

Levels of Development

Notice on the map key the term *subsistence farming*. This term means the production of food mainly for use by the farmer's own family. In less-developed countries, subsistence farming is often one of the main economic activities. In contrast, in developed countries there is little subsistence farming.

NORTH AMERICA

SOUTH AMERICA

▲ **Growing barley in Ecuador**
These farmers in Ecuador use hand tools to harvest barley. They will use most of the crop they grow to feed themselves or their farm animals.

0 miles   2,
0 kilometers   2,000
Robinson

▲ **Growing rice in Vietnam**
Women in Vietnam plant rice in wet rice paddies, using the
same planting methods their ancestors did.

**PRACTICE YOUR
GEOGRAPHY SKILLS**

1 In what parts of the world is
subsistence farming the main
land use?

2 Locate where manufacturing
and trade are the main land
use. Are they found more often
near areas of subsistence
farming or areas of commercial
farming? Why might this be so?

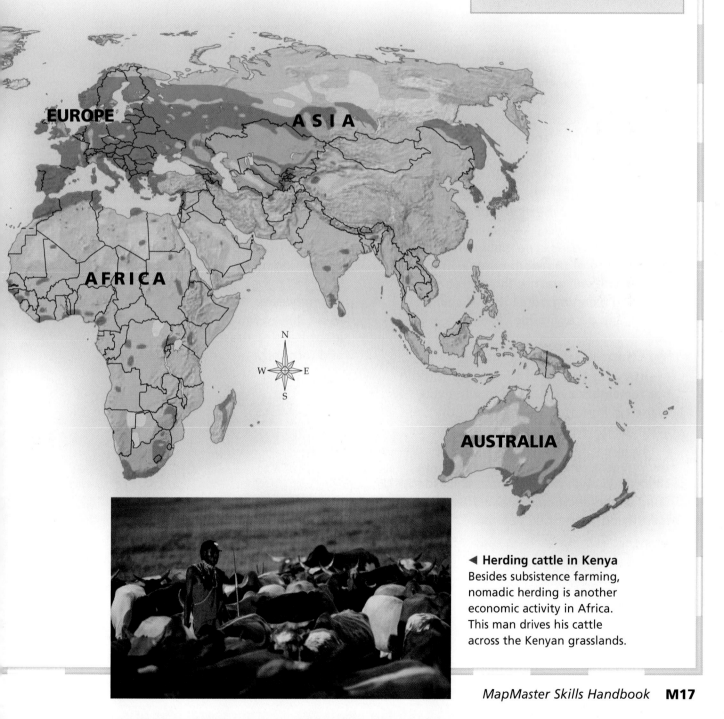

EUROPE

ASIA

AFRICA

AUSTRALIA

◄ **Herding cattle in Kenya**
Besides subsistence farming,
nomadic herding is another
economic activity in Africa.
This man drives his cattle
across the Kenyan grasslands.

How to Read Social Studies

Target Reading Skills

The Target Reading Skills introduced on this page will help you understand the words and ideas in this book and in other social studies reading you do. Each chapter focuses on one of these reading skills. Good readers develop a bank of reading strategies, or skills. Then they draw on the particular strategies that will help them understand the text they are reading.

Chapter 1 Target Reading Skill

Using the Reading Process Previewing can help you understand and remember what you read. In this chapter you will practice using these previewing skills: setting a purpose for reading, predicting what the text will be about, and asking questions before you read.

Chapter 2 Target Reading Skill

Clarifying Meaning If you do not understand something you are reading right away, you can use several skills to help clarify the meaning of the word or idea. In this chapter you will practice these strategies for clarifying meaning: rereading, reading ahead, and paraphrasing.

Chapter 3 Target Reading Skill

Identifying the Main Idea Since you cannot remember every detail of what you read, it is important that you identify the main ideas. The main idea of a section or paragraph is the most important point and the one you want to remember. In this chapter you will practice these skills: identifying stated and implied main ideas and identifying supporting details.

Chapter 4 Target Reading Skill

Using Context Using the context of an unfamiliar word can help you understand its meaning. Context includes the words, phrases, and sentences surrounding a word. In this chapter you will practice using these context clues: descriptions, definitions, comparisons, and examples.

Chapter 5 Target Reading Skill

Comparing and Contrasting You can use comparison and contrast to sort out and analyze information you are reading. Comparing means examining the similarities between things. Contrasting is looking at differences. In this chapter you will practice these skills: comparing and contrasting, identifying contrasts, making comparisons, and recognizing contrast signal words.

EUROPE and RUSSIA

Europe and Russia lie on a gigantic landmass that stretches from the Atlantic Ocean to the Pacific. The countries of this region are as diverse as their geography, with distinctive cultures and societies. Ancient civilizations that developed in Europe still influence people around the world. Today, the region contains countries with histories that stretch back hundreds of years as well as countries that were formed just a decade or two ago.

Guiding Questions

The text, photographs, maps, and charts in this book will help you discover answers to these Guiding Questions.

1. **Geography** What are the main physical features of Europe and Russia?

2. **History** How have Europe and Russia been affected by their history?

3. **Culture** How have the people of Europe and Russia been shaped by their cultures?

4. **Government** What types of government have existed in Europe and Russia?

5. **Economics** How have Russian and European economies developed into what they are today?

Project Preview

You can also discover answers to the Guiding Questions by working on projects. Several project possibilities are listed on page 208 of this book.

Investigate Europe and Russia

Europe and Russia extend across more than half the world's longitudes, from Iceland in the west at about 25° W to easternmost Siberia at 175° E. Europe is a continent made up of many countries, while Russia is one country that actually lies on two continents— Europe and Asia. Together, Europe and Russia form a rich pattern of different cultures, histories, and languages.

▲ **Amsterdam, the Netherlands**
Skating on one of the city's many frozen canals

LOCATION

1 Investigate Europe and Russia's Location

The location of an unfamiliar place can be described in relation to a familiar place. Use the map above to describe the location of Europe and Russia in relation to the United States. What ocean lies between Europe and the United States? If you were on the west coast of the United States, in what direction would you travel to get to the east coast of Russia most quickly? How close to the Equator are the two regions—Europe and Russia and the United States? How close are they to the Arctic Circle? Many people think the climates of Europe and the United States are similar. Look at the map, and explain why this might be so.

REGIONS

2 Estimate the Size of Europe and Russia

How big are Europe and Russia? To find out, compare the size of Europe and Russia together to that of the 48 states of the United States main-land. Now compare Europe alone to those states. Notice that Russia lies in two continents, Asia and Europe. The striped area shows the European part of Russia. The solid green area shows the Asian part of Russia.

Political Europe and Russia

Key

— National border
⊛ National capital
• Other city

ARCTIC OCEAN

RUSSIA

Murmansk
St. Petersburg
Moscow
Volgograd
Astrakhan
Novosibirsk
Irkutsk
Lake Baikal
Magadan
Yakutsk
Sea of Okhotsk
Vladivostok
Barents Sea
Laptev Sea
East Siberian Sea

0 miles 1,500
0 kilometers 1,500
Lambert Conformal Conic

ICELAND
Reykjavik

FAEROE ISLANDS
(Denmark)

NORWAY
Oslo

SWEDEN
Stockholm

FINLAND
Helsinki

Murmansk

St. Petersburg
Tallinn
ESTONIA
RUSSIA
Moscow

Riga
LATVIA
LITHUANIA Vilnius
KALININGRAD
(Russia)
Minsk
BELARUS

Volgograd
Astrakhan

UNITED KINGDOM
Dublin
IRELAND
London

DENMARK
Copenhagen

NETHERLANDS
The Hague
Amsterdam
Berlin
Warsaw

GERMANY POLAND
BELGIUM
Brussels
LUXEMBOURG
Luxembourg
Prague
CZECH REPUBLIC
SLOVAKIA
Kiev
UKRAINE

Paris
LIECHTENSTEIN
Bern
Vienna
Bratislava
MOLDOVA
Chişinău

AUSTRIA HUNGARY
Budapest
SWITZERLAND
Ljubljana
Zagreb
ROMANIA
Belgrade
Bucharest

FRANCE
SLOVENIA CROATIA
SAN MARINO
Sarajevo
SERBIA
BOSNIA & HERZEGOVINA
MONT.
Sofia
BULGARIA

ANDORRA
MONACO
Rome
Podgorica
Tiranë
Skopje
MACEDONIA

PORTUGAL
Lisbon
Madrid
Corsica
VATICAN CITY
ALBANIA
GREECE
Athens

SPAIN
Balearic Islands
Sardinia
ITALY
Sicily

MALTA
Valletta
Crete

AFRICA
Mediterranean Sea

ATLANTIC OCEAN
Norwegian Sea
North Sea
Baltic Sea
Bay of Biscay
Black Sea
Caspian Sea
ASIA

0 miles 500
0 kilometers 500
Lambert Conformal Conic

▲ **Moscow, Russia**
The historic building called the Kremlin is the headquarters for Russia's government.

LOCATION

3 Investigate the Countries of Europe

The landmass upon which Europe and Asia are located is known as Eurasia. Russia is the largest country in that landmass and the largest country in the world. Some of the world's smallest countries are in Europe. Name three of them. Name four countries that share a border with Germany. What are the names of the seas and oceans that surround Europe?

Physical Europe and Russia

The Matterhorn, Switzerland ▶
The Matterhorn is Switzerland's most famous mountain.

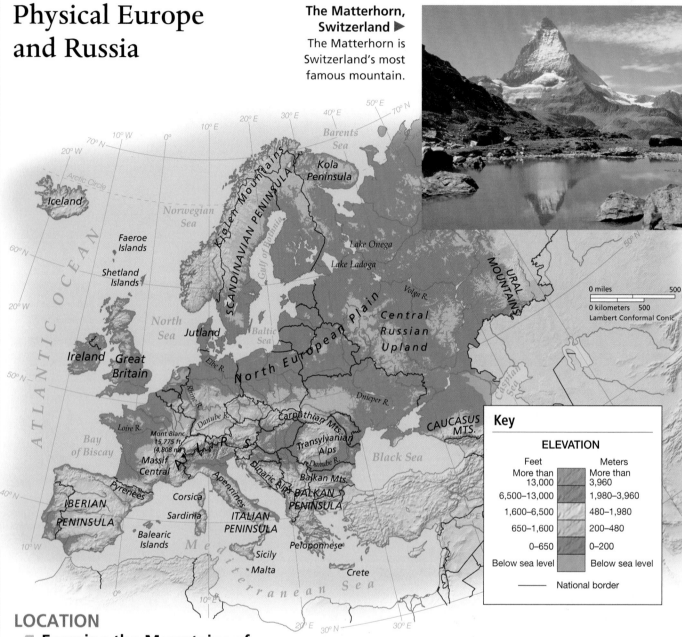

LOCATION

4 Examine the Mountains of Europe and Russia

Several mountain ranges stretch through Central and Southern Europe, from the Bay of Biscay to the Caspian Sea. Find and name four of these mountain ranges. What mountain range separates France from Spain? Now locate Russia's Ural Mountains. Most of Russia lies in Asia, east of the Ural Mountains. Most Russians, however, live in the European part of Russia, west of the Ural Mountains.

Key

ELEVATION

Feet	Meters
More than 13,000	More than 3,960
6,500–13,000	1,980–3,960
1,600–6,500	480–1,980
650–1,600	200–480
0–650	0–200
Below sea level	Below sea level

—— National border

Europe and Russia: Population Density

Population density describes how crowded a particular place is. Use the key below to determine what color on the map represents an area where many people live. What color represents an area where very few people live? Compare the parts of Europe where there are very few people with the parts of Europe where there are very many. How might the locations of these areas explain the differences?

KEY

Persons per sq. mile	Persons per sq. kilometer
More than 3,119	More than 1,204
520–3,119	200–1,204
260–519	100–199
130–259	50–99
25–129	10–49
1–24	1–9
Less than 1	Less than 1

Urban Areas
☐ 5,000,000–9,999,999
⊙ 1,000,000–4,999,999
• Less than 1,000,000
— National border

▼ **Norway**
Sami children on a snowmobile

▲ **Sergivev Posad, Russia**
Trinity Monastery of St. Sergius

PRACTICE YOUR GEOGRAPHY SKILLS

1   You begin to explore Europe from its west coast. From Portugal you fly over the headwaters of the Danube and the Rhine rivers. In what direction are you flying?

2   You board a train in Moscow and travel east. When you get to the farthest point in Siberia, you have gone about one third of the way around the world. What mountain range did you cross?

3   You are going to drive from Warsaw to Moscow. In what direction will you travel?

Focus on Countries in Europe and Russia

Now that you've investigated the geography of Europe and Russia, take a closer look at some of the countries that make up this region. This map shows all of the countries of Europe and Russia. The 14 countries you will study in depth in the second half of this book appear in yellow on the map.

Go Online
PHSchool.com

Use Web Code **ldp-1000** for the **interactive maps** on these pages.

Key

— National border

Countries with in-depth coverage

Non-feature countries

ICELAND

ATLANTIC OCEAN

NORWAY
SWEDEN

North Sea

DENMARK

IRELAND

UNITED KINGDOM

NETHERLANDS

KALINING (Ru

BELGIUM

GERMANY

POLA

LUXEMBOURG

CZECH REPUBLIC

LIECHTENSTEIN

SLOVAK

SWITZERLAND

AUSTRIA

HUNGA

FRANCE

SLOVENIA

CROATIA

PORTUGAL

ANDORRA

SAN MARINO

BOSNIA & HERZEGOVINA SER

SPAIN

MONACO

ITALY

MONTENEGRO

MACEDO

VATICAN CITY

ALBANIA

Mediterranean Sea

GRE

MALTA

▲ **United Kingdom**
Britain once headed a great empire. Today, as a member of the United Nations, the United Kingdom plays an important role in world diplomacy.

Poland ▶
Poland has undergone tremendous social, political, and economic changes since its communist government lost power in 1989. However, agriculture has remained an important part of the country's economy.

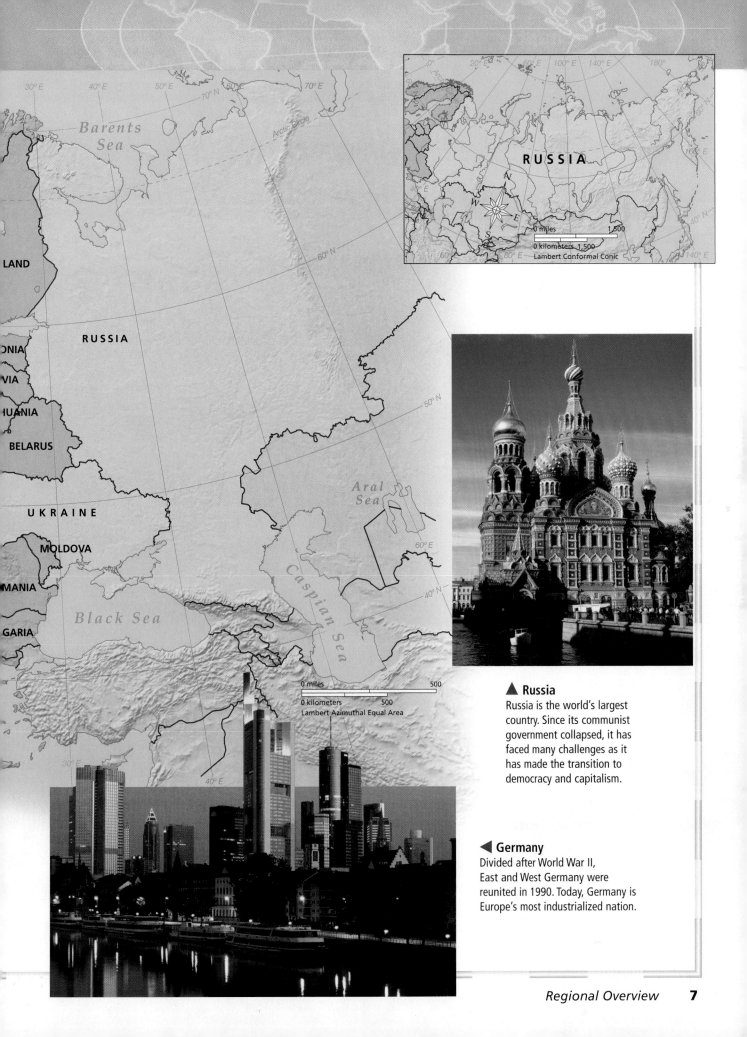

Barents
Sea

RUSSIA

RUSSIA

Arctic Circle

70° N

60° N

50° N

Aral
Sea

Caspian Sea

40° N

LAND

ONIA

VIA

HUANIA

BELARUS

UKRAINE

MOLDOVA

MANIA

GARIA

Black Sea

30° E   40° E   50° E   60° E   70° E   70° E

30° E

40° E

50° E

60° E

60° E

0 miles   500
0 kilometers   500
Lambert Azimuthal Equal Area

RUSSIA

N
W   E
S

0 miles   1,500
0 kilometers   1,500
Lambert Conformal Conic

0° | 20° E | 60° E | 100° E | 140° E | 180°

▲ **Russia**
Russia is the world's largest
country. Since its communist
government collapsed, it has
faced many challenges as it
has made the transition to
democracy and capitalism.

◀ **Germany**
Divided after World War II,
East and West Germany were
reunited in 1990. Today, Germany is
Europe's most industrialized nation.

Chapter Preview

This chapter will introduce you to the geography of Europe and Russia and show how geography affects the people who live there.

Section 1
Land and Water

Section 2
Climate and Vegetation

Section 3
Resources and Land Use

Target Reading Skill

Reading Process In this chapter you will use previewing to help you understand and remember what you read.

▶ Waves splash against the rocky coast of Cornwall in southern England.

Europe and Russia: Climate Regions

KEY

National border

‑ ‑ ‑ Disputed border

• City

Humid continental

Semiarid

Mediterranean

Humid subtropical

Marine west coast

Highland

Tundra

Subarctic

ARCTIC OCEAN

Kara Sea

Laptev Sea

East Siberian Sea

Greenland Sea

Barents Sea

RUSSIA

Arctic Circle

Norwegian Sea

St. Petersburg

Sea of Okhotsk

Moscow

Novosibirsk

Irkutsk

London

EUROPE

Paris

Rome

ATLANTIC OCEAN

Barcelona

Mediterranean Sea

ASIA

Vladivostok

PACIFIC OCEAN

AFRICA

Tropic of Cancer

0 miles   2,000

0 kilometers 2,000

Mercator

Location The climates of Europe and Russia vary widely, from subtropical in Southern Europe to tundra in Russia. **Identify** Which climate is named after a major body of water in the region? **Contrast** Study the location of this climate. How do you think this climate differs from that of Northern Europe and Russia?

Go Online
PHSchool.com Use Web Code
ldp-7111 for step-by-step
map skills practice.

Land and Water

Prepare to Read

Objectives

In this section you will

1. Learn about the size, location, and population of Europe and Russia.
2. Examine the major landforms of Europe and Russia.
3. Find out about the waterways of Europe and Russia.

Taking Notes

As you read this section, look for the main ideas about land and water. Copy the table below and record your findings in it.

Region	Landforms	Bodies of Water
Europe		
Russia		

Target Reading Skill

Set a Purpose for Reading When you set a purpose for reading, you give yourself a focus. Before you read this section, look at the headings, the maps, and the photographs to see what the section is about. Then set a purpose for reading the section. Your purpose might be to find out about the geography of Europe and Russia. As you read, use the Taking Notes table to help you achieve your purpose.

Key Terms

- **population density** (pahp yuh LAY shun DEN suh tee) *n.* the average number of people living in a square mile or a square kilometer
- **peninsula** (puh NIN suh luh) *n.* a land area nearly surrounded by water
- **plateau** (pla TOH) *n.* a large raised area of mostly level land bordered on one or more sides by steep slopes or cliffs
- **tributary** (TRIB yoo tehr ee) *n.* a river or stream that flows into a larger river
- **navigable** (NAV ih guh bul) *adj.* wide and deep enough for ships to travel through

A windmill in Friesland, the Netherlands

If you cross a field in the Netherlands (NETH ur lundz), you could be walking where sea waves once roared. Water formerly covered more than two fifths of the country. Centuries ago, the people of the Netherlands began an effort to create land where there was water. They built long walls called dikes to hold back the water. They pumped the water into canals that empty into the North Sea. In this way, they created polders (POHL durz), or patches of new land.

The polders that lie below sea level are always filling with water. Netherlanders must continually pump them out. Keeping the polders dry is important. Like much of Europe, the country's many people must find living space on a small amount of land. The richest farmlands and some cities in the Netherlands are located on polders.

Size, Location, and Population

Europe and Russia are parts of Eurasia, the world's largest landmass. This landmass is made up of two continents, Europe and Asia. The country of Russia stretches over both continents. About one fourth of Russia is in Europe; the rest is in Asia. The Ural (YOOR ul) Mountains divide Europe from Asia.

Location Trace a latitude line from the United States to Eurasia in the map titled World: Political in the Atlas. You will see that much of Europe and nearly all of Russia are farther north than is the United States. Berlin, the German capital, lies at about the same latitude as the southern tip of Canada's Hudson Bay.

A Small Continent With Many People Europe is a small continent. Only Australia is smaller. While Europe lacks size, it has 44 different countries. Many are the size of an average state in the United States. Russia, though, is the largest country in the world. It is almost twice the size of the United States.

Most of the countries of Europe have a much higher population density than other countries in the world. **Population density** is the average number of people living in a square mile or a square kilometer. The Netherlands has more than 1,236 people per square mile (477 people per sq kilometer). By comparison, the world average is about 106 people per square mile (42 people per sq kilometer). Russia, on the other hand, has a much lower population density—only about 22 people per square mile (9 people per sq kilometer).

✓ **Reading Check** **What is the largest landmass in the world?**

Rural Regions of Europe and Russia
The Ural Mountains, shown at the bottom, mark the dividing line between Europe and Asia. The inset photo shows a church situated in the highlands of northern Scotland.
Analyze Images *Use clues from the photographs to estimate which of these places has a greater population density.*

Major Landforms

Study the shape of Europe on the map below. The continent of Europe forms a **peninsula** (puh NIN suh luh), or a body of land nearly surrounded by water. The European peninsula juts out into the Atlantic Ocean. Europe also has many smaller peninsulas with bays. These bays include harbors, or sheltered bodies of water where ships dock. Good harbors enabled Western European countries to become world leaders in the shipping industry.

Now look at the small physical map of Russia on page 4. Notice how much of Russia lies on the Arctic Ocean. For most of the year, this body of water is frozen and cannot be used for shipping. Between Russia and the other countries of Europe, however, there are no physical barriers. Movement between these two regions has always been easy.

Europe: Land Regions

MAP MASTER™ Skills Activity

KEY

ELEVATION

Feet	Meters
More than 13,000	More than 3,960
6,500–13,000	1,980–3,960
1,600–6,500	480–1,980
650–1,600	200–480
0–650	0–200
Below sea level	Below sea level

Physiographic border

National border

Regions Europe is divided into four major land regions, each sharing similar characteristics. **Identify** Which region is characterized by elevations of more than 6,500 feet (1,980 kilometers)? **Compare** Which European region covers the largest area?

Go Online PHSchool.com Use Web Code ldp-7121 for step-by-step map skills practice.

Plains, Uplands, and Mountains of Europe Within the peninsula of Europe are four major land regions: the Northwestern Highlands, the North European Plain, the Central Uplands, and the Alpine Mountain System. Find these regions on the map on page 12.

The Northwestern Highlands stretch across the far north of Europe. It is a region of old mountains that have been worn down by wind and weather. Because they have steep slopes and thin soil, they are not good for farming, and few people live there. But the forests there support a successful timber industry. And people there raise goats and sheep, especially in Spain and Scotland.

Notice that the North European Plain covers more than half of Europe. These plains include most of the European part of Russia and reach all the way to France. This region has the most productive farmland and the largest cities in Europe.

In the center of southern Europe are the Central Uplands. The Central Uplands are a region of highlands, made up of mountains and plateaus. **Plateaus** (pla TOHZ) are large raised areas of mostly level land bordered on one or more sides by steep slopes or cliffs. Most of the land there is rocky and not good for farming. But the uplands have other uses, including mining, industry, and tourism.

The mountains of the Alpine Mountain System stretch from France to the Balkan Peninsula. They include the Alps, the highest mountains in the system. Some families do small-scale farming in the mountain valleys and meadows of the Alps.

Traveling in the Alps
A train carries people between alpine villages in southern Switzerland. The country has an extensive rail system.
Infer *What geographical challenges does a nation like Switzerland face when building a rail system?*

Making a Living in Siberia
The nomadic Chukchi people make their living by herding reindeer in the uplands of northeastern Siberia. The name *Chukchi* means "rich in reindeer." **Infer** *Why does it make sense for the Chukchi to be nomadic—moving from place to place—rather than to live in fixed settlements?*

Plains, Uplands, and Mountains of Russia Europe and western Russia share the North European Plain. Russia's largest cities, Moscow (MAHS kow) and St. Petersburg, are in this region. Most of Russia's industries are there, too. More people live in this region than in any other part of Russia.

Where the plains end, the uplands begin. On the eastern border of the North European Plain, you will find the Ural Mountains. To the east of the Urals is the Asian part of Russia— a region known as Siberia (sy BIHR ee uh). This region makes up about 75 percent of Russian territory, but the climate is so harsh that only about 20 percent of Russia's people live there.

If you continue east into Siberia from the Ural Mountains, you will cross the largest plain in the world—the West Siberian Plain. This low, marshy plain covers more than one million square miles (2.59 million sq kilometers). More than half of it rises only 328 feet (100 meters) above sea level. Farther east is the Central Siberian Plateau, which slopes upward from the West Siberian Plain. If you travel still farther east, you will find the East Siberian Uplands, which include more than 20 active volcanoes among the rugged mountains and plateaus.

√ **Reading Check** **Where are most of Russia's industries located?**

Waterways of Europe and Russia

Rivers and lakes provide the people who live in Europe and Russia with water and transportation.

Major Rivers High in the Alps in Switzerland (SWIT sur lund), melting glaciers create two streams that combine to form the Rhine River. Winding through forests and plains, the Rhine makes a journey of 865 miles (1,392 kilometers), from Switzerland to the Netherlands and the North Sea. The Rhine River is connected to the farthest reaches of Western Europe by canals and **tributaries** (TRIB yoo tehr eez). A tributary is a river or stream that flows into a larger river.

Another major waterway is the Danube (DAN yoob) River. The Danube is Europe's second-longest river. It begins in the Black Forest region of western Germany. It travels 1,770 miles (2,850 kilometers) to the Black Sea of southeastern Europe. Along the way, the Danube passes through nine countries.

The longest river in Europe is Russia's Volga (VOHL guh) River. It flows 2,291 miles (3,687 kilometers) through western Russia and empties into the Caspian (KASP ee un) Sea. Canals link the Volga and its tributaries to the Baltic Sea and other seas. Unfortunately, the Volga freezes along much of its length for three months of each year. During the winter months, it is not **navigable** (NAV ih guh bul), or clear enough for ships to travel through.

Set a Purpose for Reading
If your purpose is to learn about the geography of Europe and Russia, how do these paragraphs help you meet your goal?

A Historical Waterway
The Rhine flows past old castles, mills, and factories along its course through Germany. Just as they did in ancient times, ships today use the river to transport goods. **Analyze Images** *What advantages would this location have given the people who settled here?*

A Seasonal Harbor
Ships wait in the harbor of Nizhny Novgorod, Russia, on the Volga River. **Analyze Images** *Is it likely that the river was navigable at the time the photo was taken?*

Lakes Though Europe is criss-crossed by rivers, it contains few lakes compared to other regions. Russia, in contrast, has a huge number of lakes, both large and small. The world's largest freshwater lake is found in Russia. Called Lake Baikal (by KAHL), it is located in southern Russia. Lake Baikal is nearly 400 miles long and has an average width of 30 miles. It is also the world's deepest lake, with some parts reaching 5,315 feet (1,620 meters). Lake Baikal contains about one fifth of Earth's fresh water and is home to hundreds of animal and plant species. In fact, the Russian word *baikal* means "rich lake."

 **Reading Check** **What is the longest river in Europe?**

Section 1 Assessment

Key Terms
Review the key terms at the beginning of this section. Use each term in a sentence that explains its meaning.

Target Reading Skill
How did having a purpose for reading help you understand important ideas in this section?

Comprehension and Critical Thinking
1. (a) Locate Which country is located on both the continents of Europe and Asia?

(b) Compare and Contrast How does the land size of Europe differ from the land size of Russia?
2. (a) Name What are the four major land regions of Europe?
(b) Identify What are the major land regions of Russia?
(c) Draw Conclusions How have physical features affected life in Europe and Russia?
3. (a) Explain Why is the Volga River in Russia not navigable year-round?
(b) Identify Effects How might Russia's industries be affected by ships not being able to travel on the rivers all year long?

Writing Activity
Write an entry in your journal describing what you learned about the landforms and waterways of Europe or Russia.

> **Writing Tip** Remember that writing in a journal is writing you do for yourself. In a journal, you can let your ideas flow without stopping to correct your writing.

Climate and Vegetation

Prepare to Read

Objectives

In this section you will

1. Find out about the wide range of climates in Europe and Russia.
2. Learn about the major climate regions of Europe and Russia.
3. Examine the natural vegetation regions of Europe and Russia.

Taking Notes

As you read this section, look for details about factors that affect climate and vegetation. Copy the flowchart below, and write each detail under the correct heading.

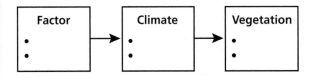

Factor	Climate	Vegetation
•	•	•
•	•	•

Target Reading Skill

Predict Making predictions about the text helps you set a purpose for reading and helps you remember what you read. Before you begin, preview the section by looking at the headings, photographs, charts, and maps. Then predict what the text might discuss about climate and vegetation. As you read this section, connect what you read to your prediction. If what you learn doesn't support your prediction, change your prediction.

Key Terms

- **rain shadow** (rayn SHAD oh) *n.* the area on the dry, sheltered side of a mountain, which receives little rainfall
- **steppes** (steps) *n.* the grasslands of fertile soil suitable for farming in Russia
- **tundra** (TUN druh) *n.* a cold, dry, treeless region covered with snow for most of the year
- **permafrost** (PUR muh frawst) *n.* a permanently frozen layer of ground below the top layer of soil

It is February in Barcelona (bahr suh LOH nuh), Spain. Twelve-year-old Pablo wakes up to the sun streaming through his bedroom window. It's another comfortable day, and the temperature is already 52°F (11°C). Pablo dresses quickly in jeans and a t-shirt and eats a breakfast of thick hot chocolate and *churros*, twisted loops of fried dough. He wants to go out and play soccer with his friends on this sunny Saturday morning.

At the very same moment, it is late afternoon in Irkutsk (ihr KOOTSK), a city in southern Siberia. Anya (AHN yuh) returns home from a day of cross-country skiing. She takes off her fur hat, gloves, boots, ski pants, and coat. The day has been sunny but cold, with an average temperature of −15°F (−26°C). Now Anya warms up with a dinner of *pelmeny* (PEL muh nee), chicken broth with meat-filled dumplings.

Boys in Spain (right) and in Siberia (below)

Achill Island, Ireland

A Wide Range of Climates

Barcelona, where Pablo lives, lies on the Mediterranean Sea. There, the summers are hot and dry, and the winters are mild. In Irkutsk, Anya's home, summers are short, and the winters are long and very cold. Temperatures in winter can drop to −50°F (−45°C). Snow covers the ground for about six months of the year.

How Oceans Affect Climate The two cities' distances from an ocean or a sea help explain their climate. Areas that are near an ocean or a sea have milder weather year-round than areas at the same latitude that are far from an ocean or sea. Look at the map below and find the Gulf Stream. Notice that it becomes the North Atlantic Current as it crosses the Atlantic Ocean. This powerful ocean current carries warm water from the tropical waters of the Gulf of Mexico to northwestern Europe. It also warms winds blowing from the west across the Atlantic Ocean. The warm waters and winds bring mild weather to much of northwestern Europe.

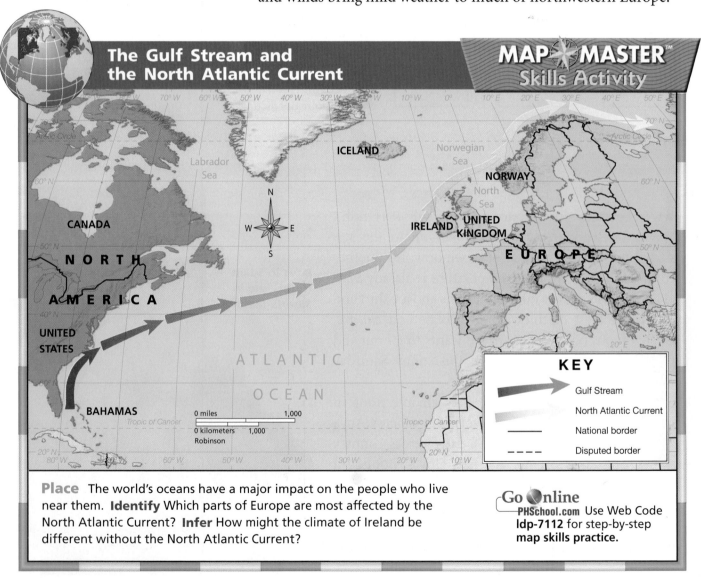

The Gulf Stream and the North Atlantic Current

MAP MASTER™ Skills Activity

KEY

→ Gulf Stream

North Atlantic Current

National border

- - - - Disputed border

Place The world's oceans have a major impact on the people who live near them. **Identify** Which parts of Europe are most affected by the North Atlantic Current? **Infer** How might the climate of Ireland be different without the North Atlantic Current?

Go Online
PHSchool.com Use Web Code **ldp-7112** for step-by-step **map skills practice.**

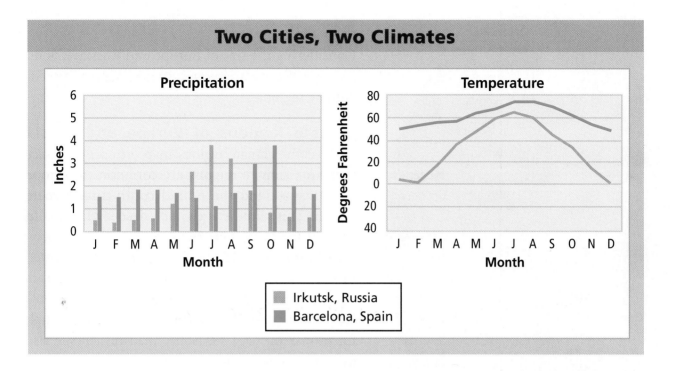

Two Cities, Two Climates

Precipitation

Inches / Month

Temperature

Degrees Fahrenheit / Month

■ Irkutsk, Russia
■ Barcelona, Spain

London, England, is farther north than any city in the continental United States, yet it has mild weather. How is this possible? The North Atlantic Current is the reason. But the most dramatic effect of the North Atlantic Current can be seen in northern Norway. Snow and ice cover most of this area in winter. Yet Norway's western coast is free of ice and snow all year. Snow melts almost as soon as it falls. Norway's ice-free ports have helped make its fishing industry one of the largest in Europe.

The ocean affects climate in other ways. Winds blowing across the ocean pick up a great deal of moisture. When these winds blow over land, they drop the moisture in the form of rain. Winds blowing from the west across the Atlantic bring a fairly wet climate to much of Western Europe.

How Mountains Affect Rainfall Mountains also affect the amount of rainfall in an area. In Europe, areas west of mountains receive heavy rainfall. These areas include parts of the United Kingdom, France, Germany, and Norway. Areas east of mountains have much lighter rainfall.

Why is this so? As winds rise up a mountain, they cool and drop their moisture. The air is dry by the time it reaches the other side of the mountain. Areas on the leeward side of a mountain, or the side away from the wind, are in a rain shadow. A **rain shadow** is an area on the dry, sheltered side of a mountain, which receives little rainfall.

✔ **Reading Check** How do mountains affect the climates of Western Europe?

■ **Graph Skills**

A city's climate is affected by its location and the geographical features that are located near it. **Identify** In which city does the temperature change most from season to season? **Draw Conclusions** What explains this city's greater range in temperature?

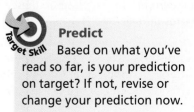

Predict
Based on what you've read so far, is your prediction on target? If not, revise or change your prediction now.

Two Very Different Climates
Much of Russia has a tundra climate, as shown in the top photo of Siberia. In contrast, London, England (at bottom), enjoys a mild climate year-round. **Infer** *How might the population densities of the places in these photos differ?*

Major Climate Regions

Considering the size of Europe and Russia, it is no surprise that this region contains many different climate regions.

Climate Regions of Europe and Russia

Look at the climate regions map on page 9. Notice that four climate regions are common to Europe and Russia. Find the humid continental climate region. This climate is characterized by long, cold winters and hot summers.

Now find Irkutsk, Russia, on the map. It is located in a huge subarctic climate region. There summers are short, and winters are long and cold. You can see how cold it is all year by looking at the temperature graph for Irkutsk on page 19. Notice that this climate also stretches across northern Europe.

Europe and Russia share two other climate regions. The northernmost areas of Europe and Russia have an arctic climate. It is very cold in these areas. On the warmest days of the short summer, temperatures sometimes barely reach 60°F (14°C). In contrast, southeastern Europe and southwestern Russia have a semiarid climate region, with hot temperatures and little rainfall.

Moderate Climate Regions of Europe
As you can see on the climate regions map, Europe has moderate climate regions that Russia does not have. For example, the marine west coast climate affects much of northwestern Europe, stretching from northern Spain to northern Norway. As you have read, winds and currents from the Atlantic Ocean keep this climate mild and rainy all year.

Another climate region surrounds the Mediterranean Sea. It is easy to remember the name of this type of climate—Mediterranean, just like the sea. Remember that Barcelona, Spain, is on the Mediterranean Sea. In the Mediterranean climate, summers are hot and dry. Winters are mild and rainy.

Finally, a band of humid subtropical climate is located in southern Europe. Warm temperatures and year-round rainfall characterize this climate.

✓ Reading Check What two climate regions are found in Europe but not Russia?

Natural Vegetation Regions

The natural vegetation, or plant life, of Europe and Russia is as varied as the climate. Vegetation regions are related to climate regions. Vegetation in Europe and Russia varies from ice cap to desert. However, the main vegetation regions are forest, grassland, tundra, and Mediterranean. Compare the climate map on page 9 with the natural vegetation map below to see how the climate and vegetation regions overlap.

Forests of Europe and Russia The natural vegetation of much of Europe is forest. However, most of these forests have been cleared to make way for farms, factories, and cities. In northern Europe, you can still find large coniferous (koh NIF ur us) forests, which have evergreen trees with cones that carry and protect the seeds. Deciduous (dih SIJ oo us) forests, which contain trees that lose their leaves in fall, cover most of Western and Central Europe.

Russia is also heavily forested. One forest, called the taiga (TY guh), covers more than 4 million square miles (10 million square kilometers). Located in Siberia, it is the largest forest in the world.

Links Across
The World

The Boreal Forest The boreal forest includes one third of all Earth's forests. The name comes from an ancient Greek god named Boreas, the god of the north wind. Russia's taiga makes up half of the boreal forest. The rest is located in the northern parts of Canada, Alaska, China, Mongolia, Scandinavia, and Scotland. Boreal forests play an important role in the environment, by filtering out carbon dioxide and other gases from the atmosphere.

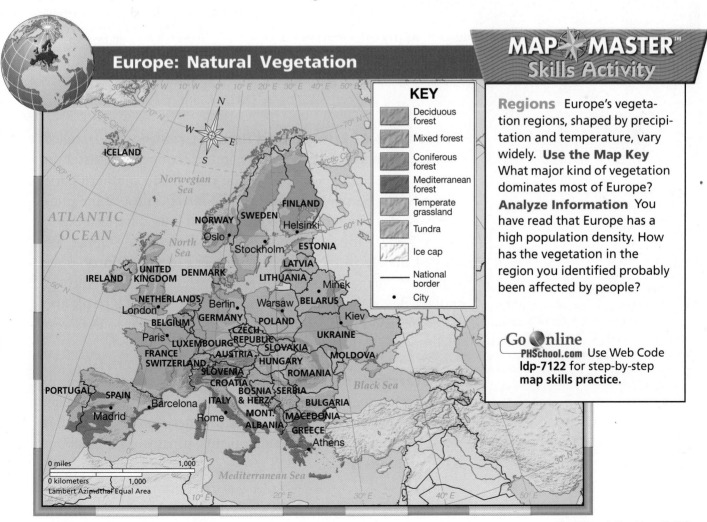

Europe: Natural Vegetation

KEY
- Deciduous forest
- Mixed forest
- Coniferous forest
- Mediterranean forest
- Temperate grassland
- Tundra
- Ice cap
- National border
- • City

MAP MASTER™
Skills Activity

Regions Europe's vegetation regions, shaped by precipitation and temperature, vary widely. **Use the Map Key** What major kind of vegetation dominates most of Europe? **Analyze Information** You have read that Europe has a high population density. How has the vegetation in the region you identified probably been affected by people?

Go Online
PHSchool.com Use Web Code **ldp-7122** for step-by-step **map skills practice.**

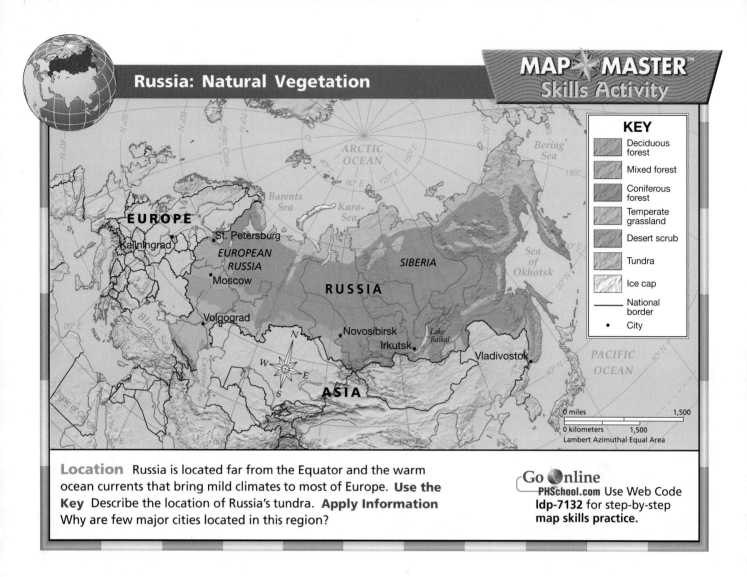

KEY

Deciduous forest

Mixed forest

Coniferous forest

Temperate grassland

Desert scrub

Tundra

Ice cap

National border

• City

Location Russia is located far from the Equator and the warm ocean currents that bring mild climates to most of Europe. **Use the Key** Describe the location of Russia's tundra. **Apply Information** Why are few major cities located in this region?

Go Online
PHSchool.com Use Web Code **ldp-7132** for step-by-step **map skills practice.**

Grasslands of Europe and Russia Grasslands, also called prairies, are a major vegetation region in Europe and Russia. In Europe, grasslands once covered the central and southern parts of the North European Plain. Like the forests, most of the prairies have also disappeared. Today, the land is used for farming.

In Russia, the grasslands are called **steppes.** Steppes are located mainly in the southwestern parts of the country. They contain a mix of grasses and low-growing vegetation such as mosses. Below that vegetation, the soil of the steppes is fertile and black and good for farming. The steppes are similar to the Great Plains of the United States.

Mediterranean Regions of Europe Just as the area of southern Europe near the Mediterranean Sea has its own climate, it also has its own vegetation region. Mediterranean vegetation is a mix of trees, scrub, and smaller plants, usually less than about 8 feet (2.5 meters) tall.

Tundra of Europe and Russia Northern parts of Europe—including northern Scandinavia and Iceland—as well as northern Russia have a tundra vegetation region. **Tundra** is a cold, dry, treeless region that is covered with snow for most of the year. There winters last as long as nine months and the ground contains **permafrost,** a layer of permanently frozen ground below the top layer of soil. During the brief season when the top surface of the permafrost thaws, grasses, mosses, and other plant life grow quickly. Few people live in the tundra region.

✓ **Reading Check** Where is the world's largest forest located?

Flowers bloom during the short Siberian summer.

Section 2 Assessment

Key Terms
Review the key terms at the beginning of this section. Use each term in a sentence that explains its meaning.

Target Reading Skill
What did you predict about this section? How did your prediction guide your reading?

Comprehension and Critical Thinking
1. (a) Describe How do oceans affect climate?
(b) Identify Effects How does the North Atlantic Current affect northern Europe?

2. (a) Recall What are the major climate regions of Europe and Russia?
(b) Draw Conclusions Why are summers in Barcelona, Spain, hot and dry?
3. (a) List What are the natural vegetation regions of Europe and Russia?
(b) Summarize How are vegetation regions and climate regions related?
(c) Generalize What geographic features might lead someone to settle in Europe, rather than in Russia?

Writing Activity
Suppose you are planning a trip to one of the cities mentioned in this section. Decide what time of year you would want to go. Based on the climate of the city, make a list of the clothes that you would pack. Then write a brief paragraph explaining why you would pack the items on your list.

For: An activity about Ireland
Visit: PHSchool.com
Web Code: ldd-7101

Using a Precipitation Map

Suppose your teacher asks you to write a report that compares the physical geography of the United States to that of Russia. You know that both countries are huge. You also know that physical geography includes many different elements, such as climate, landforms, vegetation, and precipitation—moisture in the form of rain or snow. You realize it would take a great deal of time to find information in each of these categories for both countries.

One good way to find all the information you need is to look at a set of special-purpose maps. A special-purpose map shows information about a certain topic. A precipitation map, for example, shows the total amount of precipitation an area receives in a year. By looking at a world precipitation map, you can quickly compare the United States' precipitation to that of Russia.

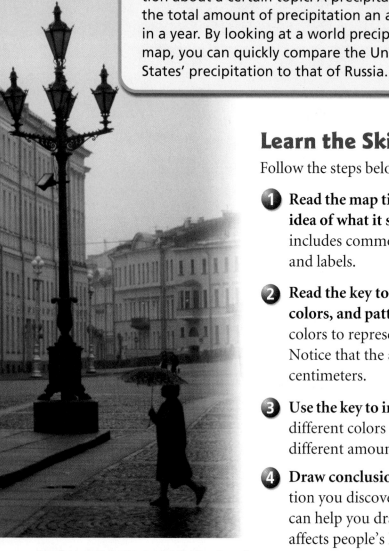

Learn the Skill

Follow the steps below to learn how to use a precipitation map.

1 **Read the map title and look over the map to get a general idea of what it shows.** Notice that a precipitation map includes common map features, such as a title, key, scale, and labels.

2 **Read the key to understand how the map uses symbols, colors, and patterns.** A precipitation map often shows colors to represent different amounts of precipitation. Notice that the amounts are indicated in both inches and centimeters.

3 **Use the key to interpret the map.** Look on the map for the different colors shown in the key. Notice where areas with different amounts of precipitation are located on the map.

4 **Draw conclusions about what the map shows.** Information you discover when you analyze a precipitation map can help you draw conclusions about how precipitation affects people's lives.

A rainy day in St. Petersburg, Russia

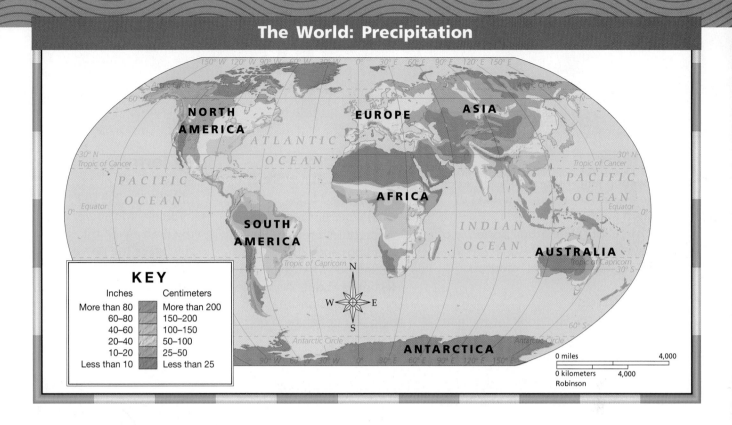

The World: Precipitation

KEY

Inches		Centimeters
More than 80		More than 200
60–80		150–200
40–60		100–150
20–40		50–100
10–20		25–50
Less than 10		Less than 25

0 miles 4,000
0 kilometers 4,000
Robinson

Practice the Skill

Use the precipitation map above to complete the following steps.

1 Become familiar with the map. What is the map's title? In general, what does it show?

2 Look at the key to see how different amounts of precipitation are shown. Familiarize yourself with the colors on the key.

3 Look for areas on the map with different amounts of precipitation. Because you want to compare the United States with Russia, find those two regions within the continents of North America, Asia, and Europe on the map. (If you need help finding the areas of the two countries, compare this map with the World: Political map in the Atlas).

4 Study the map. Use the information on it to compare precipitation in the United States and Russia. Which country has more variation in precipitation? Which country is generally drier? Write a conclusion that summarizes your comparison.

Apply the Skill

Turn to Section 2 of Chapter 1 and look at the Europe: Natural Vegetation map on page 21. Use the steps of this skill to analyze and draw conclusions about this special-purpose map.

Prepare to Read

Objectives
In this section you will
1. Learn about the natural resources of Western Europe.
2. Find out about the natural resources of Eastern Europe.
3. Examine Russia's natural resources.

Taking Notes
As you read this section, look for the natural resources located in Europe and Russia. Copy the Venn diagram below, and record your findings in it.

Natural Resources of Europe and Russia

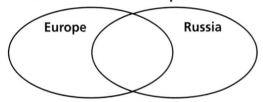

Europe   Russia

Target Reading Skill
Preview and Ask Questions Before you read this section, preview the headings and illustrations to find out what the section is about. Write one or two questions that will help you understand or remember something important in the section. Then read this section to answer your questions.

Key Terms
- **loess** (LOH es) *n.* a type of rich, dustlike soil
- **hydroelectric power** (hy droh ee LEK trik POW ur) *n.* the power generated by water-driven turbines
- **fossil fuel** (FAHS ul FYOO ul) *n.* a source of energy that forms from the remains of ancient plants and animals

A North Sea oil rig

How would you like to live and work on an ocean? Oil workers on the North Sea do just that. Their job is to pump oil from deep beneath the ocean floor. They work on a tower called an oil rig anchored over an oil field. Oil rig workers live and work as if they were on a ship. But they cannot seek the safety of a harbor when a big storm is stirring.

The North Sea, located between the United Kingdom and mainland northwestern Europe, sometimes has violent weather. Severe storms with winds of as much as 100 miles (160 kilometers) an hour are common. Waves as high as 90 feet (27 meters) batter oil rig platforms. Despite the harsh conditions, crews work around the clock to operate, inspect, and repair the rigs.

Making sure a rig operates properly is a very important job. The United Kingdom and other nations around the North Sea depend on oil and natural gas from the rigs.

Resources of Western Europe

Western Europe is a wealthy region and a world leader in economic development. Part of this wealth and success comes from Western Europe's rich and varied supply of natural resources. These natural resources include fertile soil, water, and fuels.

Fertile Soil Soil is one of Earth's most important natural resources because it is needed to grow food. Much of Western Europe is covered with rich, fertile soil, especially the region's broad river valleys.

Wind has helped create the fertile soil of the North European Plain. Over thousands of years, winds have deposited **loess** (LOH es), a type of rich, dustlike soil. This soil, combined with plentiful rain and moderate temperatures, provides for a long growing season. These conditions allow European farmers to produce abundant crops.

Tulips brighten the landscape at a flower farm in the Netherlands.

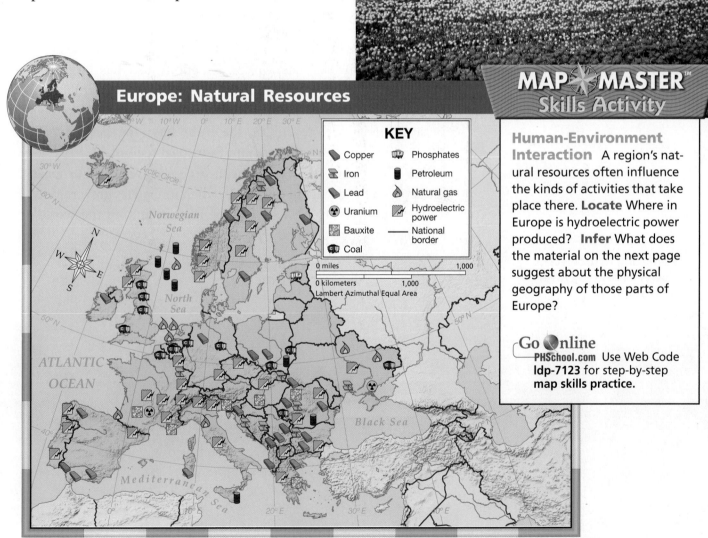

Europe: Natural Resources

KEY

Copper	Phosphates
Iron	Petroleum
Lead	Natural gas
Uranium	Hydroelectric power
Bauxite	National border
Coal	

0 miles 1,000
0 kilometers 1,000
Lambert Azimuthal Equal Area

MAP MASTER™
Skills Activity

Human-Environment Interaction A region's natural resources often influence the kinds of activities that take place there. **Locate** Where in Europe is hydroelectric power produced? **Infer** What does the material on the next page suggest about the physical geography of those parts of Europe?

Go Online
PHSchool.com Use Web Code ldp-7123 for step-by-step map skills practice.

Abundant Water Another important resource in Western Europe is water. People need water for drinking. Water nourishes crops. Water can also be used to produce electricity for industries and homes. To be used as a source of energy, water must flow very quickly. The force of water from a waterfall or a dam can be used to spin machines called turbines (TUR bynz). Spinning turbines generate, or create, electric power. Power generated by water-driven turbines is called **hydroelectric power** (hy droh ee LEK trik POW ur).

Many countries in Western Europe have favorable locations for the development of hydroelectric power. Some rivers that flow down through the mountains have been dammed to generate hydroelectric power. Norway gets almost all of its electric power from water. Hydroelectric power also keeps factories in Sweden, Switzerland, Austria, Spain, Scotland, and Portugal operating.

Fuel Deposits Like flowing water, fuel deposits are another source of energy for many industries. **Fossil fuels** are sources of energy that formed from the remains of ancient plants and animals. Fossil fuels include natural gas, oil, and coal.

Both the United Kingdom and Norway have large deposits of oil and natural gas. The United Kingdom also has large coal fields, as does Germany. The largest coal deposits in Germany are located in the Ruhr (ROOR), a region named for the Ruhr River. Because of its fuel resources, the Ruhr has long been one of Western Europe's most important industrial regions.

An abundance of coal and iron ore gave Western European industries a head start in the 1800s, when industries grew rapidly. Today, countries in Western Europe remain among the world's leading industrial powers.

Producing hydroelectric power on the Tay River in Scotland

✓ **Reading Check** How is hydroelectric power generated?

Resources of Eastern Europe

Now, shift your view from Western to Eastern Europe. Turn back to the map on page 27 showing Europe's natural resources. Notice that Eastern Europe has resources similar to those of Western Europe. Place a finger on the area just west of 50°N and 20°E. This is in southern Poland, on the border of the Czech Republic. This area is called Silesia (sy LEE zhuh). Large deposits of coal there have helped to make Silesia a major industrial center.

Ukraine (yoo KRAYN), a large country in Eastern Europe, has coal deposits, too. It also has other fuel resources—especially oil and natural gas. However, the most important resource is probably its soil. The region's black earth is very fertile. Not surprisingly, farming is an extremely important activity in Ukraine.

Eastern Europe has fewer water resources than does Western Europe. However, the nations of the Balkan Peninsula produce a large amount of hydroelectric power.

✓ **Reading Check** What is Silesia, and where is it?

Energy and Land Resources
The photo at the left shows miners on the job in a Silesian coal mine. Above, a Ukrainian woman harvests flowers to use in making perfume.
Compare and Contrast *What do mining and farming have in common? How are they different?*

Resources of Russia

Russia has a much greater supply of natural resources than does the United States. The United States has used its resources to become the richest nation on Earth. You might wonder why Russia has not done the same.

One answer is that Russia's harsh climate, huge size, and few navigable rivers have made it difficult to turn the country's resources into wealth. In addition, Russia has relatively few places that are suited for farming. Much of Russia lacks one or more of the key elements for farming: favorable climate, good soil, and plentiful water.

A tugboat pushes a barge loaded with logs along a Russian river.

Russia: Natural Resources

MAP MASTER
Skills Activity

KEY

Symbol	Resource	Symbol	Resource
Gold	Iron	Tin	Tungsten
Coal	Diamonds	Natural gas	National border
Copper	Lead	Nickel	Bauxite
Phosphates	Petroleum	Hydroelectric power	

Place Russia has some of the world's largest deposits of many energy and mineral resources. **Note** How many different resources are located in Siberia? **Predict** Study Siberia's geography. What challenges might Russians face in making use of Siberia's resources?

Go Online
PHSchool.com Use Web Code ldp-7123 for step-by-step **map skills practice.**

From Plants to Fossil Fuel

1. Peat is made of partially decayed plant material. ▶

2. Over millions of years, material ▶ built up over ancient peat deposits. The pressure of this material gradually changed the peat into brown coal.

◀ **3.** Continuing pressure gradually turned brown coal into soft coal. Soft coal is the most common coal found on Earth. It is often used in industry.

Fossil Fuels and Minerals Russia has the largest reserves, or available supply, of natural gas in the world. It is also one of the world's five leading oil producers. Scientists estimate that the country has about one third of the world's coal reserves. In addition, Russia has huge deposits of minerals, including cobalt, chromium, copper, and gold.

Russia also has the world's largest reserves of iron ore, which is used to make steel. Many of these iron ore deposits are in the part of Russia that is on the continent of Europe. That is one reason why most of Russia's industry is west of the Ural Mountains. Fueled by its natural resources, Russian factories produce automobiles, cloth, machinery, computers, and chemicals.

Forest, Fishing, and Energy Resources Russia has the world's largest forest reserves. Wood harvested from these forests is used to make paper and pulp, and it also supplies wood for houses and furniture.

Because of Russia's location on the Pacific Ocean, fish provide another abundant resource. Russians also fish the Black and Caspian seas, as well as the country's many inland lakes. The fishing industry is an important part of Russia's economy.

Finally, Russia has ample energy resources. It uses much of its fossil fuel resources to produce electricity. In addition, many Russian rivers are dammed to generate electricity in hydroelectric plants. Russia is one of the world's largest producers of electricity.

■ Diagram Skills

A man in Ireland cuts pieces of peat from the ground. **Explain** If this peat stayed in the ground, how long would it take to turn into brown coal? **Apply Information** Explain why coal is a nonrenewable resource, using information from the diagram.

Preview and Ask Questions
Ask a question that will help you learn something important from this section. Then read the section, and answer your question.

Breaking Up Old Ships
When ships are no longer seaworthy, they are broken apart like this oil tanker in the harbor of Murmansk, Russia. Breaking up ships often causes environmental and health problems. **Infer** *What specific problems might breaking up an oil tanker cause?*

Challenges to Using Russia's Resources Most of Russia's deposits of oil, natural gas, and coal are located in Siberia. Three fourths of Russia's forests are located there, too. These forests contain half of the world's reserves of softwood timber. However, Siberia is far from the population and industrial centers of the country.

Russia's huge size presents a major challenge to transporting Siberian resources to areas where they are needed. Except for the Volga, Russia's rivers are not very useful for transportation. Siberia's rivers do not flow toward Russia's most important cities. Instead, they flow north into the Arctic Ocean. In spite of these problems and the bitter-cold winter weather, Russia has found ways to move resources from Siberia. Pipelines carry oil and natural gas, and railroads transport coal to European Russia.

Extracting Russia's resources has created a new challenge—protecting the environment. Some of the world's worst cases of pollution are found in Russia, especially Siberia. Nuclear waste has been dumped into rivers for 40 years. Air pollution from factories is very severe. Besides finding ways to develop its valuable resources, Russia must also consider how to restore polluted areas.

 Reading Check **Where are most of Russia's oil, natural gas, and coal deposits located?**

Section 3 Assessment

Key Terms
Review the key terms at the beginning of this section. Use each term in a sentence that explains its meaning.

Target Reading Skill
Look at the list of questions you asked. Which ones helped you learn and remember something from this section?

Comprehension and Critical Thinking
1. (a) List Name Western Europe's major natural resources.

(b) Summarize How is water used as a natural resource in Western Europe?
2. (a) Recall Which important natural resources are located in Ukraine?
(b) Draw Conclusions Why is farming important to Ukraine?
3. (a) List Name Russia's major natural resources.
(b) Compare and Contrast How do Western Europe and Russia differ in their use of natural resources?
(c) Draw Conclusions Why is Russia not as wealthy as Western Europe?

Writing Activity
What do you think is the most important natural resource in Europe and Russia? What makes that resource so important? Write a paragraph explaining your choice. Be sure to include a main idea statement in your paragraph.

Writing Tip Before you begin writing, list all the natural resources discussed in the section. Then choose which you think is most important.

Review and Assessment

◆ Chapter Summary

Section 1: Land and Water

- Europe and Russia are part of Eurasia, the world's largest landmass.
- Both Europe and Russia have plains, uplands, and mountains.
- Europe's major rivers are the Rhine and the Danube, and Russia's is the Volga.

Section 2: Climate and Vegetation

- Oceans and mountains both affect the climates of Europe and Russia.
- The climate regions of Europe and Russia range from Mediterranean to subarctic.
- The natural vegetation of Europe and Russia is as varied as its climate and includes forest, grassland, and tundra.

London

Ukraine

Section 3: Resources and Land Use

- The resources of Western Europe include fertile soil, water, and fossil fuels.
- Eastern Europe has resources similar to those of Western Europe, including coal, oil, and natural gas.
- Russia has abundant mineral, energy, and other resources, with the majority of these resources located in Siberia.

◆ Key Terms

Use each key term below in a sentence that shows the meaning of the term.

1. population density
2. navigable
3. peninsula
4. plateau
5. tributary
6. rain shadow
7. loess
8. tundra
9. permafrost
10. steppes
11. hydroelectric power
12. fossil fuel

◆ Comprehension and Critical Thinking

13. (a) Identify Which areas of Europe and Russia are the most densely populated?
(b) Summarize What physical features encouraged people to settle in those areas?

14. (a) Define What are the European Central Uplands?
(b) List Name two uses of these uplands.
(c) Contrast How do the Central Uplands differ from the North European Plain?

15. (a) Name List two factors that affect the climates of Europe and Russia.
(b) Summarize What effect do large bodies of water have on climate in Europe and Russia?

16. (a) Describe Explain what a Mediterranean climate is.
(b) Compare and Contrast How is a Mediterranean climate similar to or different from a subarctic climate?

17. (a) Identify What are the major natural resources of Western Europe, of Eastern Europe, and of Russia?
(b) Predict What factors might influence how well a river can be used to transport resources?
(c) Identify Cause and Effect Why are Western Europe's natural resources more fully developed than Russia's natural resources?

18. (a) List Name three kinds of fossil fuels.
(b) Draw Conclusions How does the development of natural resources affect the way that people live?

◆ Skills Practice

Using a Precipitation Map In the Skills for Life activity in this chapter, you learned how to use a precipitation map. The steps you followed to learn this skill can be applied to other kinds of special purpose maps.

Review the steps you used to learn the skill. Then turn to the map titled Europe: Natural Resources on page 27. Use the map title and key to read and interpret the map. Then write a conclusion about the information the map contains.

◆ Writing Activity: Geography

Suppose you are visiting a fourth-grade classroom. You have been asked to report to the students on Europe and Russia's geography. Write a brief report on this subject. To get started, write down the various kinds of landforms and bodies of water that are discussed in the chapter. Do the same for the human and natural resources of Europe and Russia. Then explain in your report how life is similar and different for the people who live in different regions of Europe and Russia.

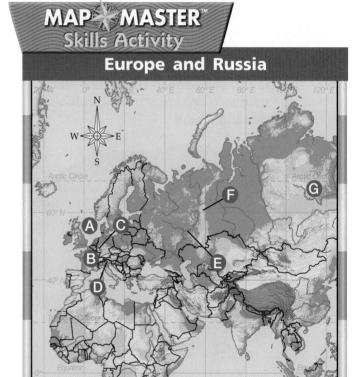

MAP MASTER™ Skills Activity

Europe and Russia

Place Location For each place listed below, write the letter from the map that shows its location.

1. France
2. Ural Mountains
3. Alps
4. Siberia
5. Rhine River
6. Volga River
7. North Sea

Go Online
PHSchool.com Use Web Code ldp-7183 for an interactive map.

Standardized Test Prep

Test-Taking Tips

Some questions on standardized tests ask you to make mental maps. Read the passage below. Then follow the tips to answer the sample question.

> Ben is playing a trivia game. One of the geography questions asks, "Which mountain range divides Russia between two continents, Europe and Asia?" What is the correct answer?

Choose the letter that best answers the question.

A Kjolen Mountains

B Ural Mountains

~~C Pyrenees~~

~~D Alps~~

TIP Rule out choices that do not make sense. Then choose the best answer from the remaining choices.

Think It Through You can rule out the Alps and Pyrenees because both are inside Europe. Which sounds more familiar to you, the Ural Mountains or the Kjolen Mountains? The correct answer is an important range and is likely to be a name you have heard. As it turns out, the Kjolen Mountains are in Scandinavia—in northern Europe. The correct answer is B.

TIP Try to picture a physical map of Europe and Russia. Then try to place each of these mountain ranges on your mental map.

Practice Questions

Use the tips above and other tips in this book to help you answer the following questions.

1. Which Russian feature covers more than 4 million square miles (10 million square kilometers)?

   A grasslands   B taiga

   C polders   D tundra

2. Because of its location near the Mediterranean Sea, Barcelona's summers are

   A mild and wet.

   B cold and snowy.

   C hot and dry.

   D short and wet.

3. The climate of the northernmost areas of Europe and Russia is called

   A marine west coast.

   B Mediterranean.

   C humid continental.

   D arctic.

4. What is the location of Siberia relative to that of Spain?

   A northeast

   B southeast

   C northwest

   D west

5. The major vegetation region of Europe and Russia that is now mainly used for farming is

   A grasslands.

   B tundra.

   C taiga.

   D Mediterranean.

Go Online
PHSchool.com

Use Web Code **lda-7101**
for a **Chapter 1 self-test.**

Chapter Preview

This chapter presents the history of Europe and Russia and shows how that history affects the region to this day.

Section 1
From Ancient Greece to the Middle Ages

Section 2
Renaissance and the Age of Revolution

Section 3
Industrial Revolution and Nationalism

Section 4
Imperial Russia to the Soviet Union

Section 5
The European Union

Target Reading Skill

Clarifying Meaning In this chapter you will focus on clarifying, or better understanding, the meaning of what you read.

▶ A bridge built in the 1100s still spans the Rhone River in Avignon, France.

MAP MASTER™
Skills Activity

ARCTIC   PEOPLES

ICELAND
(Norway)

NOVGOROD

NORWAY

SWEDEN

TEUTONIC
ORDER

SMALL RUSSIAN
STATES

GOLDEN HORDE

ATLANTIC
OCEAN

SCOTLAND

North
Sea

DENMARK

LITHUANIA

IRELAND
(England)

ENGLAND

POLAND

Caspian Sea

WALES
(England)

HOLY ROMAN
EMPIRE

FRANCE

HUNGARY

Black Sea

NAVARRE

GASCONY
(England)

VENICE

PAPAL
STATES

SERBIA

BULGARIA

BYZANTINE
EMPIRE

PORTUGAL

ARAGON

NAPLES

SARDINIA
(Aragon)

SMALL GREEK
STATES

CASTILE

MALLORCA

SICILY
(Aragon)

CRETE (Venice)

GRANADA

Mediterranean Sea

KEY

— Political border

0 miles   1,000

0 kilometers   1,000

Lambert Azimuthal Equal Area

Place In 1300, Europe was divided into a number
of states and kingdoms. **Compare and Contrast**
Compare this map with the Europe: Political map in the
Atlas. Which countries' political borders look similar in
1300 and today? Which are different? Which countries
did not exist in 1300? **Analyze Information** How can
physical geography help explain why some countries'
borders have changed little?

Go Online
PHSchool.com Use Web Code
ldp-7211 for step-by-step
map skills practice.

Section 1

From Ancient Greece to the Middle Ages

Prepare to Read

Objectives

In this section you will

1. Learn how the heritage of ancient Greece influences life today.
2. Discover the glory of the ancient Roman Empire.
3. Learn about Europe in the Middle Ages.

Taking Notes

As you read this section, look for information about ancient times and the Middle Ages. Copy the outline below and record your findings in it.

> I. The Greek heritage
> A. Democracy
> B.
> II.

Target Reading Skill

Reread Rereading is a strategy that can help you to understand words and ideas in the text. If you do not understand a certain passage, reread it to look for connections among the words and sentences. For example, rereading the second paragraph below can make it clear that marathons today are modeled after an event from ancient times.

Key Terms

- **Middle Ages** (MID ul AY juz) *n.* the time between the ancient and modern times, about A.D. 500–1500
- **democracy** (dih MAHK ruh see) *n.* a kind of government in which citizens govern themselves
- **city-state** (SIH tee stayt) *n.* a city with its own government that was both a city and an independent state
- **feudalism** (FYOOD ul iz um) *n.* a system in which land was owned by lords, but held by vassals in return for their loyalty

Runners beginning the Boston Marathon

Every April thousands of people from around the world gather in a small Massachusetts town. At noon, they begin a marathon race that requires great strength and willpower. The race ends in the city of Boston, some 26 miles (42 kilometers) away.

The Boston Marathon was inspired by an event that is said to have happened 2,500 years ago in the ancient Greek city of Athens. In 490 B.C., the people of Athens were at war with the Persians. The Athenians defeated the Persians at the Battle of Marathon. To announce their victory, an Athenian soldier named Pheidippides (fuh DIP ih deez) ran all the way to Athens, about 25 miles (40 kilometers) away. Pheidippides shouted, "Rejoice, we conquer!" as he entered the city. Then he died of exhaustion.

The Greeks loved the story, and people all over the world still run marathons. When they do, they show how history lives on. This chapter discusses three periods in the history of Europe and Russia—ancient times, modern times, and the Middle Ages, or the time between the ancient and modern times. We will see how the past affects the present in Europe and Russia.

The Greek Heritage

The Athenians and other ancient Greeks were Europe's first great philosophers, historians, poets, and writers. They invented new ideas about how the world worked and how people should live.

The Growth of Democracy One such idea was democracy, or a kind of government in which citizens, not a king or other ruler, govern themselves. In ancient times, Greece had more than a hundred city-states, or cities with their own governments that were both cities and independent states. The Greek city-states had several different kinds of government. Many of them were democracies.

One of the most famous democratic Greek city-states was Athens. Every citizen there had the right to vote on laws and government policies, or the methods and plans a government uses to do its work. Citizens were either elected or chosen at random for government positions.

Democracy was a fresh idea for the Greeks. However, it was not the same as the democracy we practice today. Most Greeks were not citizens. Only freeborn males whose fathers held Athenian citizenship were citizens of Athens. Women, slaves, freed slaves, non-Greeks, and people whose families came from other parts of Greece were not citizens. They could not vote. Still, the Greek idea that citizens should have a voice in their own government had a strong influence on people in later times.

The Golden Age of Athens Democracy reached its highest point in Athens from about 479 to 431 B.C., during Athens' "Golden Age." During that period, the arts, literature, and philosophy also flourished. The Greeks studied the nature of plants, animals, and the human body. In the process, they developed ways of thinking that still influence life today.

■ **Chart Skills**

Greek ideas that developed over two thousand years ago still influence societies around the world today. **Note** When were democratic ideals of government formed in Athens? **Apply Information** Which of these ideals can be seen in today's United States government?

The Legacy of the Greeks

Topic	Influence on Modern Society
Drama	Aristotle created the rules for drama in his work *The Poetics*. Today, playwrights and movie scriptwriters still use his ideas.
Architecture	Many modern building designs reflect the common Greek styles known as Ionic, Doric, and Corinthian.
Science	The ancient Greeks introduced many principles of modern medicine, physics, biology, and mathematics.
Politics	The democratic ideals of government by the people, trial by jury, and equality under the law were formed in Athens around 500 B.C.
History	Herodotus collected information from people who remembered the events of the Persian wars. This method of research set the standard for the way history is recorded today.

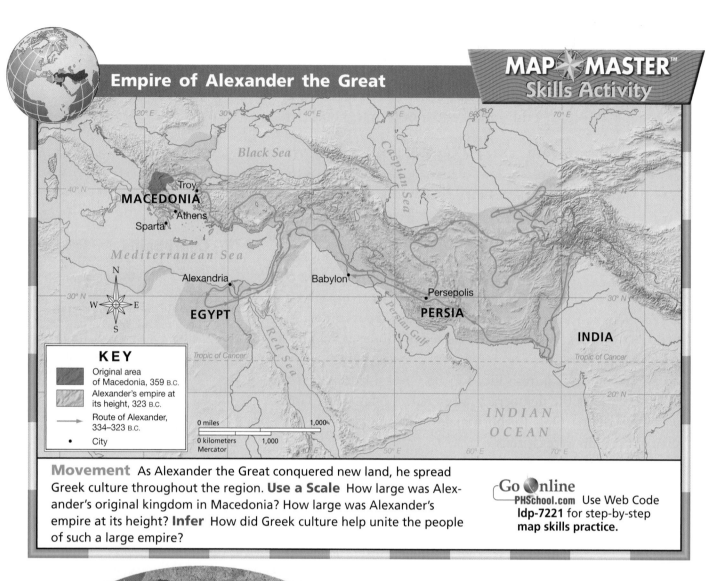

MAP MASTER™
Skills Activity

Black Sea

Caspian Sea

Troy

MACEDONIA

Athens

Sparta

Mediterranean Sea

N
W E
S

Alexandria

Babylon

Persepolis

EGYPT

PERSIA

Persian Gulf

Red Sea

Tropic of Cancer

INDIA

Tropic of Cancer

INDIAN
OCEAN

20° N

KEY

Original area
of Macedonia, 359 B.C.

Alexander's empire at
its height, 323 B.C.

Route of Alexander,
334–323 B.C.

City

0 miles   1,000

0 kilometers   1,000
Mercator

Movement As Alexander the Great conquered new land, he spread Greek culture throughout the region. **Use a Scale** How large was Alexander's original kingdom in Macedonia? How large was Alexander's empire at its height? **Infer** How did Greek culture help unite the people of such a large empire?

Go Online
PHSchool.com Use Web Code
ldp-7221 for step-by-step
map skills practice.

This ancient Italian mosaic shows Alexander the Great in battle.

The Spread of Greek Ideas A young man named Alexander, later called Alexander the Great, helped spread the ideas of the Greeks. At age 20, he became king of Macedonia (mas uh DOH nee uh) in northern Greece. But he was not satisfied with his small kingdom. In 334 B.C., Alexander set out to conquer the world. Within only ten years, he had conquered an empire almost as great in size as the United States is today. An empire is a collection of lands ruled by a single government. The map above shows Alexander's travels and the lands he conquered.

In all his new lands, Alexander established Greek cities, the Greek language, and Greek ideas. At the time of his death in 323 B.C., Greek culture linked the entire Mediterranean world. The people who next ruled the region, the Romans, also borrowed much from the Greeks.

✓ **Reading Check** What is an empire?

The Glory of Ancient Rome

Have you ever heard someone say, "All roads lead to Rome" or "Rome was not built in a day"? These expressions refer to the Roman Empire. At its peak, the Roman Empire covered a huge area, and Romans built magnificent cities and structures.

About 50,000 miles (80,500 kilometers) of hard-surfaced roads linked the cities of the Roman Empire. The Roman system of roads was one of the most outstanding transportation networks ever built. Constructed more than 2,000 years ago, many of these roads are still in use today.

The Romans also built aqueducts, or canals that carried water to the cities from distant sources. Like Roman roads, some of these aqueducts are still in use.

Roman Art and Architecture
The Colosseum (above) held as many as 50,000 people for public events. The sculpture below is of Rome's first emperor, Augustus. **Conclude** *What does the art a society produces tell you about its culture and wealth?*

The Pax Romana The Romans began building their empire soon after the death of Alexander the Great. The first emperor of Rome, Augustus, took control in 27 B.C. This began the *Pax Romana* (paks roh MAH nah), which means "Roman peace." It lasted for about 200 years. During the Pax Romana, Rome was the most powerful state in Europe and in the Mediterranean. With Rome in control, these regions remained stable.

Roman Law One of Rome's greatest gifts to the world was a system of written laws. Roman lawmakers were careful and organized. They did not rely on word of mouth to pass their laws from one generation to the next. Instead, they wrote the laws down. When a judge made a decision, he based it on written law. His decision was also put in writing to guide other judges. After a while, the law became so complex that it was difficult to learn. Various groups were appointed to gather the laws together into an organized system. Today, the legal system of almost every European country reflects the organization of ancient Roman law.

Roman laws protected all citizens. At first, citizens included only free people who lived in Rome. In time, the term came to include people all over the empire. Roman laws thus protected the rights of all citizens, not just the powerful and wealthy. Modern laws and government are based on this idea.

Christian Art
This mosaic of Jesus, at the right, decorates the dome of a monastery in Daphni, Greece. Symbols of Christianity—a cross and a fish—are shown below. Early Christians used the symbol of the fish because each letter in the Greek word for fish, *ichthys*, stood for a word describing Jesus. **Analyze Information** *Why might early Christians have depended on symbols to express their faith, rather than doing so openly?*

Beginnings of Christianity Roman emperors allowed a certain amount of religious freedom within the empire. Jews were allowed to practice their religion as long as they obeyed Roman law. For centuries, the Jewish people had believed that God would send them a messiah, or a savior, who would free them from outside rule. Many Jews were content to cooperate with the Romans, but others began resisting Roman rule. In present-day Israel, the Romans crushed their attempts to revolt.

In about A.D. 30 a spiritual leader, Jesus of Nazareth, traveled and preached throughout the region. His followers believed that God was acting through him. They later called him Jesus Christ. *Christ* means "someone anointed, or a savior sent by God." After the Romans put Jesus to death, his followers began spreading his teachings. They eventually became known as Christians. At first, they were treated poorly by Roman emperors.

After three centuries, Christianity had become so strong that a Roman emperor, Constantine, became a Christian. Within decades, it became the official religion of the Roman Empire. Many people who had suffered under Roman rule turned to the church for comfort at this time.

The Decline of Rome Over time, it grew more difficult to govern the huge Roman Empire. Germanic invaders outside the empire broke through Roman lines of defense. More than once, they terrorized and looted Rome itself.

Reread
Reread the paragraphs under Beginnings of Christianity to understand the phrase "spiritual leader."

To fight the invaders, the empire needed more soldiers. The government raised taxes to pay for the warfare. This hurt the empire's economy. The empire had also grown too large for one person to govern, so it was divided into two empires, one in the eastern Mediterranean and one in the west. The eastern empire remained strong, but the western one continued to weaken. In the A.D. 450s, invaders attacked Rome itself. Finally in A.D. 476, the western Roman Empire collapsed.

√ Reading Check **What was the Pax Romana?**

Europe in the Middle Ages

The collapse of the Roman Empire in western Europe led to a time of uncertainty. The legal system of the Roman Empire no longer protected people. The invading peoples did gradually settle down and establish kingdoms. But no kingdom was able to provide unity and security like the Roman Empire. Europe entered a long period of turmoil and warfare. Government, law, and trade broke down.

Eventually, a new structure of European society arose to provide order and security. It was based on a new political system and the Roman Catholic Church. The Roman Catholic Church was the name for the Christian church in the former western Roman Empire.

Feudalism To bring about order, people in western Europe developed feudalism, or a system in which land was owned by kinds of lords, but held by vassals in return for their loyalty. In each country, the king held the highest position. His greatest obligation was to provide security for his kingdom, which meant that he needed soldiers to build an army. Nobles provided the king with knights and foot soldiers. In exchange for knights, soldiers, and the nobles' loyalty, the king—also called a lord—gave land to the nobles—also called vassals.

The noble landholders needed people to work their estates, or manors. They gave peasants the right to farm their land in exchange for a large portion of their crops and any other income from the land. In exchange, they maintained order, enforced laws, and protected the peasants. This economic system is called manorialism. It provided a basis for the feudal political system.

The peasants who worked the land were called serfs. Serfs were not free people. They were bound to the land and could not leave without their lord's permission. But serfs were not slaves. They could not be sold away from the land.

Details from books and calendars dating from the 1400s show farming scenes at medieval manors.

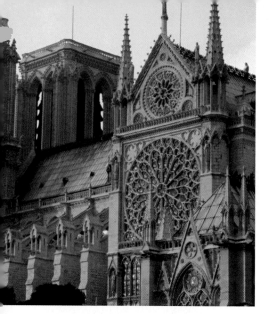

Cathedral of Notre Dame
The Notre Dame cathedral in Paris, France, dates from the 1100s. It is one of the largest and most spectacular in the world. A carved figure from the roof of the cathedral is shown at the right. **Analyze Images** *What features from the cathedral do you think were meant to inspire awe in the people who worshipped there?*

The Byzantine Empire The eastern Roman Empire, later called the Byzantine Empire, was not divided into feudal kingdoms. The empire survived largely intact in southeastern Europe and southwestern Asia until the 1400s. The Byzantine Empire followed a form of Christianity that became known as the Orthodox Christian Church. Today, this is the main form of Christianity in Russia and much of Eastern Europe.

Christianity Religious faith gave people a sense of security and community during the Middle Ages. In this period, most people's lives centered on the church. Religious ceremonies marked major events in the calendar and in the lives of individuals. Wealthy nobles and kings donated money for the construction of grand cathedrals, churches, and monasteries. In a world where most people's lives were marked by hardship and uncertainty, these grand buildings were awe-inspiring. Their brilliant stained-glass windows taught religious stories to peasants who were unable to read.

Europe Begins to Change As the centuries passed, trade increased in Europe. Towns offered opportunities to merchants and other tradespeople. Towns grew into cities. By the A.D. 1400s, a new way of life centered around cities had begun to develop in Europe.

 Reading Check **How did serfs differ from slaves?**

 Section 1 Assessment

Key Terms
Review the key terms at the beginning of this section. Use each term in a sentence that explains its meaning.

 Target Reading Skill
What word or idea did you clarify by rereading certain passages?

Comprehension and Critical Thinking
1. (a) Recall What kind of government did ancient Athens have?

(b) Contrast How was the government of ancient Athens different from today's United States government?
2. (a) List What were the most important lasting ideas of the ancient Romans?
(b) Sequence Explain how the Roman Empire declined.
3. (a) Name Which institutions brought order and security to people in the Middle Ages?
(b) Summarize How did the feudal system work?
(c) Draw Conclusions Who benefited the most from feudalism? Explain.

Writing Activity
Suppose you are a Roman governor in Britain, far from your home and family in Rome. Write a journal entry describing the things you miss about Rome.

Writing Tip Remember to write your description in the first person, using the pronouns *I* or *we*. Use vivid words to describe Rome. You might write about things such as Rome's weather, art, and architecture.

Renaissance and the Age of Revolution

Prepare to Read

Objectives

In this section you will
1. Discover what the Renaissance was like at its peak.
2. Examine the effects of increased trade and stronger rulers in the Renaissance.
3. Learn about revolutions in government and science in the 1600s and 1700s.

Taking Notes

As you read this section, look for details about the Renaissance and the Age of Revolution. Copy the chart below and record your findings in it.

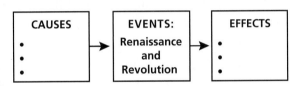

Target Reading Skill

Paraphrase When you pharaphrase, you restate what you have read in your own words. You could paraphrase the first two paragraphs of this section this way: "Marco Polo recorded his world travels in a book that influenced Christopher Columbus." As you read, paraphrase the information following each red or blue heading.

Key Terms

- **Renaissance** (REN uh sahns) *n.* a period of European history that included the rebirth of interest in learning and art
- **monarch** (MAHN urk) *n.* the ruler of a kingdom or empire, such as a king or a queen
- **revolution** (rev uh LOO shun) *n.* a far-reaching change
- **colony** (KAHL uh nee) *n.* a territory ruled by another nation

I n about A.D. 1324 an elderly explorer named Marco Polo said before he died, "I have only told the half of what I saw!" Marco Polo indeed had an interesting life. For a time, he was a messenger of the great Mongol (MAHN gul) emperor Kublai Khan (KOO bly kahn), ruler of China. Polo also traveled across burning deserts and sailed south of the Equator. He visited the Spice Islands, which were the sources of the spices cinnamon, nutmeg, and cloves that Europeans valued. He earned great riches, only to be robbed on his way home to Italy.

Marco Polo and Kublai Khan

These stories were published in a book we know today as *The Travels of Marco Polo*. Two hundred years later, Marco Polo's book inspired Christopher Columbus, another explorer. When Columbus sailed west from Europe, he was searching for a new route to the rich lands Marco Polo had described: China, Japan, and India.

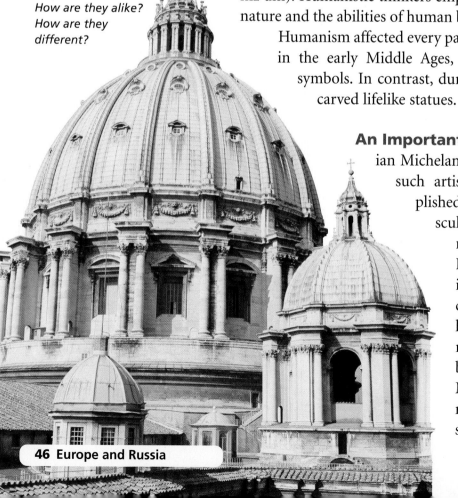

Works of Michelangelo
Michelangelo used themes from the Bible in many of his art works. Above is his sculpture of Moses. As an architect, Michelangelo worked on the dome of St. Peter's, the church of the Pope, in Rome. **Compare and Contrast** *Compare the photo of St. Peter's with that of Notre Dame on page 44. How are they alike? How are they different?*

Glories of the Renaissance

Columbus's search for a new route to the riches of the East was only one example of the movement sweeping Europe. The changes began in Italy in the 1300s and spread over the continent. Traders bought and sold goods across the region. The rich grew even richer. They had the time to enjoy art and learning—and the money to support artists and scholars. This period is called the Renaissance (REN uh sahns), or the rebirth of interest in learning and art. The Renaissance reached its peak in the 1500s.

Looking to the Past In trying to understand the world around them, Renaissance thinkers re-examined, or looked at once again, the ideas of Greek and Roman thinkers. People learned again about the ancient world's great poetry, plays, ideas, buildings, and sculpture. What they learned changed them. Writers began writing fresh, powerful poetry. The wealthy built glorious new buildings and filled them with breathtaking paintings.

Humanism: A New View Recall that during the Middle Ages much of Europe was in chaos, and religion was a way to bring order to people's lives. Renaissance thinkers began to focus on improving this world rather than hoping for a better life after death. This new approach to knowledge was called humanism (HYOO muh niz um). Humanistic thinkers emphasized the importance of human nature and the abilities of human beings to change the world.

Humanism affected every part of Renaissance life. For example, in the early Middle Ages, statues had been carved as stiff symbols. In contrast, during the Renaissance period artists carved lifelike statues.

An Important Renaissance Artist The Italian Michelangelo (my kul AN juh loh) was one such artist. Michelangelo was an accomplished painter, poet, architect, and sculptor. His lifelike statues were remarkably realistic and detailed. In some, you can see veins bulging in the hands. Or the drape of a cloak across the sculpted person looks so real that it appears to be made of cloth rather than of marble. Like other Renaissance artists, Michelangelo's work gave art a new importance. During the Renaissance, the role of art changed.

Art came to be seen as an important way to understand man, God, and nature. You can read about another important Renaissance figure, Leonardo da Vinci (lee uh NAHR doh duh VIN chee) in the box below.

Printing Spreads the Renaissance An important invention encouraged the spread of the Renaissance. Around 1450, the printing press was invented in Germany. Before printed books, books were made by carefully copying them by hand—a process that took a very long time. With the printing press, books could be made quickly.

Printed books made in large quantities could reach far more people than could books copied by hand. For that reason, the spread of printing had two important effects. First, it increased literacy, or the ability of people to read and write. Second, it allowed ideas of the Renaissance, written in books, to spread to large numbers of people. To understand the difference that the printing press made, consider this example. Before the printing press, there were a few thousand hand-copied books in Europe. Within 50 years after the printing press was invented, there were about 9 million books in Europe.

✔ **Reading Check** What is literacy?

Leonardo da Vinci: Renaissance Man

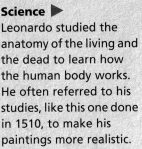

◀ **Painting**
Leonardo's *Mona Lisa* (1503–1506) is one of the most famous paintings in the world. The lady is believed to have been a merchant's wife. The style of her portrait and the misty background behind her continue to influence artists today.

Inventions ▶
Leonardo built machines of all kinds, but was especially interested in the possibility of human flight. He studied birds and drew imaginary flying machines. This helicopter-like machine, designed in 1487, was inspired by a child's toy.

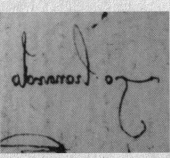

Science ▶
Leonardo studied the anatomy of the living and the dead to learn how the human body works. He often referred to his studies, like this one done in 1510, to make his paintings more realistic.

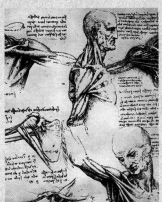

Mirror Writing ▶
Leonardo used "mirror writing"—writing from right to left—in his journals. No one is sure why, but some believe that because he was left-handed, he found it easier to write from right to left. This signature says "Io, Lionardo" or "I, Leonardo."

By the mid-1400s, European merchants like the one shown here sold a wide variety of goods, some from as far away as China. **Identify** What items in the diagram were made in Germany? **Analyze Information** What kinds of people most likely bought things from merchants such as this one? Why do you think so?

More Trade, Stronger Rulers

During the Renaissance, traders began to travel more often outside of Europe. In the 1400s, Portuguese explorers traveled along the western coast of Africa. There they traded in gold, ivory, and slaves. This trade was very profitable. Some Portuguese traders traveled as far east as the Indian Ocean.

Then in 1492, a discovery brought even more possibilities for wealth. While searching for a shortcut to the Indian Ocean spice trade, Christopher Columbus landed in the Americas. He claimed the lands for Spain. Other Spanish explorers soon followed.

While Portugal grew rich from spices, Spain grew wealthy from American gold and silver. Other European countries grew envious. By the 1600s, France, England, and the Netherlands took a growing share of the riches to be gained from overseas trade and settlement.

The Effects of Trade Europeans raced to the Americas in search of wealth. Precious metals, such as gold and silver, and trade goods, such as fur and tobacco, poured into Europe. Much of the wealth went to European **monarchs** (MAHN urks), or rulers such as kings and queens. Some of it went to traders and merchants. These people formed a new social class. They became the middle class, the class between the privileged nobles and the lowly peasants or farmers. The taxes paid by prosperous merchants and traders made monarchs even wealthier. Soon, kings no longer needed the support of feudal lords. Feudalism declined, local lords grew weaker, and kings gained power.

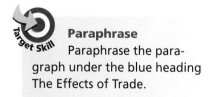

Paraphrase
Paraphrase the paragraph under the blue heading The Effects of Trade.

The Age of Monarchs The period in European history from the 1600s to the 1700s can be called the Age of Monarchs. During this time, many European monarchs became absolute monarchs, meaning that they exercised complete power over their subjects.

One such monarch was France's King Louis (LOO ee) XIV, who ruled from 1643 to 1715. One of Europe's most powerful kings, Louis XIV ruled at a time when France was a leading world power. Like other kings of his time, Louis was an absolute monarch. As he said, "I am the state." His wishes were law, and no one dared to disagree with him. Like other European monarchs, Louis believed that his power to rule came from God. To oppose him was the same as opposing God.

Louis used his power to make people pay heavy taxes. These taxes, in part, paid for his very expensive lifestyle. But Louis also wanted to make France strong. Other rulers wanted their countries to be strong as well. Over time, these monarchs made their countries stronger and more unified. As these changes took place, people began thinking again about government. Should the monarchs have such great power? What should the role of the government be?

✓ **Reading Check** **What is an absolute monarch?**

A Wealthy Monarch
Louis XIV, king of France, rides a horse in this painting from the mid-1600s. He built the palace of Versailles, shown below, to be his personal residence as well as the center of France's government.
Analyze Images *How does Versailles reflect Louis XIV's lifestyle? What does it say about his vision of government?*

Antoine Laurent Lavoisier (1743–1794) is considered one of the founders of modern chemistry. He was the first scientist to recognize oxygen as an element, and he gave it its name. He was also an important public servant. He built workhouses, savings banks, and canals to improve the lives of people in his district.

During the French Revolution, people turned against Lavoisier and other people who were wealthy or had been part of the government. In 1793, Lavoisier was arrested and given an unfair trial. On May 8, 1794, he and 28 others were executed. Lavoisier is shown in this 1788 painting by Jacques-Louis David with his wife Marie-Anne, who helped her husband in his lab.

Revolutions in Government

The 1600s and 1700s are often called the Age of Revolution. A revolution is a far-reaching change. European thought, beliefs, and ways of life all changed. This period was the beginning of the modern age of science and democracy that we know today.

The English Revolution One revolutionary change was that people began to believe that kings should not have all the power. For example, in England, King Charles I refused to share power with Parliament (PAHR luh munt), the elected legislature. Parliament then went to war with the King. Charles I was defeated, tried in court, and then put to death. No English ruler could ever again claim absolute power.

The American and French Revolutions The idea that people should have a say in government spread to North America, where Great Britain had several colonies. A colony is a territory ruled by another nation. In 1776, 13 of the colonies rebelled against the British king because they felt that the laws applied to them were not fair. The colonists defeated the British and formed the independent nation of the United States.

In 1789, 13 years after the Americans declared their independence, a revolution occurred in France. In order to create a democracy, the French people used extreme violence to overthrow their government. They did this in the name of freedom, equality, and brotherhood. The French Revolution created chaos in France. It also inspired new, radical theories about political and economic change. Ideas born in the French Revolution continued to influence Europeans long after the revolution ended.

✓ **Reading Check** What revolutions took place during the 1600s and 1700s?

This painting captures the scene of angry colonists pulling down a statue of British King George III after declaring independence in 1776.

Revolutions in Science

For centuries, Europeans had based their view of the world on their religious faith. Scientists had studied nature to explain how the world fit with their religious beliefs. Slowly, scientists began to change their approach. Influenced by humanism and the Renaissance, scientists began to observe nature carefully and record only what they observed. Then they based their theories on facts instead of making the facts fit their religious beliefs. This change in outlook is called the Scientific Revolution.

The Scientific Method It is difficult to pinpoint the exact beginning of the Scientific Revolution. Yet many sources agree that it started at least in part with the work of a scientist named Copernicus (koh PUR nih kus), who lived during the Middle Ages. Before Copernicus, people believed that Earth was the center of the universe. Copernicus shocked the world by suggesting that the sun was the center of the universe, and that Earth moved around the sun. Over time, he was proved to be right. His theories sparked other scientists to look at the world in different ways.

Copernicus and other scientists needed new procedures to test their ideas. These procedures make up what is called the scientific method, in which ideas are tested with experiments and observations. Scientists will accept an idea only if it has been tested repeatedly. The chart on the right shows the steps of the scientific method. Using the scientific method, scientists made dramatic advances.

Other Scientific Developments Some of the greatest advances were in the fields of chemistry and medicine. Before the 1600s, chemistry as we know it today did not exist. Instead, the main idea of chemistry was that any metal could be turned into gold. A scientist named Robert Boyle changed that. Boyle's ideas about temperatures and the behavior of gases set the stage for modern chemistry.

New ideas in medicine came about at that same time. People made efforts to learn about the human body, both inside and out. An English doctor named William Harvey discovered how blood circulates inside the body. The Dutch inventor Antonie van Leeuwenhoek (ahn TOH ne van LAY vun hook) developed techniques for making lenses for microscopes. He used his microscopes to study small lifeforms, such as insects and bacteria.

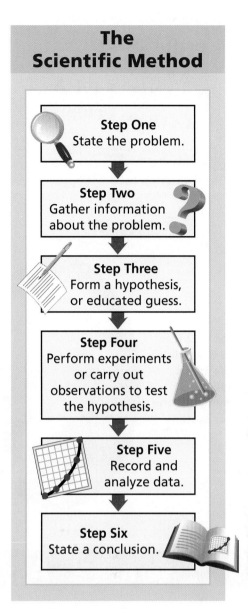

The Scientific Method

Step One
State the problem.

Step Two
Gather information about the problem.

Step Three
Form a hypothesis, or educated guess.

Step Four
Perform experiments or carry out observations to test the hypothesis.

Step Five
Record and analyze data.

Step Six
State a conclusion.

■ Diagram Skills

Though the scientific method is simple, it greatly changed the way science is done. **Explain** What is a hypothesis? How is it tested? **Apply Information** What was Copernicus's hypothesis about the universe?

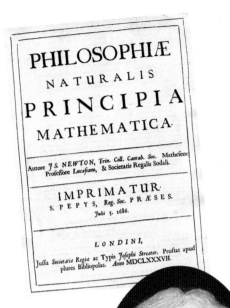

Isaac Newton and the title page of his book about gravity and the solar system

These and other developments led to a new way of thinking among scientists. With each new discovery, scientists began to see the universe as a giant machine. They believed this machine worked in a regular way, with set rules. They also believed that they could eventually learn everything about it.

Isaac Newton One of the greatest scientists of the Scientific Revolution was Isaac Newton. You may have heard a story about Newton, in which he saw an apple fall from a tree. He wondered if the force that pulled the apple to the ground was the same force that kept the moon in orbit around Earth.

To test this idea, Newton invented a new branch of mathematics called calculus (KAL kyoo lus). He had to invent calculus because the mathematics that existed at the time could not be used to explain his ideas. Using calculus and a few simple laws, Newton was able to demonstrate how the moon and planets move. Newton's laws and his mathematics are still used in science today.

By the end of the Age of Revolution, the nations of Europe were bustling with trade and bursting with new scientific ideas. Europe was about to begin a new kind of revolution. This time it would be an economic one.

√ **Reading Check** What did Isaac Newton invent?

Section 2 Assessment

Key Terms
Review the key terms at the beginning of this section. Use each term in a sentence that explains its meaning.

 Target Reading Skill
Paraphrase the text under the blue heading Isaac Newton above.

Comprehension and Critical Thinking
1. (a) Define What was the Renaissance?
(b) Identify Causes What invention helped spread the ideas of the Renaissance?

2. (a) Recall What was Christopher Columbus searching for when he landed in the Americas?
(b) Identify Effects How did Europeans' desire for wealth lead to voyages of exploration?
3. (a) Explain Why are the 1600s and 1700s called the Age of Revolution?
(b) Summarize How did the thinking of European scientists change during this period?
(c) Make Inferences How did humanism and advances in art help bring about changes in science?

Writing Activity
Marco Polo's writings excited readers and made them want to explore the places he had visited. Think about a place that you have visited. What makes it special? Describe in detail the features that you especially liked. Write about the place in a way that would make a reader want to go there.

For: An activity about Leonardo da Vinci
Visit: PHSchool.com
Web Code: ldd-7202

Industrial Revolution and Nationalism

Prepare to Read

Objectives

In this section you will

1. Learn how the Industrial Revolution changed peoples' lives.
2. Examine how nationalism and war can be related.

Taking Notes

As you read this section, look for details about how life changed as a result of the Industrial Revolution. Copy the chart below and record your findings in it.

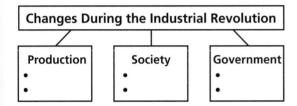

Changes During the Industrial Revolution

Production	Society	Government
•	•	•
•	•	•

🎯 Target Reading Skill

Summarize You can better understand a text if you pause to restate the key points briefly in your own words. A good summary includes important events and details, notes the order in which the events occurred, and makes connections between the events or details. Because a summary leaves out less important details, it is shorter than the original text.

Key Terms

- **Industrial Revolution** (in DUS tree ul REV uh LOO shun) *n.* the life-changing period in the 1800s when products began to be made by machines in factories
- **textile** (TEKS tyl) *n.* a cloth product
- **imperialism** (im PIHR ee ul iz um) *n.* the pursuit of economic and political control over foreign territories
- **nationalism** (NASH uh nul iz um) *n.* pride in one's country
- **alliance** (uh LY uns) *n.* an agreement between countries to protect and defend each other

It was dawn. Thick, black smoke rose from the tall smokestack of the factory. The smoke and the roar of machines signaled that the factory workday had begun. Inside, women and children worked at rows of machines that wove cotton thread into cloth. Their work was dirty, noisy, and dangerous. The day before, a worker had severely injured his hand in a machine. Today, another worker stood in his place. Both were only 13 years old. But the machines kept going. Workers fed them thread for 12 hours every day—six days a week. Vacations did not exist, and there were few breaks.

Factories like this one could be found all across Europe in the early 1800s. They were a result of the **Industrial Revolution**, a life-changing period when goods changed from being made by hand to being made by machines in factories. Industrialization caused great suffering at first, but in time brought an easier way of life to people all over the world.

Workers grind razors at a factory in Sheffield, England, in 1866.

Improvements in Making Cloth
For generations, people used spinning wheels like the one above to spin cloth. After the Industrial Revolution, huge machines called "spinning mules" in factories like the one at the right produced cloth cheaper and more quickly. **Evaluate Information** *How do you think the shift from using simple tools to complex machinery affected the average worker?*

The Industrial Revolution

Until the late 1700s, nearly all goods were made by hand. People made what they needed, or bought it from a craftsperson or at a store for a high price. The Industrial Revolution—a revolution in the way goods were made and in the ways people lived and worked—changed all that.

Changes in Production The first machines of the Industrial Revolution were invented in Great Britain to speed up the weaving of **textiles, or cloth products.** Large factories housed the machines. Factory work was very different from work done by hand. For example, a person weaving cloth would first spin the thread, then dye it, and then weave it. He or she might work on every step of the finished product. In contrast, in a factory each worker tended a specific machine, which performed a specific job over and over again. The machine worked much faster than a person could. This meant that goods could be made quickly and much more cheaply than they had been by hand.

This new factory system was improved by new inventions in machinery, transportation, and communication. Other new inventions also brought about improvements in agriculture. Food could be grown in larger quantities by fewer people, and transported quickly to supply factory workers in the cities.

Changes in Society Because Great Britain's factories were so successful, business people in other countries began to build factories. By 1900, factories produced many of the goods made in the United States and Western Europe.

The Industrial Revolution changed life in almost every way. Inventions created to fuel the Industrial Revolution were soon used in everyday life. Improved transportation meant that people could travel more quickly and often more cheaply. Better communications meant that people separated by long distances could talk to one another almost instantly.

Yet not all of the effects of the Industrial Revolution were positive. For hundreds of years, families had farmed the land. Now they moved to industrial centers to work in factories. Cities grew rapidly. People lived in cramped, dirty housing. Because of unclean and crowded conditions, diseases spread rapidly.

Factory work was also difficult. Factory owners took advantage of workers. Wages were low. Factory conditions were not safe. However, workers slowly began to form labor unions and to demand better working conditions. In the early 1900s, governments began passing laws to protect workers. Over time, conditions improved and wages rose. The Industrial Revolution helped give working people a greater voice in government. Many European nations became more democratic as a result.

■ Timeline Skills

Important inventions of the late 1700s and early 1800s had a major impact on industry and society.
Note When was the spinning jenny invented?
Apply Information Which inventions helped improve transportation?

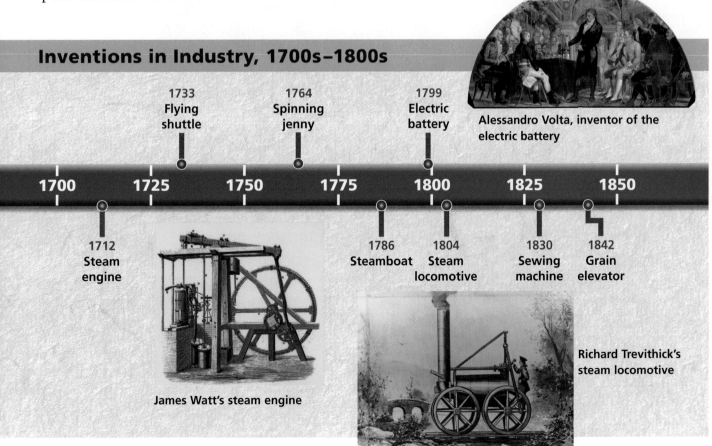

Inventions in Industry, 1700s–1800s

1733 Flying shuttle

1764 Spinning jenny

1799 Electric battery

Alessandro Volta, inventor of the electric battery

1700 — 1725 — 1750 — 1775 — 1800 — 1825 — 1850

1712 Steam engine

1786 Steamboat

1804 Steam locomotive

1830 Sewing machine

1842 Grain elevator

James Watt's steam engine

Richard Trevithick's steam locomotive

Textile Mill

Weaving, or making cloth from threads or yarns, is one of the oldest crafts in the world. It was also the first to take advantage of the inventions that fed the Industrial Revolution. Water, and then steam, powered the first textile factories and their machines. In England, this new form of manufacturing produced goods for trade and export, and wealth and power for the nation.

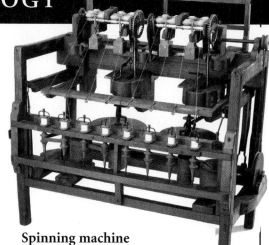

Spinning machine
A water-powered spinning machine (called a water frame) was invented by Sir Richard Arkwright.

Weaving loom

Some jobs were done by children.

The bell is used to signal the beginning and end of the workday, and the lunch break.

4 Belts, attached to pulleys, power the mill's many machines.

Spindles hold the cotton thread.

3 Gears transfer power to different parts of the mill.

1 Water flows under the mill, turning the wheel.

2 As the wheel turns, it spins the gears.

Water wheel
Flowing water turns the mill wheel, driving gears that cause the overhead shafts to turn. These shafts drive belts that power the machines.

ANALYZING IMAGES
Near what geographical feature must this textile mill have been located?

Changes in Government At the same time, though, European governments were becoming more aggressive abroad. Beginning in the 1600s, many European nations had followed the policy of **imperialism,** or the practice of taking control of foreign territories as colonies in order to form an empire. Colonies provided the raw materials, such as cotton, wood, and metals, that industry needed. Colonies also supplied markets for European goods. Finally, European countries hoped to spread their influence over people in those colonies by converting them to their own religions.

The late 1800s are called the Age of Imperialism. During this time, the nations of Belgium, France, Italy, Spain, Portugal, Germany, and the United Kingdom colonized most of Africa. Some of these countries also took over much of Southeast Asia and many South Pacific islands. In time, struggles among the colonial powers would bring disaster to Europe.

✓ **Reading Check** **Why are the late 1800s called the Age of Imperialism?**

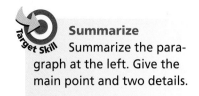

Summarize Summarize the paragraph at the left. Give the main point and two details.

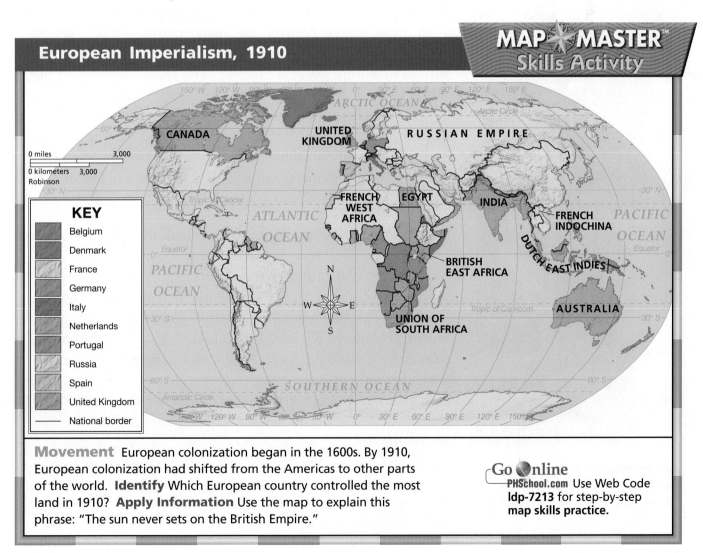

European Imperialism, 1910

MAP MASTER™ Skills Activity

KEY

- Belgium
- Denmark
- France
- Germany
- Italy
- Netherlands
- Portugal
- Russia
- Spain
- United Kingdom
- National border

0 miles 3,000
0 kilometers 3,000
Robinson

CANADA, UNITED KINGDOM, RUSSIAN EMPIRE, ARCTIC OCEAN, ATLANTIC OCEAN, FRENCH WEST AFRICA, EGYPT, INDIA, FRENCH INDOCHINA, PACIFIC OCEAN, BRITISH EAST AFRICA, DUTCH EAST INDIES, UNION OF SOUTH AFRICA, AUSTRALIA, SOUTHERN OCEAN

Movement European colonization began in the 1600s. By 1910, European colonization had shifted from the Americas to other parts of the world. **Identify** Which European country controlled the most land in 1910? **Apply Information** Use the map to explain this phrase: "The sun never sets on the British Empire."

Go Online
PHSchool.com Use Web Code **ldp-7213** for step-by-step map skills practice.

A Century of War and Nationalism

At the start of the 1900s, the people of Europe were filled with **nationalism,** or pride in their countries. Nationalism can be either a destructive or a constructive force, depending on what it leads people to do. It can make one nation harm another in an effort to get ahead. It can also prevent nations from working with one another. Then, hatred and warfare can erupt between countries. Between 1900 and 1950, destructive nationalism played a part in causing two world wars and the deaths of millions of people.

World War I During the early 1900s, European nations feared one another. Each nation was afraid another would invade, or try to take over, its territory. To protect themselves, nations made **alliances** (uh LY un sez), or agreements with one another. In such alliances, a nation promises to protect its friends if someone attacks them. Soon, Europe was divided into two major alliances. On one side were Germany, Austria-Hungary, and Turkey. On the other side were Great Britain, France, and Russia.

In 1914, fighting between the alliances broke out into what is now called World War I. Over the course of the war, most of the nations of Europe became involved. The United States—on the side of Great Britain, France, and Russia—also joined the war in 1917. The alliance of Germany, Austria-Hungary, and Turkey was defeated, but at an enormous cost. By the end of the war in 1918, more than 9 million soldiers had been killed. About 13 million civilians, or non-soldiers, had also died. Europe had lost almost an entire generation of young men.

World War II But the flame of nationalism still burned. In 1939, another war broke out. This war was called World War II. As in World War I, there were two alliances. On one side were the Axis Powers—Germany, Italy, and Japan. These countries sought to increase their national wealth and power by means of military conquest. They quickly captured most of Europe and parts of China and the South Pacific. Germany also attacked the Soviet Union.

The Allies—Great Britain, the Soviet Union, France, and China—opposed the Axis Powers. In 1941, the United States joined the Allies. More than 50 nations took part in this war, which was the most destructive ever fought. More people died, more property was damaged, and more money was spent than in any other war in history. The fighting finally ended in August of 1945. The Allies had won.

During World War I, countries on both sides of the fight used posters to promote their causes.

Two Paths Emerge in Europe After World War II, the Soviet Union and the United States emerged as the world's two superpowers. These nations had very different ideas about government and its role in society. Both nations used their ideas to influence people around the world.

After the war, much of Europe was in ruins. It was time to rebuild. The nations of Western Europe allied themselves with the United States. They also grew together as a region. With the shared values of peace and prosperity, they worked together to restore the economies and standards of living that had been shattered by war.

The nations of Eastern Europe, in contrast, took a different path. Many of the nations of Eastern Europe followed the example of the Soviet Union. Their economies failed to recover after the war, and their governments suspended many of their people's freedoms. You will read more about the Soviet Union and its influence on Eastern Europe in the next section.

Eastern and Western Europe remained divided, with very different governments and standards of living, until the 1990s. You will read about their recent history in Chapters 4 and 5.

The United States led an effort called the Marshall Plan to rebuild the economies of Europe. In this photo, a parade in Greece celebrates the delivery of Marshall Plan food supplies.

✓ Reading Check **Which countries made up the Axis Powers? Which made up the Allies?**

Section 3 Assessment

Key Terms
Review the key terms at the beginning of this section. Use each term in a sentence that explains its meaning.

Target Reading Skill
Summarize the information in the paragraphs on this page.

Comprehension and Critical Thinking
1. (a) Recall Where did the Industrial Revolution begin?

(b) Find the Main Idea How did the Industrial Revolution change the way that goods were made?
(c) Identify Effects How did this change affect the lives of Europeans?
2. (a) Describe Give an example of destructive nationalism.
(b) Identify Cause and Effect How did nationalism help to cause World War I and World War II?
(c) Predict How might nationalism be used in the future as a creative force for peace?

Writing Activity
After World War II, colonies in Africa and Asia demanded their freedom. Suppose you were a citizen of a colony of one of the European nations. Write a paragraph explaining why you would want your country to be independent.

> **Writing Tip** Use the following topic sentence to help you organize your thoughts: It is important for people to control their own destiny.

Problem Solving

Marco Polo dressed in clothes worn by the Tatars, a nomadic tribe of eastern Asia

In 1275, Marco Polo arrived at the court of Kublai Khan in China. The Mongol leader appointed Marco Polo governor of Yangchow, a busy Chinese city. After three years had passed, Marco Polo wanted to return to Venice. He had enemies within the court. The khan was getting older. Marco Polo worried that when the khan died, those enemies would have him killed. But the khan refused to let him return to Venice.

One year, a Mongol princess was promised as a bride to the Persian khan. Marco Polo proposed that he accompany the princess on the journey, to keep her safe. He knew that at the end of the trip he could escape to Venice. The khan agreed, and Marco Polo set out by sea with the princess and hundreds of men. The trip was dangerous, and most of the men died. But it might have been even more dangerous to go by land, because of robbers.

Solving a problem requires a range of skills. You must first state the problem clearly and identify the possible solutions. Then you must think about the likely outcome of each solution and choose the best option. In the passage above, Marco Polo identified and solved two problems.

Learn the Skill

Follow the steps below to learn how to solve problems.

1 Identify the problem. State the problem in a direct, complete, and accurate way. Your statement should contain facts, not opinions. The facts should be directly related to the problem.

2 List possible solutions. There may be more than one way to solve the problem. Identify all possible solutions.

3 Review the possible solutions. Identify the resources that would be needed to carry out each solution. Also identify consequences of each solution.

4 Choose the best solution. Decide which solution is the most effective, or the easiest to carry out. What will the likely outcome be?

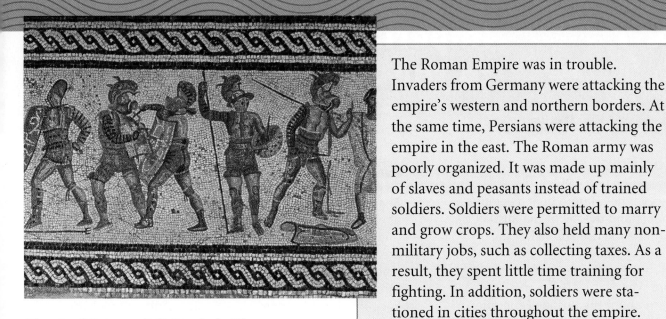

Mosaic of Roman gladiators in battle

The Roman Empire was in trouble. Invaders from Germany were attacking the empire's western and northern borders. At the same time, Persians were attacking the empire in the east. The Roman army was poorly organized. It was made up mainly of slaves and peasants instead of trained soldiers. Soldiers were permitted to marry and grow crops. They also held many non-military jobs, such as collecting taxes. As a result, they spent little time training for fighting. In addition, soldiers were stationed in cities throughout the empire. When attacks on the empire occurred, it was difficult to gather the soldiers together in one place for defense. Finally, the government had not kept the roads in repair, so travel was very difficult.

Practice the Skill

Read the passage above. Use the steps from Learn the Skill to identify the Roman Empire's problem and possible solutions.

1 Identify the Roman Empire's problem. State the problem in a clear sentence or two.

2 Identify possible solutions. Does the passage bring to mind any obvious solutions? Does it suggest any solutions that aren't as obvious?

3 Review the possible solutions. What kind of resources would each solution require? Think of what the possible outcome would be for each solution.

4 Identify the solution you think is best. Explain why you think it is the best one, and what its outcome would be.

Bronze statue of a Roman soldier

Apply the Skill

Reread the passage titled Revolutions in Government on page 50. Then use the steps in this skill to identify the problem described in the passage, note its possible effects, and explain the solutions used.

Imperial Russia to the Soviet Union

Prepare to Read

Objectives

In this section you will

1. Discover how Russia built its empire.
2. Understand the fall of the Russian tsars.
3. Examine the rise and fall of the Soviet Union.
4. Learn the causes and effects of the Cold War.
5. Learn about the Russian Federation today.

Taking Notes

As you read this section, look for important dates in Russia's development as an empire. Copy the timeline below and record your findings on it.

1200   1900

Target Reading Skill

Read Ahead Reading ahead can help you understand something you are not sure of in the text. If you do not understand a certain word or passage, keep reading. The word or idea may be clarified further on. For example, in the last paragraph below you may not be sure what is meant by the word *expansion*. As you read the section, that word will be clarified by the text.

Key Terms

- **westernization** (wes tur nuh ZAY shun) *n.* the adoption of western European culture
- **tsar** (zahr) *n.* a Russian emperor
- **revolutionary** (rev uh LOO shuh neh ree) *adj.* ideas that relate to or cause the overthrow of a government, or other great change
- **communism** (KAHM yoo niz um) *n.* a political system in which the central government owns farms, factories, and offices

Catherine the Great

The Russian court under Catherine the Great was dazzling. Catherine loved the arts, literature, philosophy, and French culture. She dreamed of creating a great nation, as glorious as France had been under Louis XIV.

Early in her rule, she made many efforts to improve the lives of the Russian people. She built schools and hospitals and gave people more religious freedom. She also became interested in ideas about liberty. Catherine did not bring freedom to all of her people, but she did make Russia a great empire. By the time of her death in 1796, she had expanded Russia southward to the Black Sea and westward into parts of Poland.

The history of Russia is a story with four themes: invasion and expansion, harsh treatment of the common people, slow **westernization,** or the process of becoming more like Western Europe, and autocratic (aw toh KRAT ik) government. An autocratic government is one in which one person has absolute power. As you read Russia's story, notice how these four themes appear again and again.

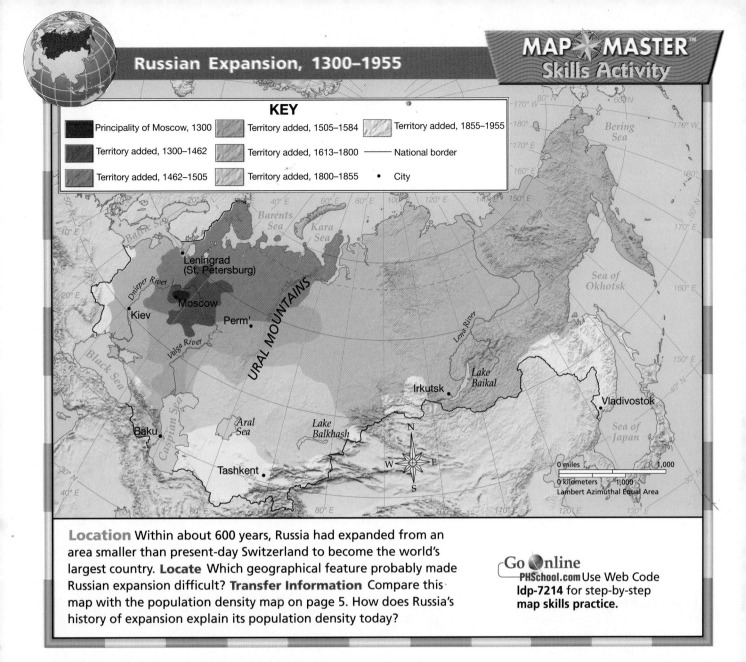

KEY

■ Principality of Moscow, 1300	Territory added, 1505–1584	Territory added, 1855–1955
Territory added, 1300–1462	Territory added, 1613–1800	—— National border
Territory added, 1462–1505	Territory added, 1800–1855	• City

Location Within about 600 years, Russia had expanded from an area smaller than present-day Switzerland to become the world's largest country. **Locate** Which geographical feature probably made Russian expansion difficult? **Transfer Information** Compare this map with the population density map on page 5. How does Russia's history of expansion explain its population density today?

Go Online
PHSchool.com Use Web Code
ldp-7214 for step-by-step
map skills practice.

Building a Vast Empire

Russia's story begins long before Catherine the Great. Many centuries before, various groups of people known as Slavs (slahvz) lived in small settlements. The Slavs lived in the region that eventually became the Russian Empire. In the 1200s, Mongol invaders from Asia swept in and conquered them.

The Rise of Moscow The prince of Moscow made clever agreements with the Mongols that helped him grow rich and powerful. By the 1330s, he had become the strongest ruler in the region. Slowly Moscow conquered surrounding territory. By the end of the 1400s, Moscow had freed itself entirely from Mongol rule. The map above shows how the small principality, or territory ruled by a prince, of Moscow grew into a huge country.

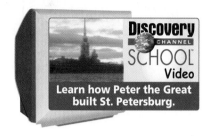

Learn how Peter the Great built St. Petersburg.

The Rise of the Tsars In the 1540s, Ivan IV became the leader of Moscow. He called himself **tsar** (zahr), or emperor. Ivan IV expanded Moscow's control of the territories to its south and east. He earned the name Ivan the Terrible for his cruelty both to those he conquered and to his own people.

After the death of Ivan the Terrible, Russia entered the Time of Troubles. During that period, the Russians endured about 20 years of civil wars and invasions by the Poles.

Finally, in 1613, Michael Romanov (ROH muh nawf) became tsar. During his reign, order was restored to Russia. The Romanovs continued expanding Russian territory throughout the 1600s and continued to rule Russia for more than 300 years.

Peter the Great Peter the Great came to power in 1689. Peter began bringing Western European ideas and culture to Russia. He hired foreign professors, scientists, and advisors, and encouraged Russians to adopt European customs. He also established new schools and reorganized his government and the army.

Peter believed that Russia needed good seaports to become a world power. He conquered land on the Baltic (BAWL tik) and Black seas, and moved the capital to St. Petersburg. Later tsars continued to expand Russian territory. Russia gained control over territories in present-day Poland, Turkey, China, and Sweden. With so many lands under its rule, Russia became an empire.

Invasion Being an empire did not mean that Russia was safe from invasion. A French army under Napoleon Bonaparte invaded Russia in 1812. Fierce fighting erupted as Napoleon's army approached Moscow. Napoleon's invasion plan, which did not take into account Russia's early winter, resulted in disastrous losses for the French. Of the 100,000 soldiers that reached Moscow, only about 10,000 survived.

√ Reading Check **Why did Peter the Great want to control land on the Baltic Sea?**

Napoleon's First View of Moscow
Napoleon and his troops approach Moscow in 1812 in this historical painting. **Analyze Images** *Which figure in the painting is Napoleon? How can you tell?*

Europe and Russia

The Fall of the Tsars

Russia had become a powerful empire, but the lives of most of its people had not improved. For hundreds of years, the tsar made all the important decisions. Below the tsar, Russian society was divided into two main groups. The first was a small number of landowners. The second group was a large number of very poor serfs. Tensions between the two groups began to rise.

Freeing of the Serfs In 1855, Alexander II became tsar. He soon freed the serfs and gave them their own land. He also gave towns more control over their own affairs. However, Alexander's son, Alexander III, reversed many of his father's reforms. Once again, the tsar ruled with absolute power.

Rumblings of Revolution In 1894, Nicholas II became tsar. He would be the last Russian tsar. Russia was badly beaten in a war with Japan in 1904 and 1905, and unrest grew among peasants, workers, and a small middle class. In 1905, thousands of workers in St. Petersburg marched to the tsar's Winter Palace. They wanted to appeal directly to the tsar for reforms. Troops stopped them and fired into the crowd, killing hundreds. This mass killing was known as Bloody Sunday.

Tsar Nicholas II was forced to agree to establish the Duma (DOO mah), a kind of congress. The people elected its members. In theory, the Duma shared power with the tsar. In fact, the Duma had very little power. Some progress toward reform was made, but many people wanted more.

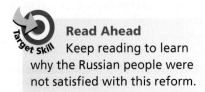

Read Ahead Keep reading to learn why the Russian people were not satisfied with this reform.

✓ **Reading Check** **What event is known as Bloody Sunday?**

Promoting Communism
At the top, Lenin gives a speech to a crowd in Moscow in 1918. The poster above promotes communism, reading, "You are still not a member of the cooperative? Sign up immediately!" **Synthesize** *What about communism might have appealed to poverty-stricken Russians?*

The Rise of the Soviet Union

On an afternoon in April 1917, a small group of Russians gathered at a German railroad station. Among them was a man named Vladimir Ulyanov, who was also called Lenin. Earlier, the Russian government had imprisoned Lenin for spreading ideas that they believed were **revolutionary,** or ideas that could cause the overthrow of a government. Later, the government gave him permission to leave Russia.

Now the Germans were taking Lenin back to Russia. The Germans made two rules. First, no member of Lenin's group could leave the train, and second, none of them could talk to any Germans during their journey. The Germans, like the Russians, knew that ideas could be more powerful than any army. At the time, Germany was at war with Russia and hoped that Lenin would cause changes in Russia. And he did.

The Russian Revolution To understand why the Germans helped Lenin, you need to go back to 1914. That year, Russia entered World War I against Germany. Millions of Russian soldiers were killed or wounded. At home, people suffered severe food and fuel shortages. By March 1917, the Russian people began rioting. Troops were sent to put down the uprising. They joined the rioters instead. Tsar Nicholas II was forced to give up his throne. The tsar and his family were held as prisoners, and were later killed by Lenin's followers. A weak government took over.

In November 1917, after his return to Russia, Lenin and his supporters pushed the weak government aside. Lenin knew that Russians wanted peace more than anything else. In March 1918, Russia signed an agreement with Germany and withdrew from World War I. Under Lenin's leadership, Russia also agreed to give up the Baltic republics, a large area of its territory that had been occupied by the Germans. This was just what the Germans had hoped for.

As the new leader of Russia, Lenin wanted to establish a communist government. **Communism** (KAHM yoo niz um) is a political system in which the central government owns farms, factories, and offices. No one person can own factories or land. Each person is supposed to work and share equally in the rewards of this work.

The idea of communism appealed greatly to many Russians. For hundreds of years, Russia's poor had suffered terrible hardships while the rich lived in luxury. Lenin promised that everyone would be equal and enjoy a better standard of living, but he broke that promise. Instead, the government took all power and most of the wealth for itself.

Building a Communist State The treaty with Germany ended the war, but peace still did not come to Russia. After the Communists came to power, there was a terrible civil war. On one side were Lenin's followers. On the other side were many groups who opposed them.

The Russian civil war lasted three years and cost millions of lives. Eventually, the Communists won. In 1922, Lenin created the Union of Soviet Socialist Republics (USSR), also called the Soviet Union. The Soviet Union was made up of Russia and several smaller republics under Russian control. It included most of the territory of the old Russian Empire. And as in the old empire, most of the people in the smaller republics were not Russian.

Lenin began turning the Soviet Union into a communist country. He jailed and even killed people who opposed him, calling them enemies of the revolution. Lenin died in 1924. Josef Stalin became the next leader. Under Stalin's form of Soviet communism, the government tried to control all aspects of citizens' lives.

Stalin's Dictatorship Josef Stalin was a dictator (DIK tayt ur), a leader who has absolute power. Stalin did not care about the suffering his decisions caused the Russian people. For example, he wanted to develop more industry in the Soviet Union. He knew that the increased number of factory workers would require great amounts of food. Therefore, Stalin forced the peasants to give their farm products to the government. Many peasants opposed the plan. As punishment, Stalin sent millions of peasants to prison camps in Siberia. Most died there. Stalin eventually succeeded in industrializing Russia. But all of the Soviet Union lived in terror of Stalin.

World War II Stalin signed an agreement with the Germans in 1939. It stated that the two countries would not go to war against each other. Despite the agreement, the Germans invaded the Soviet Union two years later. Three million German soldiers, with tanks and airplanes, advanced deep into the Soviet Union.

For a time, a German victory appeared likely. Many Soviet cities were destroyed. Millions of soldiers died or were captured. But the Soviet people fought bravely. By 1943, the Soviets had begun pushing the Germans out of Russia. Two years later, Soviet troops had captured Berlin, the capital of Germany.

✓ **Reading Check** Why was Stalin called a dictator?

Ending World War II
In the photo at the top, a Russian soldier celebrates the Soviet victory in Berlin by raising the Soviet flag. Above, the leaders of the Soviet Union, the United States, and the United Kingdom meet to discuss their countries' roles in the post-war world. **Recognize Causes** *How did the Soviet Union's role in World War II help it become a world power?*

A Nuclear Threat
By the 1980s, the superpowers had built enough powerful nuclear weapons to destroy the entire world. The top photo shows the explosion of a nuclear bomb. The bottom photo shows the universal yellow and black symbol of fallout shelters—underground rooms meant to protect people from fallout, or dangerous particles, after a nuclear explosion.
Sequence *What events led to the buildup of nuclear weapons by the Soviet Union and the United States?*

The Cold War

As you have read, after World War II the United States and the Soviet Union were so powerful that people called them superpowers. Relations between the superpowers became extremely tense. However, the two sides never fought each other. This time of tension without actual war is called the Cold War. It lasted roughly from 1945 until 1991 and shaped events within the two nations and around the world.

Causes of the Cold War The first cause of the Cold War was the situation in Eastern Europe. During World War II the Soviet army moved westward to Berlin, freeing the Eastern European countries that the Germans had conquered. But after the war, the Soviet troops did not leave. They forced those countries to become communist. Trade and most contact with the West were cut off. British leader Winston Churchill said that it was as if an "iron curtain" had fallen across Eastern Europe, dividing the East from the West.

Second, the Soviets tried to expand their power beyond Eastern Europe. They encouraged rebels in other nations to turn to communism. The United States was determined to stop this. The superpowers often backed opposing sides in conflicts in Latin America, Asia, and Africa. They also built powerful nuclear (NOO klee ur) weapons to use against each other.

Collapse of an Empire The Soviet Union's economy grew weak during the Cold War. The government had invested most of its money in heavy industries and weapons. It did not produce enough basic consumer goods, such as food and clothing. Also, the government's central control of the economy was not working.

Many of the Soviet people had lost faith in the communist system by the early 1980s. They were still poor and no longer believed the government's promises. One Soviet leader responded. Mikhail Gorbachev (mee kah EEL GAWR buh chawf), who took power in 1985, made many changes in the Soviet system. He allowed more personal freedom. He also reduced the government's control of the economy.

When people who have lived under harsh rule are given a taste of freedom, they often want more. This happened across Eastern Europe and the Soviet Union by the late 1980s. Eastern European countries abandoned communism. The Soviet republics demanded their independence. Finally, at the end of 1991, the Soviet Union broke apart.

✓ **Reading Check** **What was the "Iron Curtain"?**

The Russian Federation

After the breakup of the Soviet Union, all of its republics became independent nations. By far the largest of these, the republic of Russia changed its name to the Russian Federation. A federation is a union of states or republics. In a federation, each member agrees to give certain powers to a central government. The Russian Federation includes Russians and peoples of many different ethnic groups. However, the Russian Federation is smaller in size than the old Soviet Union.

The Russian Federation made efforts to build a free-market economy, or an economy in which producers compete freely for consumers' business. It sold its state-owned factories and businesses to private individuals. It also tried to become more democratic. The transition away from a communist system was difficult, however. Russia experienced economic chaos.

Russia also experienced conflicts among its ethnic groups. Many of the non-Russian peoples were tired of being ruled by Russians, who are the majority in Russia. The republic of Tatarstan, for example, negotiated with the Russians to have more rights. The republic of Chechnya (CHECH nee uh), however, has fought bitterly for its independence. Russia today faces many challenges to building a new way of life.

Russian president Vladimir Putin in 2000

✓ **Reading Check** **Why did the Russian Federation sell businesses to private individuals?**

Section 4 Assessment

Key Terms
Review the key terms at the beginning of this section. Use each term in a sentence that explains its meaning.

Target Reading Skill

What word or idea were you able to clarify by reading ahead?

Comprehension and Critical Thinking
1. (a) Name Who was the first Russian leader to begin westernization?
(b) Draw Conclusions Why did he encourage Russians to adopt western customs?

2. (a) Define What was the Russian Duma?
(b) Identify Causes Why did Tsar Nicholas II create the Duma?
3. (a) Explain Why had Lenin been imprisoned by the Russian government?
(b) Sequence How did Lenin become Russia's leader?
4. (a) Define What is a federation?
(b) Summarize How did the Russian Federation try to westernize its economy?

Writing Activity
Today, some people in Russia want to return to their lives under communist rule. Write a paragraph arguing either for or against returning to communism.

For: An activity about Leo Tolstoy
Visit: PHSchool.com
Web Code: ldd-7204

The European Union

Prepare to Read

Objectives

In this section you will
1. Learn about the history of the European Union.
2. Understand the purpose of the European Union.
3. Examine the structure of the European Union.
4. Find out what the future holds for the European Union.

Taking Notes

As you read this section, look for details about the European Union. Copy the concept web below and record your findings in it.

European Union

Target Reading Skill

Reread or Read Ahead
Both rereading and reading ahead can help you understand words and ideas in the text. If you do not understand a word or passage, use one or both of these techniques. In some cases, you may wish to read ahead first to see if the idea is clarified later on. If it is not, try going back and rereading the original passage.

Key Terms

- **euro** (YUR oh) *n.* the official currency of the European Union
- **single market** (SIN gul MAHR ket) *n.* a system in which goods, services, and capital move freely, with no barriers
- **foreign minister** (FAWR in MIN is tur) *n.* a government official who is in charge of a nation's foreign affairs

Robert Schuman worked to repair war-torn Europe.

At the end of World War II, Europe lay in ruins. Many of the nations of Europe had been at war with one another for years. Europeans needed to work together to bring about peace, rebuild their nations, and strengthen their shattered economies.

A French government official named Robert Schuman had a plan. He wanted European nations to work together to control their coal and steel industries. He proposed a new organization called the European Coal and Steel Community (ECSC). Six nations—Belgium, France, Italy, Luxembourg, the Netherlands, and West Germany—joined the group in 1951.

Over time, this small group grew into a much larger group, with many more roles and responsibilities. Today, it is called the European Union (EU), and has 27 member states. Many additional countries are waiting to become members.

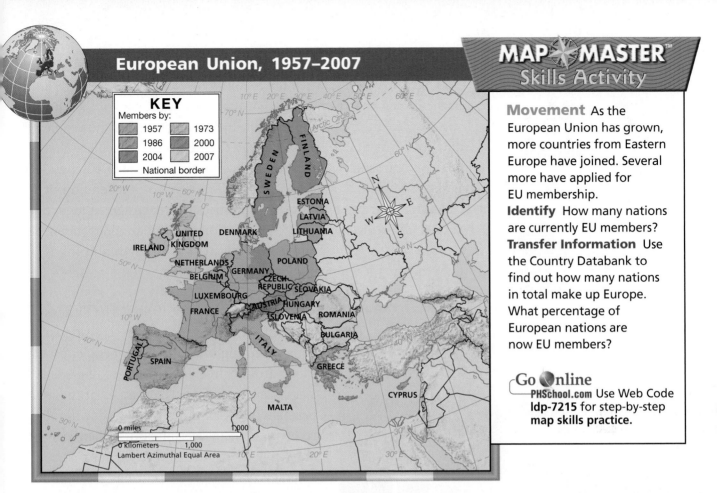

European Union, 1957–2007

KEY

Members by:
- 1957
- 1986
- 2004
- 1973
- 2000
- 2007
- National border

Movement As the European Union has grown, more countries from Eastern Europe have joined. Several more have applied for EU membership.
Identify How many nations are currently EU members?
Transfer Information Use the Country Databank to find out how many nations in total make up Europe. What percentage of European nations are now EU members?

Go Online
PHSchool.com Use Web Code **ldp-7215** for step-by-step map skills practice.

History of the European Union

The ECSC created the European Economic Community (EEC) in 1957. The EEC expanded the ECSC, giving it greater economic powers. It also added the power to make social policies.

Expanding Membership Throughout the 1970s and 1980s, more and more nations wanted to join the EEC. The United Kingdom, Ireland, and Denmark joined in 1973. Greece followed in 1981. Portugal and Spain joined in 1986. Soon, the member nations began working on a new plan for an even stronger union.

The EEC Becomes the EU In 1992 the member nations of the EEC signed the Maastricht (MAH strikt) Treaty. This treaty, which went into effect the next year, established the European Union. It also laid out the plan for EU nations to adopt a single currency, or money. Europe's common currency is called the **euro,** (YUR oh). By 2001, twelve countries had adopted the euro. Denmark, Sweden, and the United Kingdom chose not to adopt the euro.

At first, only banks and other businesses used the euro. In 2002, nations adopting the euro withdrew their own coins and paper bills from circulation and began using euros instead.

✓ **Reading Check** What is the currency of the European Union?

What Does the European Union Do?

The EEC was created when the memory of a terrible war was fresh in the minds of all Europeans. For that reason, the goal of the EEC was to make future wars impossible by binding together the people and governments of Europe. Today the EU works to achieve that goal by cooperating to promote economic and social progress. Unlike the United States or Russia, the EU is not a federation of states. It is a group of individual countries that have agreed to give certain powers to the EU. Each EU nation remains an independent nation. But by working together, the EU has strength and influence that no individual nation could have alone.

A Market With Two Currencies
A Spanish market lists prices in both euros (top) and pesetas, the old Spanish currency. Many European markets used both currencies before changing over completely to euros. **Generalize** *What are some advantages of having just one currency throughout several countries?*

Common Social Policies The citizens of all EU member nations are considered equal. Throughout the EU, people can move around freely without needing special visas or permits. They can even move permanently to another EU nation without receiving official permission. When new nations join the EU, however, it may be several years before their citizens gain all of these rights.

EU member nations also establish common policies in areas such as education, the environment, and fighting crime. For example, EU nations have similar policies for combating poverty. EU nations also follow over 200 environmental guidelines set up by the EU.

Finally, the EU strives to protect European heritage and culture. European students are encouraged to learn foreign languages and study in other EU countries. The EU also sponsors cultural projects—such as theater, dance, and film—that are produced by EU member nations working together.

Common Economic Policies EU member nations can trade freely with one another without having to pay tariffs, or taxes, on international trade. In effect, the EU has a **single market,** or a system in which goods, services, and capital move freely, with no barriers. EU nations also cooperate to create jobs for citizens in all countries throughout the EU.

All EU member nations help plan and contribute to the EU's central budget. A special bank manages this budget, which pays for all of the EU's expenses.

Common Government and Foreign Policies

The EU has many different roles relating to government and foreign policy. It creates laws that govern its member nations. It also signs treaties with non-EU countries and organizations. Most of these treaties have to do with trade or industry. Finally, the EU oversees policies that have to do with crime and the national security of the region.

A court called the Court of Justice ensures that the EU's policies are applied fairly in every EU member nation. It settles any legal disputes between member nations, EU organizations, or EU citizens. The Court is made up of one judge from each EU member state.

Things the EU Does Not Handle Recall that all EU member nations still remain independent countries. Although EU member nations work together, they keep control over many of their countries' own policies. For example, each nation decides how best to handle its own healthcare, national defense, education, and housing policies. Still, member nations try to make policies that agree with the policies made by other member nations.

✓ **Reading Check** **What is the court that ensures EU policies are applied fairly?**

A Seat of Government
The European Parliament is located in Strasbourg, France. **Infer** *What challenges might EU nations have faced in deciding on where to locate its parliament?*

Structure of the European Union

The EU has three main policy-making institutions. These institutions are the European Parliament, the Council of the European Union, and the European Commission.

European Parliament The European Parliament passes the majority of the EU's laws. It is the only EU institution that meets and debates in public. It is elected by all the citizens of the EU and represents their interests.

The number of representatives to Parliament differs according to the size of each country. When the Parliament meets, the representatives are assembled by political party, not by nation.

Council of the European Union The Council of the European Union is made up of the foreign ministers from individual EU nations. A **foreign minister** is a government official who is in charge of a nation's foreign affairs, or relations with other nations. The Council represents the separate national interests of the member nations.

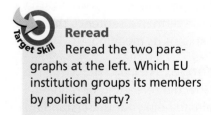

Reread
Reread the two paragraphs at the left. Which EU institution groups its members by political party?

Members of the EU discuss energy resources with non-EU members.

Other EU Institutions The European Commission represents the interests of the whole EU community. It is made up of several different offices, each overseeing a certain area of policy. Each EU member nation sends representatives to the Commission. Other EU institutions perform services such as monitoring the EU's income and spending, advising on economic policy, and overseeing long-term investment.

✓ **Reading Check** Which institution in the EU represents each nation's national interests?

Future of the European Union

In just over 50 years, the EU has enjoyed great success. It has brought peace and prosperity to almost 500 million Europeans.

The EU continues to expand. In 2004, ten nations from Eastern and Southern Europe joined. By 2006, several more countries had applied to join and were working to meet EU requirements. Bulgaria and Romania became members of the EU in 2007. To join, new members must accept existing EU laws, values, and policies. The EU will continue to draw its strength from following its own rules and honoring its traditions. Its long-term goal is to bring all the democracies of Europe together. This process will be a careful and gradual one.

✓ **Reading Check** What must a nation do to join the EU?

Section 5 Assessment

Key Terms
Review the key terms at the beginning of this section. Use each term in a sentence that explains its meaning.

 Target Reading Skill
How did rereading or reading ahead help your understanding?

Comprehension and Critical Thinking
1. (a) Name Which three nations in the EU did not adopt the euro?
(b) Infer Why might these countries not have wanted to adopt a single currency?

2. (a) List What are some examples of the EU's social policies?
(b) Analyze Information What do these policies tell you about how the EU views its citizens?
3. (a) Recall What are the EU's main policy institutions?
(b) Draw Conclusions Why do you think the representatives in Parliament are assembled by political group and not by nation?
4. (a) Recall What must new members of the EU accept before they can join the EU?
(b) Infer Why might some European countries not want to join the EU?

Writing Activity
Suppose that you are a citizen of a nation that is interested in joining the European Union. Write a letter to your local newspaper describing both the benefits and the disadvantages of joining.

Writing Tip A letter should begin with an overview sentence or two. After describing the benefits and disadvantages, end the letter with a closing statement.

◆ Chapter Summary

Section 1: From Ancient Greece to the Middle Ages

- The first great philosophers, historians, and writers were the ancient Greeks.
- Ancient Romans created a system of written laws that are still in use today.
- In the Middle Ages, many people found order and security in feudalism and Christianity.

Section 2: Renaissance and the Age of Revolution

- The ideas, writing, and art of the ancient world later inspired Renaissance scholars and artists.
- Explorers began to travel beyond Europe in search of wealth.
- Revolutions in government and science changed European ways of life.

Section 3: Industrial Revolution and Nationalism

- The Industrial Revolution changed the way that goods were made and how people lived and worked.
- Workers began to demand better working conditions and a voice in government.
- Europe experienced a century of war and nationalism in the 1900s.

Section 4: Imperial Russia to the Soviet Union

- By the 1900s, Russia was a huge empire.
- Following the Russian Revolution, Vladimir Lenin came to power and a communist state was established.
- The Cold War was a time of great tension between the United States and Russia that lasted for nearly 50 years.
- After the collapse of the Soviet Union, the Russian Federation was formed.

Section 5: The European Union

- The European Union was officially created in 1992.
- The European Union works to achieve common security and economic goals.
- Three main institutions create European Union policy.
- The European Union continues to expand.

Euro bills and coins

◆ Key Terms

Match the vocabulary words with their correct definitions.

1. Industrial Revolution
2. euro
3. foreign minister
4. alliance
5. Renaissance
6. tsar

A   a Russian emperor

B   a government official who is in charge of relations with other nations

C   the currency of the European Union

D   the period of history when products began to be made by machines in factories

E   a period of history that included the rebirth of interest in learning and art

F   an agreement between countries to protect and defend each other

◆ Comprehension and Critical Thinking

7. (a) List Name two important ideas given to us by the ancient Greeks.
(b) Synthesize How did Alexander the Great spread Greek ideas?

8. (a) Recall When did the Renaissance reach its peak?
(b) Explain To what culture did Renaissance scholars and artists look for inspiration?
(c) Contrast How did the art of the Renaissance differ from the art of the Middle Ages?

9. (a) Name In what ways did people suffer as a result of industrialization?
(b) Draw Conclusions Why did labor unions begin to form during the Industrial Revolution?
(c) Identify Effects How did changes in society during the Industrial Revolution lead to changes in government?

10. (a) Explain Why was there rioting in Russia in 1917?
(b) Identify Effects How did Lenin use the power of ideas to persuade Russians to follow him?

11. (a) Explain How did Russia gain more territory and become an empire?
(b) Summarize Why did the Russian people come to oppose the tsars?
(c) Contrast How was Russia under the tsars different from the Soviet Union under communism?

12. (a) Recall What are the main goals of the European Union?
(b) Analyze Why might EU member nations prefer to handle some issues, such as health-care, education, and housing policies, on their own?

◆ Skills Practice

Problem Solving In the Skills for Life activity in this chapter, you learned how to solve problems. Review the steps you followed to learn this skill. Then turn to the section titled Changes in Society on page 55 of this chapter. Identify the problem that factory workers faced. Then explain how the problem was solved.

◆ Writing Activity: Math

Rome's emperor Hadrian had a wall built from coast to coast across northern England, in order to defend his empire's land. The wall extends 73 miles (118 kilometers) from Wallsend in the east to Bowness in the west. There are many towers and gates along the wall. About every seven miles there is a fort. Calculate how long it would have taken an army to march the entire length of the wall, if their marching speed was three miles per hour. Write a paragraph explaining your opinion on whether a wall would work as a type of defense.

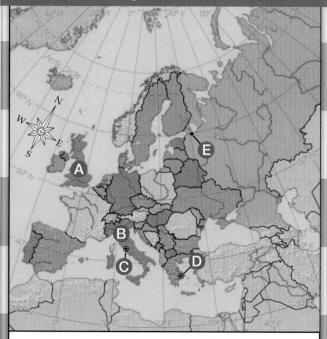

MAP MASTER™
Skills Activity

Europe and Russia

Place Location For each place listed below, write the letter from the map that shows its location. Use the maps in the Regional Overview to help you.

1. Athens
2. Rome
3. Italy
4. Great Britain
5. St. Petersburg

Go Online
PHSchool.com Use Web Code **ldp-7225** for an interactive map.

Standardized Test Prep

Test-Taking Tips

Some questions on standardized tests ask you to find main ideas or topic sentences. Read the paragraph below. Then follow the tips to answer the sample question.

> In 334 B.C., Alexander the Great set out from Greece to conquer the world. Within ten years, his empire extended from Egypt to northern India. He founded many new cities across these lands. Greek culture linked the whole Mediterranean world by the time of his death in 323 B.C.

Pick the letter that best answers the question.

Which topic sentence is missing from this paragraph?

A Alexander the Great was a great soldier, thinker, and artist.

B Alexander the Great was one of the world's greatest military minds.

C The accomplishments of Alexander the Great were enormous.

D Alexander's conquest spread Greek language, culture, and ideas.

TIP Some paragraphs have a topic sentence that states the main idea. All the other sentences in the paragraph support this point.

Think It Through What is the main point of the paragraph? You can eliminate C because it is too general. Answer A may or may not be true, but even if it is true, it doesn't completely describe every sentence in the paragraph. That leaves B and D. Alexander was a great military mind, but the paragraph includes other accomplishments as well. The correct answer is D.

TIP Make sure that you read each answer choice carefully. Carelessness can easily cost points on a multiple-choice test.

Practice Questions

Use the tips above and other tips in this book to help you answer the following questions.

1. In a feudal system, there is a special relationship between

   A knights and foot soldiers.

   B lords and vassals.

   C peasants and knights.

   D peasants and kings.

2. Which of the following would not be discussed under the topic sentence, Renaissance sculptors made powerful lifelike statues?

   A the work of Michelangelo

   B the importance of human beings to Renaissance artists

   C the role of printing in the Renaissance

   D the 1500 sculpture named *David*

3. After World War II, Eastern Europe was under the influence of which country?

   A the Soviet Union

   B France

   C Germany

   D the United States

4. What type of leader was Joseph Stalin?

   A president

   B tsar

   C prime minister

   D dictator

Go Online
PHSchool.com

Use Web Code **lda-7201**
for a **Chapter 2 self-test.**

From Pearl in the Egg
By Dorothy Van Woerkom

Prepare to Read

Background Information

In Europe in the Middle Ages, a typical day for a person your age was quite different than it is for you. For one thing, a child at that time was considered much closer to being an adult than is a child today. This is because people had shorter life expectancies. More people in those days died of diseases that today can be cured.

Pearl in the Egg was the name of a real girl who lived in the 1200s. Historians know little about her. Dorothy Van Woerkom has written a book of historical fiction about Pearl. Her descriptions of Pearl's life are based on what historians know about life in England in the 1200s. At that time, people in Europe were just beginning to use family names. Usually they gave themselves names that described their work or their families in some way.

In this part of Pearl's story, you will read about a typical day in her life.

Objectives

In this selection you will

1. Learn about the everyday life of a young serf in the Middle Ages.
2. Understand the importance of work on a feudal manor.

---

rushlight (RUSH lyt) *n.* a lamp made with grease and part of a rush, or swamp plant

Pearl set the bowl of cabbage soup down on the floor near the rushlight. She knelt beside the box of straw that was her father's bed. She wiped his forehead, listening to his heavy breathing.

"Please, Fa," she coaxed. She broke off a piece from a loaf of black bread and dipped it into the soup. She placed it on his lips, letting the soup trickle into his mouth. She ate the chunk of bread, and dipped another.

dripping (DRIP ing) *n.* fat and juices drawn from cooking meat

"I will be in the fields until the nooning," she said, "so you must try to eat a little now. See, I have put a bit of dripping in the soup."

She forced the warm, mild liquid down his throat until the bowl was half empty. She drank the rest herself, chewing hungrily on the lump of fat that the sick man had not been able to swallow.

Again she wiped his face, and then she blew out the light. She crossed the smooth dirt floor, and pulled a sack from a peg on the wall near the door as she left the hut. Outside, the sky was gray with the dawn. Ground fog swirled around her feet. The air smelled of ripening grain and moist earth.

serfs (surfs) *n.* peasant farmers who worked the land as the slaves of a wealthy landowner

From other huts of mud and timber, serfs hurried out into the early morning mist. Some, like Pearl, would spend the day in their own small holdings in the fields. It was the time for harvesting their crops, which would feed their families through the winter. Others, like Pearl's older brother, Gavin, had already left for work in the manor fields to bring in Sir Geoffrey's crops.

Sir Geoffrey was lord of the manor, which included his great stone house and all the land surrounding it. He owned this tiny village. He even owned most of the people in it. A few, like the baker, the miller, and the soapmaker, were freemen and free women. They worked for themselves and paid the lord taxes. For tax, Sir Geoffrey collected a portion of everything they produced. No one in the village had money.

But the serfs were not free. They could never leave the manor, or marry without the lord's permission. They could not fish in the streams or hunt in the forest. They owned only their mud huts and small gardens, called holdings, and an ox or cow, or a few geese or sheep. The serfs also paid taxes. Each year they gave Sir Geoffrey a portion of their crops. He took a share of their eggs; if a flock of sheep or geese increased, he took a share; and if a cow had a calf, he took that also. On certain days of the week each family had to send a man—and an ox if they had one—to help plow the lord's fields, harvest his crops, and do their work. Each woman had to weave one garment a year for the lord and his family.

A page from a French book dating from around 1460 shows people planting seeds.

The sun was up when Pearl reached the long <u>furrows</u> of her field, where the flat green bean pods weighed down their low bushes. She bent to see if the leaves were dry. Wet leaves would wither when she touched them.

furrows (FUR ohz) *n.* grooves in the earth made by a plow

The sun had dried them. Pearl began filling her sack, wondering how she could finish the harvest all by herself before the first frost. She had other plots to work as well.

Now that their father was ill, twelve-year-old Gavin was taking his place for three days each week in the manor fields. Sir Geoffrey would get his crops safely in! But if the frost came early, or if the only one left at home to work was an eleven-year-old like Pearl, that was of small matter to Sir Geoffrey.

Pearl stood up to rub her back. A serf's life was a hard life. Her father's was, and his father's before him. She sighed. Who could hope to change it?

Old <u>Clotilde</u> came swaying up the narrow path between her field and Pearl's. She waved her empty sack by way of greeting and squatted down among her plants.

"How be your Fa this morning?" she asked Pearl.

Clotilde (kluh TILD)

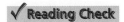
Reading Check

Why does Pearl work alone in her family's holdings?

A painting of nobles hunting illustrates this manuscript, created in 1515.

bowmen (BOH mun) *n.* men with bows and arrows; archers

defiant (dee FY unt) *adj.* bold or resistant

"He took some soup. But he wanders in his head. He thinks I am my mother, though she's been dead three summers now."

"Ah, and he'll join her soon, Big Rollin will." Clotilde's wrinkled face was nearly the same dirty gray as her cap. "They all do, soon as they take a mite of sickness. For the likes of us to stay alive, we must stay well! Get the priest for him! He won't plow these fields again."

Before Pearl could reply, the shrill blare of a hunting horn sounded across the meadow, followed by the baying of hounds on the trail of a wild boar. Startled to their feet, the serfs watched the terrified boar running in and out among the rows of crops.

"Run, lest you get trampled!" Clotilde screamed, dashing down the path toward the forest. The others followed her. Someone pulled Pearl along as she stumbled forward, blinded by angry tears, her fingers tightly gripping her sack.

The hounds came running in pursuit of the boar. Behind the hounds rode the hunting party of twenty horsemen, led by Sir Geoffrey. At the rear was another man Pearl recognized. Jack, one of Sir Geoffrey's <u>bowmen</u>, had come upon her one day as she scrounged for dead branches near the edge of the forest. He had baited her with cruel words, rudely ruffling her hair with the shaft end of an arrow.

"Jack's my name. What's yours?" he had demanded, taking pleasure in her discomfort. For answer she had spat at him, and he had pressed the arrow's metal tip against her wrist until she'd dropped her bundle. Laughing, he had scattered the branches with his foot and grabbed her hair.

"Spit at me again, girl, and that will be the end of you!" Though his mouth had turned up in a grin, his eyes had been bright with anger. His fingers had tightened on the nape of her neck, bending her head back. She stared up at him, frightened, but <u>defiant</u>.

"Perhaps you need a lesson in manners right now," he'd said, raising his other hand. He probably would have struck her, but for the rattle of a wagon and the tuneless whistle signaling someone's approach. He had let her go with a suddenness that had left her off balance, and had stalked away.

Shaken, Pearl had turned to see Sir Geoffrey's woodcutter driving out of the forest with a wagonload of wood for the manor house.

Now Pearl shuddered at the memory; but Jack was taking no notice of her. His eyes were on the boar and on his master. If the boar became maddened during the chase and turned on one of the hunters, Jack was ready with his arrows to put an end to the beast.

Over the meadow they galloped, and onto the fields. They churned up the soft earth, trampled down the precious bean plants, crushed the near-ripe ears of the barley and oats, tore up the tender pea vines. They chased the boar across the fields and back again, laughing at the sport.

When they had gone, Pearl ran back to her field. She crawled in the turned-up earth, searching for unbroken bean pods. The other serfs were doing the same.

"What is the matter with us?" she demanded of Clotilde, "Why do we stay silent, with spoiled crops all around us, just so Sir Geoffrey will have his sport?"

"Shish!" Clotilde warned, looking quickly around to see who might have heard. "Do you want a <u>flogging</u> for such bold words? Hold your tongue, as you see your elders do."

For the rest of the morning they worked in silence. At midday, Pearl picked up her half-filled sack. It should have been full by now. She glared fiercely across the meadow at the manor house, but she held her tongue.

Pearl returned home to find that her father had worsened. When she could not rouse him, she went for the priest.

About the Selection

Pearl in the Egg: A Tale of the Thirteenth Century, with illustrations by Joe Lasker, was published in 1980. Pearl in the Egg and Matil Makejoye, another character who appears in the book, were listed in the king's account books as minstrels in the court of King Edward I. The story of Pearl's life is fiction, but it is based on the life of real people in the 1200s.

flogging (FLAHG ing) *n.* a beating or whipping

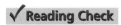

Reading Check

What stopped Jack from hitting Pearl?

Review and Assessment

Thinking About the Selection

1. **(a) Recall** What did the serfs use to pay their taxes?
(b) Explain Why did the serfs give Sir Geoffrey a portion of their crops every year?
(c) Infer The feudal system existed for more than 400 years. Why do you think it lasted for such a long time?
2. **(a) Explain** What did Clotilde mean when she said, "Do you want a flogging for such bold words?"

(b) Predict Based on what you know about Pearl, how do you think she might act the next time she sees the lord or one of his men?

Writing Activity
Write a Short Story
Write a preface to Pearl's story telling how she received the name Pearl in the Egg. Or write a short story in which Pearl awakens in 2005. She is still 11 years old, and her father is still ill. Describe her reaction to today's world.

About the Author

Dorothy Van Woerkom (b. 1924) was born in Buffalo, New York. She was an elementary school teacher before becoming a writer. She is most noted for her folktale translations and her religious stories. She often rewrites folktales, sometimes changing the characters' names and the settings, but keeping the plot.

Chapter Preview

This chapter will introduce you to the cultures of Europe and Russia.

Section 1
The Cultures of Western Europe

Section 2
The Cultures of Eastern Europe

Section 3
The Cultures of the Russian Federation

Target Reading Skill

Identify Main Ideas In this chapter you will focus on finding and remembering the main idea, or the most important point, of sections and paragraphs.

▶ The golden domes of the Annunciation Cathedral brighten up the sky above Moscow, Russia.

MAP MASTER™
Skills Activity

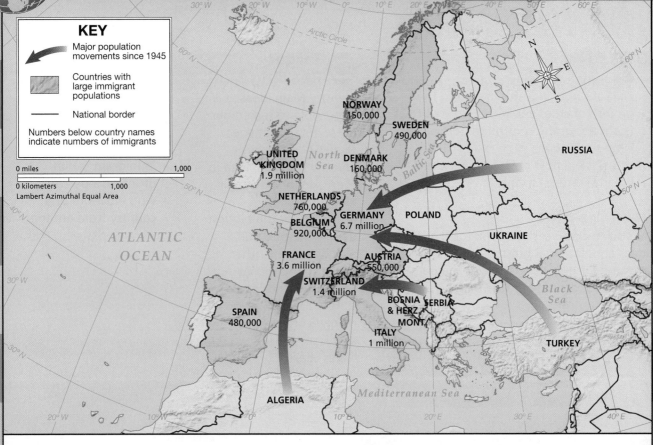

KEY

Major population
movements since 1945

Countries with
large immigrant
populations

National border

Numbers below country names
indicate numbers of immigrants

0 miles — 1,000
0 kilometers — 1,000
Lambert Azimuthal Equal Area

NORWAY
150,000

SWEDEN
490,000

North Sea

DENMARK
160,000

Baltic Sea

RUSSIA

**UNITED
KINGDOM**
1.9 million

NETHERLANDS
760,000

GERMANY
6.7 million

POLAND

BELGIUM
920,000

UKRAINE

FRANCE
3.6 million

AUSTRIA
550,000

*ATLANTIC
OCEAN*

SWITZERLAND
1.4 million

*Black
Sea*

SPAIN
480,000

**BOSNIA
& HERZ.** **SERBIA**
MONT.

ITALY
1 million

TURKEY

Mediterranean Sea

ALGERIA

Movement Every year, the countries of Western Europe attract large
numbers of immigrants. **Identify** How many people have moved to France
from other countries? **Predict** If the economies of North Africa and Eastern
Europe improve, how might that affect migration to Western Europe?

Go Online
PHSchool.com Use Web Code
ldp-7311 for step-by-step
map skills practice.

The Cultures of Western Europe

Prepare to Read

Objectives

In this section you will
1. Find out how industry has led to the growth of cities and increased wealth.
2. Learn about the cultural centers of Western Europe.
3. Understand how open borders affect life in Western Europe.

Taking Notes

As you read this section, look for the main ideas and details about the cultures of Western Europe. Copy the web diagram below and record your findings in it.

Western European Cultures

Target Reading Skill

Identify Main Ideas It is impossible to remember every detail that you read. Good readers identify the main idea in every section. The main idea is the most important or the biggest point—the one that includes all the other points in the section. Sometimes this idea is stated directly. As you read, record the main ideas of this section in the Taking Notes chart.

Key Terms

- **urbanization** (ur bun ih ZAY shun) *n.* the movement of populations toward cities
- **immigrant** (IM uh grunt) *n.* a person who moves to one country from another

A high-speed train travels across Europe.

As the train speeds down the track, the passengers hear hardly a whisper. As the passengers sit in their comfortable seats, they can look out the window at the highway next to the railroad. They know that the cars are traveling at least 60 miles (96 kilometers) per hour, but the cars seem to be moving backward. That's because the train is traveling three times faster than the cars—about 180 miles (289 kilometers) per hour.

Would you like to take a trip like that? You can if you go to France, which has some of the world's fastest trains. Great Britain also has speedy rail travel. Some British trains reach speeds of 140 miles (225 kilometers) per hour. In Western Europe, high-speed trains have made travel between countries easy and fast. Someone in a European country can be in another country in hours. Such easy movement through Western Europe affects the entire culture of the region.

Growth of Industry

Most Western European countries are prosperous, or wealthy. This prosperity is based on strong economies. The economies of Western Europe have grown because of productive industries and high-quality services.

A Farming Revolution

The Industrial Revolution of the late 1700s sped up the development of industry in Western Europe. Before the Industrial Revolution, most people worked on farms. They could grow little beyond their basic food needs. Over time, new and better farm machines were able to do tasks that once required many workers. Farmers also learned ways to improve soil quality and fight insects. With these advances, farms could produce more and better crops with fewer laborers.

This revolution in farming grew out of the Industrial Revolution. Factory-made farm equipment and chemicals helped each farmer to grow more. Thus, as the need for farm workers declined, the need for industrial workers grew. Many people began moving to cities, where factories were located.

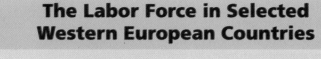

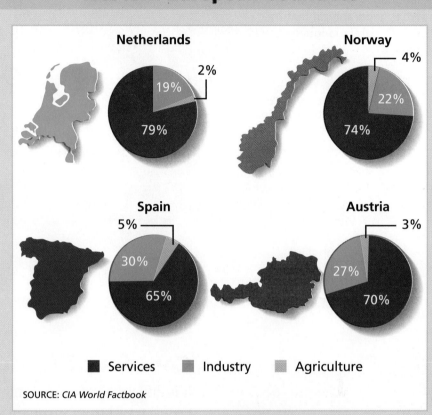

The Labor Force in Selected Western European Countries

Netherlands — 2%, 19%, 79%

Norway — 4%, 22%, 74%

Spain — 5%, 30%, 65%

Austria — 3%, 27%, 70%

■ Services ■ Industry ■ Agriculture

SOURCE: *CIA World Factbook*

The Growth of Cities

Urbanization (ur bun ih ZAY shun), or the movement of populations toward cities, was a trend throughout the 1800s and 1900s. Following World War II, it increased rapidly. The United States provided billions of dollars to help Western Europe recover from the war. With this help, the region's industries came back stronger than ever. And even more people left rural areas to work in cities.

Today, the majority of Western Europeans have a comfortable life. They earn good wages working in factories or in service industries such as banking and food service.

✓ Reading Check **How was farming transformed?**

▌ Diagram Skills

The economies of most Western European countries today are based on service industries. **Identify** Which country has the highest percentage of its labor force in services? **Compare** In what ways are the labor forces in all four countries similar?

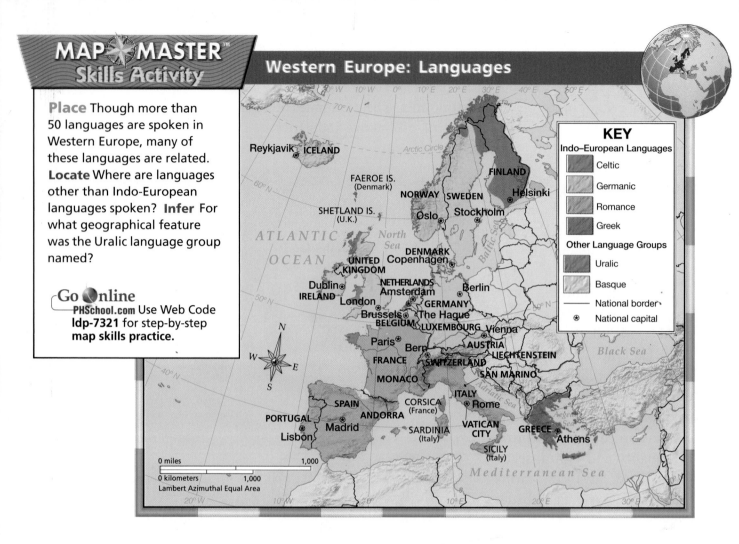

Western Europe: Languages

Place Though more than 50 languages are spoken in Western Europe, many of these languages are related. **Locate** Where are languages other than Indo-European languages spoken? **Infer** For what geographical feature was the Uralic language group named?

Go Online
PHSchool.com Use Web Code **ldp-7321** for step-by-step **map skills practice**.

KEY

Indo–European Languages
- Celtic
- Germanic
- Romance
- Greek

Other Language Groups
- Uralic
- Basque
- National border
- ⊛ National capital

Centers of Culture

It is difficult to travel far in Europe without coming across a city. People travel from small towns and villages to cities to find jobs. Some people go to cities to attend school. People also travel to cities to enjoy cultural attractions. These include museums, concerts, restaurants, nightclubs, theaters, and stores.

A modern entrance was added to the over-400-year-old Louvre Museum in Paris, France.

The Old and the New Most Western European cities are a mix of the old and the new. Both public buildings and houses from the Middle Ages are a common sight. They stand next to modern apartments and office buildings. Cars and buses drive along cobblestone streets once used by horse-drawn carriages. Monuments honor leaders who lived hundreds of years ago. Market plazas dating back to medieval times still thrive today.

Vibrant Cities Each city in Western Europe is different from every other city. However, they all share certain characteristics. The majority of Western Europeans live and work in cities. Cities are also the centers of Western European culture.

Let's take a look at some Western European capital cities. Paris, the capital of France, attracts scholars, writers, and artists from all over the world. England's capital, London, is known for its important financial center as well as for its grand historic buildings and lovely parks. The Spanish capital city of Madrid (muh DRID) is known as a place with a vibrant street life, a place where people meet on café terraces to relax outdoors after work. As a cultural and economic center for the Spanish-speaking world, the city is rich in both business and the arts. The German capital, Berlin, is always full of activity and attracts many visitors to its theaters and museums.

Work and Leisure Let's focus on life in Germany for a moment. Most visitors to Germany think that the Germans are efficient. In other words, Germans do their work without waste or extra effort. Visitors get this idea from what they see. German cities, streets, and buses are kept clean. Hotels are well run. German cars are well designed. Travel is swift on an excellent system of highways. Travel is equally fast on high-speed trains.

But life in Germany is not all hard work and fast-paced activity. Many workers enjoy as much as six weeks of vacation each year. Skiing, hiking, and camping are popular recreational activities throughout the country's mountains and highlands. The country's many rivers, as well as the North and Baltic seas, are good for swimming and boating. Those who prefer city life enjoy the museums, concerts, and plays. Life is similar in countries throughout Western Europe.

The European Union and the Arts One of the goals of the European Union is to support Europe's cultural community. Although different from one another geographically and politically, European nations often share a common history and cultural heritage. They all belong to the European community. The EU organizes concerts, cultural events, exhibits, and conferences to bring Europeans together. The EU's goal is to respect individual cultures, while encouraging cooperation among them.

European City Scenes
A trolley passes by historical buildings in Amsterdam, the Netherlands, in the top photo. The photo above shows Germany's Parliament building, called the Reichstag, in Berlin. It was built in 1995 after the country was reunified. **Infer** *Why do you think the German government chose a modern style of architecture for its new Parliament building?*

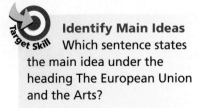

Identify Main Ideas Which sentence states the main idea under the heading The European Union and the Arts?

Links Across
Time

Immigrants in the United Kingdom The United Kingdom's immigrant population today reflects its history as a world power. In 2004, almost half of the immigrants came from countries—including Pakistan, India, and Nigeria—that were once under British rule. In the future, the UK's immigration patterns are expected to change. As more countries from Eastern and Central Europe join the EU, large numbers of people from those regions are expected to immigrate to the UK and other Western European countries.

To achieve that goal, the EU finances programs that help cultural development and encourage cultural exchange. One of the programs that the EU funds is the DEBORA (Digital Access to Books of the Renaissance) project. It gives Internet users access to documents from the Renaissance. The books and materials dating from the 1500s are stored in libraries throughout Europe. However, access to these collections is often limited. With the EU's support, Internet technology now makes viewing the collections possible. The EU helps museums, libraries, and other cultural institutions make these collections accessible to more people. By doing so, it helps connect people to their cultural heritage.

Changing Immigration Patterns Although life in Western Europe is good now, it was not always so. In the 1800s and early 1900s, millions of Western Europeans left Europe. Most went to the United States, Canada, and South America. They left in search of more opportunities and better lives.

Since World War II, patterns of human movement have been reversed. Large numbers of people stopped leaving Western Europe. Industry continued to expand in the postwar years and more workers were needed. As a result, people from other countries began moving to Western Europe.

Today's Immigrants Today, about 6 percent of workers in Western Europe are **immigrants** (IM uh grunts), or people who move to one country from another. Most of the immigrants in Western Europe are from Eastern Europe, North Africa, South Asia, and the Middle East. The four largest countries in the European Union—France, Germany, Italy, and the United Kingdom—all have large immigrant populations.

More than 6 million immigrants live in France, making up more than 10 percent of the total population. Algerians make up the largest group of immigrants. In 2005, the number of immigrants in Germany accounted for about 12 percent of its total population, or more than 10 million people. Many of Germany's immigrants come from Poland, Turkey, and the former Yugoslavia, with smaller numbers of other Europeans and Asians.

About 4 percent of Italy's population is foreign-born, with Romanians, Moroccans, and Albanians being the largest groups. Most of the United Kingdom's 5 million immigrants come from Ireland, India, Pakistan, and Central and Eastern Europe. They make up about 9 percent of the country's population.

Blending Cultures Immigrants do not leave their cultures behind when they leave their homelands. They bring their languages, religious beliefs, values, and customs to their new homes. But most immigrants make changes in their ways of life. They may change the way they dress. They may try new foods and discover new ways of cooking. Most immigrants learn the language of their new country.

In many ways, immigration has changed the cultures of Western Europe. In countries like the United Kingdom and France, people from many different backgrounds live and work together. They learn about one another's ways of life. In the process, the cultures blend and change. In this way, many Western European countries have become multicultural.

✔ **Reading Check** What does the European Union hope to gain by supporting the arts?

Video
Learn how soccer brings Europeans together.

Faces of Western European Immigration
The photos from left to right show Africans in France, Caribbean Islanders in the UK, a Turkish woman in Germany, and a South American in Italy. All are immigrants.
Analyze Images *What details in the photographs show cultural traditions that these people have brought with them?*

Goods are transferred from a train to a truck in Munich-Reim, Germany.

Open Borders

You read that on a high-speed train, travelers can go from one country to another in a matter of hours. Ideas, goods, and raw materials can travel quickly as well. In addition to the closeness of the countries and the good train service, Western Europe is becoming more prosperous because goods and people can now flow freely across its borders.

Adding to the ease of movement across the borders is the use of a single European currency, the euro, which you read about in Chapter 2. Think about how different it was when a traveler had to stop at every country's border to show a passport and to change money to the local currency. Since 2002, the euro has replaced old currencies such as the French franc, the German mark, and the Italian lira.

Adopting the euro is one step in a series of efforts to move Europe toward both economic and political unity. Even the colorful design of the euro coins and bills reflects this effort. They do not have any famous people on them. Instead, they symbolize European unity by featuring a map of Europe, flags of the EU member nations, and bridges, gateways, and windows. The open exchange of ideas, goods, and money is an outcome of the European Union and has helped Western Europe thrive.

✓ **Reading Check** Which factors have created a prosperous Western Europe?

 Section 1 Assessment

Key Terms
Review the key terms at the beginning of this section. Use each term in a sentence that explains its meaning.

Target Reading Skill
State the main ideas in Section 1.

Comprehension and Critical Thinking
1. (a) **Recall** What is Western Europe's prosperity based on?

(b) **Identify Effects** How has the growth of industry affected cities in Western Europe?
2. (a) **List** Which four Western European countries have large immigrant populations?
(b) **Summarize** How have immigrants changed the cultures of Western Europe?
3. (a) **Explain** Why is it easy to travel among Western European countries?
(b) **Make Generalizations** How would life be different for travelers in Western Europe if borders were not open?

Writing Activity
Write down two facts about Western Europe that you were surprised to learn. How has this new information changed the way you think about Western Europe or its people?

For: An activity on the European Union
Visit: PHSchool.com
Web Code: ldd-7301

The Cultures of Eastern Europe

Prepare to Read

Objectives

In this section you will

1. Learn about the different ethnic groups in Eastern Europe.
2. Understand the impact of foreign domination on the region.
3. Find out about ethnic conflict in Eastern Europe.
4. Learn about Eastern Europe's cultural centers.

Taking Notes

As you read, create an outline of this section. The outline below has been started for you.

> I. Eastern Europe's ethnic groups
>   A. Slavic heritage
>   1.
>   2.
>   B. Non-Slavic groups
> II.

Target Reading Skill

Identify Supporting Details The main idea of a section is supported by details that explain or develop the main idea with reasons or examples. The main idea of the section titled Eastern Europe's Ethnic Groups is stated in the first sentence of the first paragraph under the heading Slavic Cultures. As you read, note the details following each of the blue headings that tell more about the cultures of Eastern Europe.

Key Terms

- **migration** (my GRAY shun) *n.* movement from place to place
- **ethnic group** (ETH nik groop) *n.* a group of people who share the same ancestors, culture, language, or religion
- **dialect** (DY uh lekt) *n.* a version of a language found only in a certain region

---

If you look at a map of Europe as it was one hundred years ago, you may notice something odd. Many of today's Eastern European countries are missing. Until 1918, three large empires ruled most of this region.

Eastern Europe formed a crossroads between east and west. To the east lay the Russian and Ottoman empires. To the west lay Germany and Austria. There were few mountains or other natural barriers to keep invaders out of Eastern Europe. For example, Russia, Prussia, and Austria moved into Poland and divided it among themselves in 1795. Poland did not become independent again until the end of World War I in 1918.

Movement throughout much of Eastern Europe has always been easy. For thousands of years, various groups have entered or crossed this region. This movement from place to place, called **migration** (my GRAY shun), is still happening today.

A European map from 1911

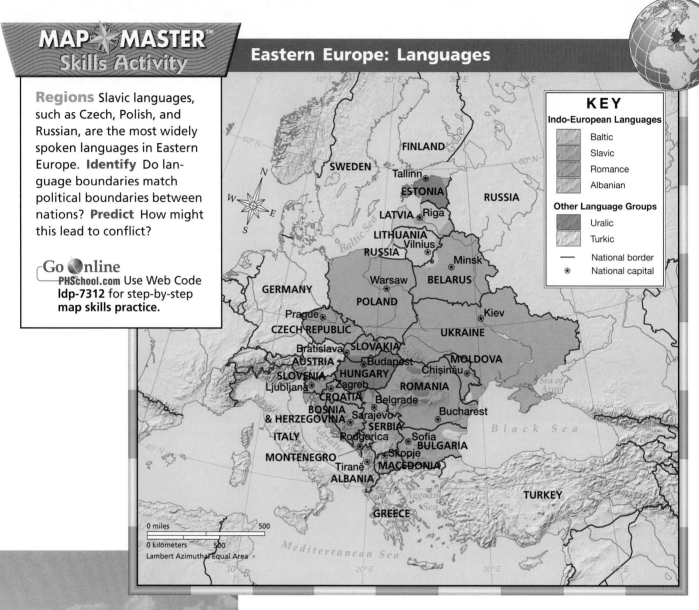

Regions Slavic languages, such as Czech, Polish, and Russian, are the most widely spoken languages in Eastern Europe. **Identify** Do language boundaries match political boundaries between nations? **Predict** How might this lead to conflict?

Go Online
PHSchool.com Use Web Code **ldp-7312** for step-by-step **map skills practice.**

KEY

Indo-European Languages
- Baltic
- Slavic
- Romance
- Albanian

Other Language Groups
- Uralic
- Turkic

— National border
⊛ National capital

Lambert Azimuthal Equal Area

0 miles 500
0 kilometers 500

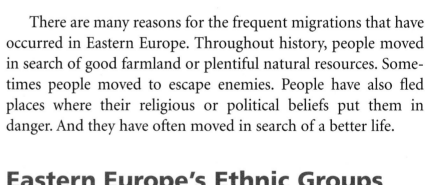

There are many reasons for the frequent migrations that have occurred in Eastern Europe. Throughout history, people moved in search of good farmland or plentiful natural resources. Sometimes people moved to escape enemies. People have also fled places where their religious or political beliefs put them in danger. And they have often moved in search of a better life.

Eastern Europe's Ethnic Groups

One of the groups that migrated across Eastern Europe long ago was the Slavs (slahvz). These people first lived in present-day Poland, Slovakia (sloh VAH kee uh), and Ukraine. By the 700s, the Slavs had spread south to Greece, west to the Alps, north to the Baltic Sea, and east into Russia.

A Roma family

Slavic Cultures Today, descendants of Slavs make up most of Eastern Europe's ethnic groups. An **ethnic group** is a group of people with a shared culture, language, or religion that sets them apart from their neighbors. Two thousand years ago, there was a single Slavic language. As the Slavs separated and moved to different areas, different Slavic languages developed. Today, about ten Slavic languages are spoken in Eastern Europe. These include Czech, Polish, and Russian.

Some countries in Eastern Europe are almost entirely Slavic-speaking. These countries include Poland, Croatia (kroh AY shuh), Slovenia (sloh VEE nee uh), and the Czech Republic.

However, even two people who speak the same Slavic language may not speak the same dialect. A **dialect** (DY uh lekt) is a version of a language that can be found only in a certain region.

There are also major religious differences among descendants of Slavs. Most follow the Eastern Orthodox faith or Roman Catholicism. Others may be Protestant or Muslim.

Other Ethnic Groups Many other ethnic groups live in Eastern Europe as well. About 90 percent of the people of Hungary belong to an ethnic group called the Magyars (MAG yahrz). In Romania, most people are Romanians. Similarly, in Albania, most people are Albanian. Roma, sometimes called Gypsies, and Germans live in several of the countries of Eastern Europe.

✓ **Reading Check** Name three Slavic languages that are spoken in Eastern Europe.

Identify Supporting Details
What details in these paragraphs give examples of Slavic languages?

Worshiping in Different Ways
Below, hundreds of Muslims pray at a mosque in Bosnia. At the left, women participate in a religious ceremony in an Eastern Orthodox church in Macedonia.
Synthesize *Though these Eastern Europeans practice different religions, what other cultural traditions might they share?*

Regions This book uses the term *Eastern Europe* to describe the region including the former Yugoslavia and the nations dominated by the Soviet Union after World War II. **Identify** Which nation is physically in the eastern half of Europe, but is not part of what we call Eastern Europe? **Apply Information** Why is this country not considered part of Eastern Europe?

Go Online
PHSchool.com Use Web Code ldp-7322 for step-by-step map skills practice.

KEY
— National border
⊛ National capital
• Other city

0 miles 400
0 kilometers 400
Lambert Azimuthal Equal Area

Foreign Domination

As you read at the beginning of this section, Eastern Europe is a region with a history of foreign domination. As you read in Chapter 2, most of Eastern Europe came under Soviet control following World War II. Communist leaders, influenced by the Soviet Union, led the governments of most Eastern European countries.

As in the Soviet Union, the Communists tried to control almost every aspect of people's lives. They took private land, and punished people for criticizing the government. They discouraged traditional expressions of culture such as religion. However, they did not succeed in destroying Eastern European culture. Instead, the cultural traditions you have read about brought people together. In Poland, for example, the Roman Catholic faith unified people in opposition to the Soviets. In Ukraine, people continued to speak Ukrainian even though Russian was the official language.

✓ **Reading Check** What country influenced Eastern Europe's leaders?

Ethnic Conflict

Eastern Europe's long history of migration and foreign domination have made it an ethnically diverse region. At times, that diversity has brought ethnic conflict. Ethnic conflict in the region has been resolved both peacefully and violently.

Czechs and Slovaks: A Peaceful Division Czechoslovakia (chek uh sloh VAH kee uh) had two main ethnic groups. The Czechs lived mostly in the western regions of Bohemia and Moravia. The Slovaks lived mostly in the eastern region of Slovakia. Hungarians, Ukrainians, Germans, and Poles lived in both areas.

Czechoslovakia was taken over by Communists, heavily influenced by the Soviet Union, after World War II. From the 1960s to the 1980s, students and writers formed groups protesting communism and calling for a return to democracy. Vaclav Havel, a playwright, explained his reasons for staying in Czechoslovakia.

> **"I am Czech. . . . This is my language, this is my home. I don't feel myself to be patriotic, because I don't feel that to be Czech is to be something more than French, English, or European, or anybody else. . . . I try to do something for my country because I live here. "**
>
> —*Vaclav Havel*

Such protests helped end communism in Czechoslovakia. However, Czechs and the Slovaks disagreed about how to run the newly democratic country. In 1993, they agreed to peacefully separate into two countries—the Czech Republic and Slovakia.

Yugoslavia: A Violent Division Unlike in Czechoslovakia, ethnic differences in the former country of Yugoslavia (yoo goh SLAH vee uh) led to violence and the breakup of the country. You will read more about this conflict in Chapter 5.

✓ **Reading Check** Who is Vaclav Havel?

The Velvet Revolution
Crowds celebrate Czechoslovakia's transition to a democratic government, which took place in a peaceful movement called the Velvet Revolution. Playwright Vaclav Havel, shown below, became the country's first president. **Infer** *Why was Czechoslovakia's change in government called the "Velvet Revolution"?*

Prague: A Historic City
Prague's buildings are a rich mix of architectural styles, including Renaissance, Gothic, and modern. Many of Prague's historic buildings house art collections. **Apply Information** *What role do you think tourism plays in the economy of the Czech Republic?*

European Centers of Culture

As in Western Europe, Eastern Europe's cities are important centers of life and culture throughout the region. These cities have thrived particularly since the fall of communist governments in the region in the 1980s.

Prague: A City Rich in Culture Prague (prahg) is the capital of the Czech Republic. Though people settled in the region thousands of years ago, the city first developed in the A.D. 800s. The Vltava (VUL tuh vuh) River winds its way through the city. Prague Castle, built in the late 800s, sits high on a hill overlooking the city. Houses dating back hundreds of years line the narrow streets of the historic city center.

Prague has always been an important center of culture. Antonín Dvořák (AHN toh nin DVAWR zhahk) and several other famous Czech composers lived in Prague. Today, their music is performed every year at a spring music festival in the city. The composer Wolfgang Mozart, an Austrian, also lived and wrote some of his famous pieces in Prague.

Prague is well known for its many theaters. It is also an important center for art, with its many museums and galleries.

Budapest: Queen of the Danube

Budapest (BOO duh pest) is Hungary's capital and its largest city. The Danube River runs through the city and separates it into two regions, Buda and Pest. These two regions, once separate cities, were joined together in 1873. Budapest got the nickname "Queen of the Danube" because of the beauty of the Danube and the hills surrounding the city.

Hungarian composers Béla Bartók (seated at left) and Zoltán Kodály (seated at right), with other Hungarian musicians, in the early 1900s

The history of Budapest stretches back to pre-Roman times. Ruins of Roman houses and baths can still be seen in Budapest. Today, it is a bustling capital city where more than one fifth of all Hungarians live. Unlike many Eastern European cities, Budapest remained a thriving cultural center even during communist times. This was because Hungary had stronger ties to Western Europe than other Eastern European countries had.

Like Prague, Budapest has produced famous composers such as Béla Bartók (BAY lah BAHR tawk) and Franz Liszt (frahntsz list). It is also an important center of art, theater, and scientific research.

 **Reading Check** **What is the capital of the Czech Republic?**

Section 2 Assessment

Key Terms
Review the key terms at the beginning of this section. Use each term in a sentence that explains its meaning.

Target Reading Skill
State the details that support the main idea on page 95.

Comprehension and Critical Thinking
1. (a) Locate Where did Slavs first live in Europe?
(b) Generalize What are some differences among Slavic groups?

(c) Summarize How did Poles use their culture to oppose the Soviet Union?
2. (a) Note Give an example of an Eastern European ethnic conflict that was solved peacefully.
(b) Conclude Why were the groups in this conflict able to come to an agreement without violence?
3. (a) Identify Name two important Eastern European cities that are centers of culture.
(b) Predict How might EU membership affect life in these two cities?

Writing Activity
Write a paragraph about ethnic diversity in Eastern Europe. In your paragraph, explain how ethnic diversity can enrich a country's culture and how it can create challenges as well.

Writing Tip Begin your paragraph with a topic sentence that states your main idea. Be sure to include examples that support your main idea.

Mr. St. Jean's debate class was discussing immigration. Mr. St. Jean had chosen that topic because he knew people had strong—and often opposing—opinions about the subject. For example, he pointed out that some people believe that when a country's economy is not doing well, immigration should be limited. They reason that immigrants might take jobs from people who have lived in the country for many years. Mr. St. Jean asked his class to think about this issue. Should countries limit immigration? And if so, what should the limits be?

Asiya thought about her own family. They had emigrated from Algeria to France. Her mother worked in a restaurant, and her father worked in a library. She did not think her parents had taken jobs from any French people. And if they had stayed in Algeria, they would not have had as good a life as they had in France. She decided to argue in favor of immigration.

A French border guard checks for illegal immigrants.

When you support a position, you present the reasoning and the evidence that back up your opinion or statement.

Learn the Skill

To learn how to support a position, follow the steps below:

1 **Write a statement that summarizes the position you want to support.** In general, a position is a broadly stated opinion that can be supported with facts. For her position statement, Asiya wrote, *Countries should not limit immigration.*

2 **Identify at least three reasons that support your position.** You may want to make notes or create a chart. Add as many details as you can to strengthen your argument. Use examples.

3 **Support each reason with accurate evidence.** Use reliable sources to strengthen your argument.

4 **Organize your reasons and supporting evidence.** Explain the connections between pieces of information, such as cause and effect.

5 **Add a reasoned conclusion.** Your conclusion should restate your position and summarize your reasons for it.

Practice the Skill

Reread the passages about immigration and culture on pages 88–89. Then decide what *your* position is about immigration. Use the steps in Learn the Skill to support your position.

1 Prepare to write a statement summarizing your position by first jotting down your ideas about immigration. Think about these questions as you decide on your position: Why do people emigrate? Why do some countries welcome immigrants? Why do other countries sharply limit immigration? How do immigrants affect the countries they move to? Now choose a position, and write a statement that summarizes it.

2 Add at least three reasons to explain why you hold your position. Clarify your reasons with examples or other details.

3 Research your position using reliable sources. Add additional reasons, details, and examples.

4 Review the information you have gathered and organize it in order to strengthen your argument. Does one reason lead to another?

5 Summarize your position about immigration in a one-sentence conclusion.

I support immigration because....

I do not support immigration because....

Apply the Skill

Reread the passage titled Growth of Industry on page 85. Use the steps you have learned in this lesson to identify and support a position on whether the trend toward urbanization in Europe is a positive or a negative thing.

The Cultures of the Russian Federation

Prepare to Read

Objectives

In this section you will
1. Learn about Russia's ethnic groups.
2. Find out about Russia's culture and its educational system.

Taking Notes

As you read this section, look for information about how cultural expression differed in the Soviet Union and Russia. Copy the table below and record your findings in it.

Cultural Expression	
Soviet Union	Russia
•	•
•	•
•	•
•	•

Target Reading Skill

Identify Main Ideas
Identifying main ideas can help you remember what you read. Sometimes the main idea is not stated directly. To find the main idea, add up all the details in the paragraphs and then state the main idea in your own words. Carefully read the details in the two paragraphs below. Then state the main idea of that section.

Key Terms

- **heritage** (HEHR uh tij) *n.* the customs and practices passed from one generation to the next
- **propaganda** (prahp uh GAN duh) *n.* the spread of ideas designed to support a cause or hurt an opposing cause

Moscow's St. Basil's Cathedral was built in the 1500s.

For many years, Russians passing the Church of Saints Cosmas and Damian in Moscow never heard a choir. They never saw a bride and groom leave the church. They never heard religious services. The only sound they heard was the hum of machines printing government documents. The government of the Soviet Union owned the church and used it as a printing shop. In the Soviet Union, the government tried to prevent people from practicing religion.

In 1991, the Soviet Union collapsed. Two years later, Russians who had never given up their faith took back their church. Now the Church of Saints Cosmas and Damian is filled with people singing songs of worship. In recent years, hundreds of other churches in Moscow have reopened their doors. The same return to religion can be seen in places of worship across all of Russia.

Russia's Ethnic Groups

The Russian Orthodox religion is a branch of Christianity closely related to the Eastern Orthodox Church. It has been a powerful bond among many Russians for hundreds of years. It is part of the Russian **heritage** (HEHR uh tij), or the customs and practices that are passed from one generation to the next.

Russia's ethnic culture is another part of the Russian heritage. More than 80 percent of Russian citizens belong to the ethnic group of Russian Slavs. These people generally speak the Russian language. Most of them live in the western parts of the Russian Federation. However, Russia is also home to many non-Russian ethnic groups.

Both of the families at the right live in Siberia.

Russia: Languages

KEY

Indo–European
- Slavic
- Iranian

Altaic
- Turkic
- Mongolic
- Tungusic

Other language groups
- Uralic
- Caucasian
- Other
- Uninhabited
- National border
- ⊛ National capital
- • Other city

Kaliningrad, St. Petersburg, Moscow ⊛, Nizhniy Novgorod, Volgograd, Novosibirsk, Irkutsk, Vladivostok, Lake Baikal

ARCTIC OCEAN, Barents Sea, Bering Sea, Sea of Okhotsk, Sea of Japan, PACIFIC OCEAN, Black Sea, Caspian Sea

0 miles 1,000
0 kilometers 1,000
Lambert Azimuthal Equal Area

Place Altaic languages, originating in Asia, are spoken in Russia today along with Indo-European and other languages. **Locate** In what parts of Russia are Altaic languages spoken? **Analyze Information** How has Russia's location on two continents shaped its culture?

Go Online
PHSchool.com Use Web Code **ldp-7313** for step-by-step map skills practice.

Buddhism in Russia
A Buddhist monastery in southern Siberia reflects the Tibetan heritage of the people who live there.
Compare and Contrast *Compare this photo with the ones on page 93. Besides religion, what other cultural differences might there be among the three groups?*

Other Ethnic Groups More than 60 non-Russian ethnic groups live in Russia. Most of them live far from the heavily populated western areas. People speaking languages related to Finnish and Turkish live near the Ural and Caucasus (KAW kuh sus) mountains. Armenians and Mongolians live along Russia's southern edges. The Yakuts (yah KOOTS) live in small areas of Siberia. These groups speak languages other than Russian.

They also follow different religions. Muslims make up Russia's second-largest religious group, after Russian Orthodox. Many followers of Buddhism (BOOD iz um) live near Russia's border with China.

Ethnic Majorities Recall that the Soviet Union was made up of many republics. Each Soviet republic was the homeland of a large ethnic group. When the Soviet Union came apart, the non-Russian republics broke away and formed their own countries. For example, Armenia is a former Soviet republic with a majority of ethnic Armenians. It gained its independence in 1991.

Other ethnic groups remained part of Russia, sometimes unwillingly. Many of them have called for more rights to rule themselves. Some have even called for independence. These efforts have brought much ethnic tension. Yet despite this great tension, fighting has broken out only between Russia and one other ethnic group—the Chechens. You will read about their independence movement, and the Russian government's repression of it, in Chapter 5.

The government of the Russian Federation has tried to keep the country unified. It has given many ethnic groups the right to rule themselves. However, it must work hard to turn the nation's ethnic diversity into an asset, rather than a source of conflict.

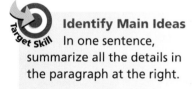

Identify Main Ideas In one sentence, summarize all the details in the paragraph at the right.

✔ **Reading Check** What is Russia's largest religious group?

The Space Age Begins

When the Soviet Union launched the first artificial satellite on October 4, 1957, it took the world by surprise. Less than four years later, the Soviet Union shocked the world again by sending the first human being into space. On April 12, 1961, twenty-seven-year-old Cosmonaut Yuri Gagarin spent one hour and 48 minutes in space. Gagarin completed a single orbit in the spacecraft *Vostok I,* before returning to Earth.

Yuri Gagarin
Yuri Gagarin completed two years of secret training before the flight.

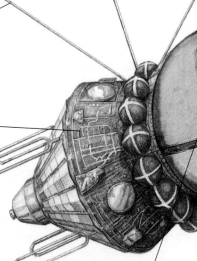

Antennas allowed Gagarin to communicate with Soviet scientists at home.

The spacecraft's instruments and main engine were located in this section, which separated from the capsule before landing.

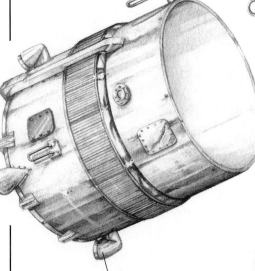

Gagarin was just a passenger in the capsule. He could not control the spacecraft.

Four jets at the base of this section helped turn and tilt the spacecraft as it headed for orbit.

Upon re-entry, only the capsule section of the 14.4-foot- (4.4-meter-) long spacecraft was left.

When the spacecraft reached orbit, this section, containing additional fuel, was released.

This section, containing fuel to lift the heavy spacecraft, was released within two minutes after liftoff.

Blasting off
Vostok I takes off with Yuri Gagarin on board. After 15 minutes, Gagarin reported, "The flight is proceeding normally. I feel well."

ANALYZING IMAGES
In which section of *Vostok I* did the cosmonaut sit?

Elaborately decorated Fabergé eggs like this one were made in St. Petersburg in the late 1800s.

Russian Culture and Education

Russia has produced many great artists. Russia's artistic heritage includes outstanding architecture, fine paintings, great plays, and intricate art objects like Fabergé (FAB ur zhay) eggs.

Russian Artists The novelist Leo Tolstoy (TOHL stoy) wrote powerful stories of life in Russia in the 1800s. Peter Tchaikovsky (chy KAWF skee) composed moving classical music. Russian painters, such as Wassily Kandinsky (VAS uh lee kan DIN skee), were leaders in the modern art movement in the early 1900s. Creating works of art has been a tradition among Russians.

Under Soviet communism, the creation of new works of art nearly came to a halt. The Soviet government believed that the purpose of art was to serve political goals. The government only approved art that supported its propaganda campaigns. **Propaganda** is the spread of ideas designed to support some cause or to hurt an opposing cause.

The Soviet Union broke apart in 1991. With the collapse of Soviet communism, the Russian people eagerly returned to their artistic traditions. Creating new works was once again possible.

Artistic Traditions in Russia

Cinema ▶
Motion pictures came to Russia in 1896. The cinema was extremely popular there before the 1917 revolution and during World War I. After the revolution, Soviet leaders used the cinema to spread communist ideas. The golden age of Russian cinema was the 1920s, although filmmaking techniques continued to develop under Stalin.

A 1929 Russian movie poster

Painting ▲
Russian painter Wassily Kandinsky (1866–1944), above, was an influential abstract artist. Abstract artists do not try to depict things the way that they appear to the eye. His style ranged from pure bursts of color to exact geometric shapes.

Tolstoy and Chekhov in 1901

◀ **Literature**
Russian literature is rich and varied, from the short stories of Nikolay Gogol to the novels of Leo Tolstoy and the plays of Anton Chekhov. Often writing in a harsh political environment, Russian authors have influenced writers all over the world with their wit, expressiveness, and insight into the human mind.

St. Petersburg: A Cultural Symbol The second-largest city and the largest seaport in Russia, the city of St. Petersburg lies on the Gulf of Finland and is an important center of Russian culture. Visitors to the city can clearly see the mixture of Russian and other European cultures. St. Petersburg was founded by Peter the Great in 1703. His goal was to create a Russian city as beautiful as any Western European city. He employed Western architects to design the city. St. Petersburg was the capital of Russia for more than 200 years before it was renamed Leningrad in 1924. In September 1991, its name was changed back to St. Petersburg.

Because of its grand architecture and many canals, St. Petersburg was once called Venice of the North. The Neva (NEE vuh) River winds gracefully through the city. Along the river's banks are palaces and public buildings hundreds of years old. St. Petersburg's grandest sight, the Winter Palace, is on the Neva. The palace has more than 1,000 rooms and was the winter home of Russia's tsars. Part of the palace is now the Hermitage (HUR muh tij) Museum. Built in 1764, it houses one of the world's finest art collections of Russian, Asian, and European art.

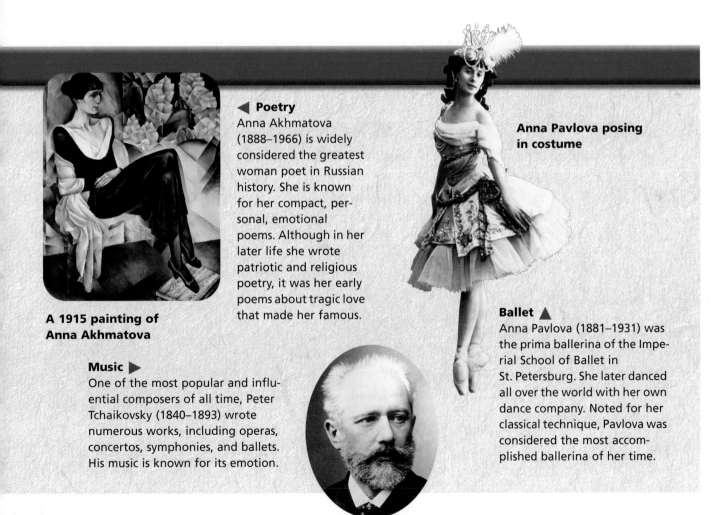

A 1915 painting of Anna Akhmatova

◀ **Poetry**
Anna Akhmatova (1888–1966) is widely considered the greatest woman poet in Russian history. She is known for her compact, personal, emotional poems. Although in her later life she wrote patriotic and religious poetry, it was her early poems about tragic love that made her famous.

Anna Pavlova posing in costume

Ballet ▲
Anna Pavlova (1881–1931) was the prima ballerina of the Imperial School of Ballet in St. Petersburg. She later danced all over the world with her own dance company. Noted for her classical technique, Pavlova was considered the most accomplished ballerina of her time.

Music ▶
One of the most popular and influential composers of all time, Peter Tchaikovsky (1840–1893) wrote numerous works, including operas, concertos, symphonies, and ballets. His music is known for its emotion.

Children learning computer skills in a Russian school

Russia's Educational System One of the strengths of the Soviet Union was its free public education system. Under that system, the number of Russians who could read and write rose from about 40 percent to nearly 100 percent. Higher education was also free for Soviet citizens.

The Russian Federation continued free public schooling for children between ages 6 and 17. When students finish ninth grade, they can choose to continue their education in a secondary school or a vocational school. Secondary schools emphasize academic subjects such as mathematics and science, while the vocational schools prepare students for careers in industry and agriculture. Schools are updating their old courses of study, which used to emphasize only one official point of view.

These changes show that Russia is trying to recover the riches of its past even as it prepares for a new future. Religion and art, two important parts of Russia's cultural heritage, can now be freely expressed. And Russia's young people, unlike their parents, can grow up deciding their future for themselves.

 **✓ Reading Check** Who founded the city of St. Petersburg?

Section 3 Assessment

Key Terms
Review the key terms at the beginning of this section. Use each term in a sentence that explains its meaning.

Target Reading Skill
State the main ideas in Section 3.

Comprehension and Critical Thinking
1. (a) **Recall** What is Russia's major ethnic group?
(b) **Identify Point of View** Why do some ethnic groups in Russia seek independence?

(c) **Draw Conclusions** How has Russia's ethnic mix created challenges for the new Russian government?
2. (a) **List** Give some examples of the ways in which Russians are reconnecting with their past.
(b) **Identify Effects** How have political changes in Russia led to changes in education?
(c) **Predict** How might the lives of young people in Russia today be different from those of their parents' generation?

Writing Activity
Suppose that you are visiting St. Petersburg. Write a postcard to your family describing the works of art, architecture, and other expressions of Russian culture that you have seen.

For: An activity on Russian cities
Visit: PHSchool.com
Web Code: ldd-7303

Celebrating Carnival in London

◆ Chapter Summary

Section 1: The Cultures of Western Europe

- Industry has made many Western European countries wealthy.
- Western European cities are the cultural centers of their countries.
- Goods, materials, and ideas can travel easily and quickly across Western Europe.

Section 2: The Cultures of Eastern Europe

- Long ago, many ethnic groups migrated across Eastern Europe.
- Under foreign domination, some expressions of Eastern European culture were discouraged.
- Ethnic conflict has influenced the modern history of Eastern Europe.
- Prague and Budapest are important cultural centers of Eastern Europe.

Section 3: The Cultures of the Russian Federation

- Russia has more than 60 different ethnic groups.
- Russia has a rich cultural heritage.

A Fabergé egg from Russia

◆ Key Terms

Each of the statements below contains a key term from the chapter. If the statement is true, write *true*. If it is false, change the term to make it true.

1. A tariff is a different version of a language.

2. Propaganda is the spread of ideas designed to support a cause.

3. Someone who moves to one country from another is an immigrant.

4. People in the same ethnic group share the same ancestors, culture, or religion.

5. Heritage is the customs and practices passed from one generation to the next.

6. Diversification is the movement of populations toward cities and the resulting city growth.

7. Migration is a movement from place to place.

Review and Assessment (continued)

◆ Comprehension and Critical Thinking

8. (a) List Name three cities in Western Europe.
(b) Summarize What features make cities in Western Europe centers of culture?

9. (a) Explain What does the concept of open borders mean?
(b) Infer Why do Western Europeans generally have a higher standard of living than do Eastern Europeans?

10. (a) Identify Who were the Slavs?
(b) Synthesize How does Slavic culture live on in Eastern Europe today?

11. (a) Recall Name two of Czechoslovakia's ethnic groups.
(b) Compare and Contrast How was the breakup of Czechoslovakia different from the breakup of Yugoslavia?
(c) Draw Conclusions Why was Czechoslovakia able to break up peacefully?

12. (a) Note About how many ethnic groups live in Russia?
(b) Analyze How have non-Russian ethnic groups reacted to recent changes in Russia?

13. (a) Recall When did the Soviet Union break apart?
(b) Find Main Ideas How has life changed for the Russian people since the collapse of the Soviet Union?
(c) Predict What might the future hold for the Russian people?

◆ Skills Practice

Supporting a Position In the Skills for Life activity in this chapter, you learned how to support a position. Review the steps you followed to learn this skill. Then turn to the section titled Ethnic Majorities on page 102. Read about Russia's republics. Decide whether you support or oppose independence for Russia's republics and then support your position.

◆ Writing Activity: Language Arts

Suppose you had friends who were visiting Europe and Russia for the first time. What information would you want to share with them? Create a brief travel guide that your friends could use to plan their trip. Mention interesting places and activities, and provide background information on the cultures of the people they will meet.

MAP MASTER™ Skills Activity

Europe and Russia

Place Location For each place listed below, write the letter from the map that shows its location.

1. France
2. Ukraine
3. Russia
4. Germany
5. Slovakia
6. St. Petersburg

Go Online
PHSchool.com Use Web Code **ldp-7363** for an **interactive map.**

Standardized Test Prep

Test-Taking Tips

Some questions on standardized tests ask you to analyze graphic organizers. Study the concept web below. Then follow the tips to answer the sample question at the right.

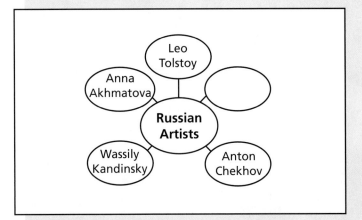

TIP Preview the question. Keep it in mind as you study the information in the web.

Pick the letter that best answers the question.
Another name that belongs on this web is

A Peter the Great.

B Tsar Nicholas II.

C Pablo Picasso.

D Peter Tchaikovsky.

TIP Be sure that you read all four options. If you don't read each one, you can't be certain that you've found the best choice.

Think It Through What other name belongs in the web? The center of the web says Russian Artists—meaning painters, writers, musicians, dancers, and so on. You can rule out A and B, because both are political figures in Russian history. That leaves C and D. You may know that Picasso is Spanish. That leaves Tchaikovsky, answer D.

Practice Questions

Use the tips above and other tips in this book to help you answer the following questions.

1. Advances in farming about 200 years ago led to
   A the Velvet Revolution.
   B increased immigration.
   C the growth of cities.
   D open borders in Western Europe.

2. Which group's descendants make up most of Eastern Europe's ethnic groups?
   A the Romanians
   B the Albanians
   C the Russians
   D the Slavs

3. More than 80 percent of Russian citizens belong to this ethnic group.
   A Russian Slavs   B Mongolians
   C Yakuts   D Buddhists

Study the concept web and answer the question that follows.

4. What other country belongs on the web?
   A Hungary
   B Romania
   C Austria
   D Czech Republic

Use Web Code **lda-7303** for a **Chapter 3 self-test.**

Chapter Preview

This chapter focuses on key countries in Western Europe: the United Kingdom, France, Sweden, Italy, and Germany.

Country Databank

The Country Databank provides data and descriptions of each of the countries in Western Europe.

Target Reading Skill

Using Context In this chapter you will focus on using context to help you understand unfamiliar words. Context includes the words, phrases, and sentences surrounding the word.

▶ Boats on one of the many canals in Venice, Italy

KEY

— National border
⊛ National capital
• Other city

0 miles   500
0 kilometers   500
Lambert Azimuthal Equal Area

Place Western Europe stretches from just north of Africa to the Arctic Circle, and from the Atlantic Ocean to the Mediterranean Sea. **Identify** Which countries lie partly within the Arctic Circle? **Apply Information** How do the climates of these countries differ from those countries that border the Mediterranean Sea?

Go **Online**
PHSchool.com Use Web Code **ldp-7411** for step-by-step **map skills practice.**

Introducing
Western Europe

Guide for Reading

This section provides an introduction to the 24 countries of Western Europe.

- Look at the map on the previous page and then read the paragraphs to learn about each nation.
- Analyze the data to compare the countries.
- What characteristics do most of these countries share?
- What are some key differences among the countries?

Viewing the Video Overview

View the World Studies Video Overview to learn more about each of the countries. As you watch, answer these questions:

- What are the four major geographic regions of Western Europe?
- What are the major bodies of water and why are they important?

Explore the geography of Western Europe.

Andorra

Capital	Andorra la Vella
Land Area	181 sq mi; 468 sq km
Population	68,403
Ethnic Group(s)	Spanish, Andorran, French, Portuguese
Religion(s)	Roman Catholic
Government	parliamentary democracy
Currency	euro
Leading Exports	tobacco products, furniture
Language(s)	Catalan (official), Spanish, French, Portuguese

The small country of Andorra (an DAWR uh) lies high in the eastern Pyrenees mountain range between France and Spain. France and Spain together ruled Andorra from the 1200s until the first full elections were held in 1993. Today, a 28-member legislature governs the country. Andorra's main source of income is its tourist industry. Most tourists come from France, Italy, or Spain to shop in the tax-free stores or to ski. Andorra's wealthiest citizens are its hotel owners.

The town of Andorra la Vella, Andorra

Austria

Capital	Vienna
Land Area	31,945 sq mi; 82,738 sq km
Population	8.2 million
Ethnic Group(s)	German, Croatian, Slovene, Hungarian, Czech, Slovak, Roma
Religion(s)	Roman Catholic, Protestant, Muslim, Jewish
Government	federal republic
Currency	euro
Leading Exports	machinery and equipment, motor vehicles and parts, paper and paperboard, metal goods, chemicals, iron and steel, textiles, foodstuffs
Language(s)	German (official), Croatian, Slovenian

Austria (AWS tree uh) borders several countries including the Czech Republic, Germany, Hungary, Italy, and Slovenia. In 1273, Austria came under the control of the Hapsburg Empire. Present-day Austria was established in 1918 after the fall of the Austro-Hungarian Empire during World War I. In 1938, Germany took control of Austria. Austria regained full independence 17 years later, in 1955. Having few natural resources, Austria imports large amounts of fossil fuels and energy from Russia.

A poster for the 1924 Commercial Fair in Brussels, Belgium

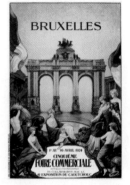

Belgium

Capital	Brussels
Land Area	11,672 sq mi; 30,230 sq km
Population	10.3 million
Ethnic Group(s)	Fleming, Walloon
Religion(s)	Roman Catholic, Protestant
Government	federal parliamentary democracy under a constitutional monarch
Currency	euro
Leading Exports	machinery and equipment, chemicals, diamonds, metals and metal products
Language(s)	Dutch (official), French (official), German (official)

Belgium (BEL jum) is a small country bordered by Germany, France, Luxembourg, and the Netherlands. It only takes about four hours to cross Belgium by car or by train. Belgium is one of the most densely populated countries in Europe. More than 95 percent of its citizens live in cities. The city of Antwerp is Belgium's main commercial center and Europe's second-largest port. Antwerp is important because Belgium has few natural resources and depends on the export of goods and services from other countries.

Denmark

Capital	Copenhagen
Land Area	16,368 sq mi; 42,394 sq km
Population	5.4 million
Ethnic Group(s)	Scandinavian, Inuit, Faeroe, Southwest Asian, Central Asian
Religion(s)	Protestant, Roman Catholic, Muslim
Government	constitutional monarchy
Currency	Danish krone
Leading Exports	machinery and instruments, meat and meat products, dairy products, fish, chemicals, furniture, ships, windmills
Language(s)	Danish (official)

Denmark (DEN mahrk) is the southernmost country in the region of northern Europe known as Scandinavia (skan duh NAY vee uh). Denmark contains many hundreds of islands, including self-governing Greenland. Greenland, located in the North Atlantic Ocean, is the world's largest island. Denmark itself is one of the flattest countries in the world. More than 65 percent of its land is used to raise crops. The North Atlantic current creates a damp but usually mild climate. These conditions help to make the region's farming profitable.

Introducing Western Europe

A brown bear in Lappi, Finland

Finland

Capital	Helsinki
Land Area	11,610 sq mi; 305,470 sq km
Population	5.2 million
Ethnic Group(s)	Finnish, Swedish, Sami, Roma, Tartar
Religion(s)	Protestant, Russian Orthodox
Government	republic
Currency	euro
Leading Exports	machinery and equipment, chemicals, metals, timber, paper, pulp
Language(s)	Finnish (official), Swedish (official), Sami

Bordered by Norway, Sweden, and Russia, Finland (FIN lund) is a low-lying country that can be divided into three geographic zones. There is a low-lying coastal strip in the south and west, where most of the cities are located. The interior of Finland is made up of vast forests and woodlands. This area also contains more than 60,000 lakes. Finland's third region is thinly wooded or barren and lies north of the Arctic Circle. The climate is extreme there. Temperatures fall well below zero degrees Fahrenheit during the six-month winter.

France

Capital	Paris
Land Area	210,668 sq mi; 545,630 sq km
Population	59.8 million
Ethnic Group(s)	French, North African, German, Breton, Basque
Religion(s)	Roman Catholic, Protestant, Jewish, Muslim
Government	republic
Currency	euro
Leading Exports	machinery and transportation equipment, aircraft, plastics, chemicals, pharmaceutical products, iron and steel, beverages
Language(s)	French (official), Provençal, German, Breton, Catalan, Basque

Located between the English Channel and the Mediterranean Sea, France (frans) is bordered by Italy, Switzerland, Germany, Belgium, and Spain. France has a long history of wars, invasions, and foreign occupations. Though it suffered great damage during both world wars, France is currently an economic leader among the nations of Europe. France helped to establish the European Union. It is the fourth-largest exporter in the world. Paris, the capital, is considered to be one of the world's great cultural centers.

Germany

Capital	Berlin
Land Area	134,835 sq mi; 349,223 sq km
Population	83 million
Ethnic Group(s)	German, Turkish, Southeast Asian
Religion(s)	Protestant, Roman Catholic, Muslim
Government	federal republic
Currency	euro
Leading Exports	machinery, vehicles, chemicals, metals and manufactured goods, foodstuffs, textiles
Language(s)	German (official), Turkish

Germany (JUR muh nee) is located in Central Europe, with coastlines on the Baltic and North seas. It is bordered by nine countries, including France, Poland, and Austria. Germany was divided into two countries from 1949 to 1990. Today the country faces problems such as unemployment and an aging population. Germans are also still working to rebuild the former East Germany. However, Germany, an EU member, is now an economic leader. It is the second-largest exporter in the world. Germany's economy—based mainly on services and industry—is Europe's largest.

Greece

Capital	Athens
Land Area	50,502 sq mi; 130,800 sq km
Population	10.6 million
Ethnic Group(s)	Greek, Albanian, Turkish
Religion(s)	Eastern Orthodox, Muslim
Government	parliamentary republic
Currency	euro
Leading Exports	food and beverages, manufactured goods, petroleum products, chemicals, textiles
Language(s)	Greek (official), Turkish, Macedonian, Albanian

Greece (grees) is located in southern Europe. It is made up of the southern tip of the Balkan Peninsula and more than 2,000 islands. It is surrounded by the Aegean, Ionian, and Mediterranean seas. Greece's landscape is dominated by mountains and coastlines. Greece is famous for its ancient culture, which influenced the development of the modern world. Today, Greece is a member of the EU. However, it has one of the weakest economies in that organization. Efforts to strengthen the Greek economy have been slowed by government policies and conflicts with Greece's neighbors.

Iceland

Capital	Reykjavík
Land Area	38,707 sq mi; 100,250 sq km
Population	279,384
Ethnic Group(s)	Norse, Celtic
Religion(s)	Protestant, Roman Catholic
Government	constitutional republic
Currency	Icelandic króna
Leading Exports	fish and fish products, animal products, aluminum, diatomite, ferrosilicon
Language(s)	Icelandic (official)

Iceland (EYES lund) is an island in northern Europe, between the Greenland Sea and the North Atlantic Ocean. Located just south of the Arctic Circle, Iceland's climate is generally cold. However, the warm waters of the Gulf Stream keep its ports ice-free in the winter. Iceland's varied landscape includes volcanoes, glaciers, fjords, and hot springs. More than half the population of Iceland lives in or near Reykjavík, the capital city. Fishing is the country's largest industry. The people of Iceland enjoy a high standard of living and a strong economy.

Introducing Western Europe

Ireland

Capital	Dublin
Land Area	26,598 sq mi; 68,890 sq km
Population	3.9 million
Ethnic Group(s)	Celtic, English
Religion(s)	Roman Catholic, Protestant
Government	republic
Currency	euro
Leading Exports	machinery and equipment, computers, chemicals, pharmaceuticals live animals, animal products
Language(s)	Irish Gaelic (official), English (official)

Ireland (EYER lund) is located in the North Atlantic Ocean off the west coast of Britain. It is an independent republic that occupies most of the island of Ireland. About one sixth of the island is Northern Ireland, which is part of the United Kingdom. Despite decades of violent conflict with Northern Ireland, Ireland's economy has grown at a remarkable rate in recent years. Its low taxes have brought in businesses from around the world. It is a member of the European Union and helped launch the euro currency. Often called the Emerald Isle, Ireland is known for its rolling green hills and mild, damp climate.

Italy

Capital	Rome
Land Area	113,521 sq mi; 294,020 sq km
Population	57.7 million
Ethnic Group(s)	Italian, Sardinian
Religion(s)	Roman Catholic
Government	republic
Currency	euro
Leading Exports	fruits, vegetables, grapes, potatoes, sugar beets, soybeans, grain, olives, beef, dairy products, fish
Language(s)	Italian (official), German, French, Rhaeto-Romanic, Sardinian

Italy (IT ul ee) is a peninsula in southern Europe. It lies in the Mediterranean Sea northeast of Tunisia. Italy also includes Sicily, Sardinia, and several other islands. Italy has a long and influential history. As the center of the Roman Empire, it was once a world leader. A system of law developed in Rome more than 2,000 years ago still influences law and citizenship in many countries today. Modern Italy became a democratic republic in 1946. Italy, a founding member of the European Union, has a strong economy based largely on manufacturing and industry.

Liechtenstein

Capital	Vaduz
Land Area	62 sq mi; 160 sq km
Population	32,842
Ethnic Group(s)	Alemannic, Italian, Southwest Asian
Religion(s)	Roman Catholic, Protestant
Government	hereditary constitutional monarchy
Currency	Swiss franc
Leading Exports	small specialty machinery, dental products, stamps, hardware, pottery
Language(s)	German (official), Alemannic dialect, Italian

Liechtenstein (LIK tun styn) is a small country in the Alps of central Europe, between Austria and Switzerland. Despite its small size, Liechtenstein has a strong free-enterprise economy and a high standard of living. It has a low tax rate, which attracts businesses from other countries. It also has many banks, with laws that protect international investors. Liechtenstein is closely tied to Switzerland, which provides the smaller country's defense. Liechtenstein uses Switzerland's franc as its national currency. Tourists visit Liechtenstein to ski, climb, and hike in the mountains.

Luxembourg

Capital	Luxembourg-Ville
Land Area	998 sq mi; 2,586 sq km
Population	448,569
Ethnic Group(s)	Celtic, French, German, Portuguese, Italian, Slavic
Religion(s)	Roman Catholic, Protestant, Jewish, Muslim
Government	constitutional monarchy
Currency	euro
Leading Exports	machinery and equipment, steel products, chemicals, rubber products, glass
Language(s)	French (official), German (official), Luxembourgish (official)

Luxembourg (LUK sum burg) is bordered by France, Germany, and Belgium. Luxembourg became wealthy from steel production before World War II and today is a financial center. Its capital city has more banks than any other city in the world. Luxembourg is also the home of important EU organizations. The people of Luxembourg enjoy high income, low unemployment, and few social problems. More than 90 percent of the population lives in cities. Tourists visit Luxembourg to see its forests, mountains, and historic castles.

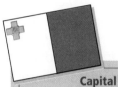

Malta

Capital	Valletta
Land Area	122 sq mi; 316 sq km
Population	397,499
Ethnic Group(s)	Maltese
Religion(s)	Roman Catholic
Government	republic
Currency	Maltese lira
Leading Exports	machinery and transport equipment, manufactured goods
Language(s)	Maltese (official), English (official)

Malta (MAWL tuh) is a group of islands south of Italy in the Mediterranean Sea. Only three islands of this rocky archipelago are inhabited. Malta fell under British rule in 1814, and the United Kingdom defended Malta through World War I and World War II. In 1964, Malta gained its independence and ten years later became a republic. Since that time, Malta has become an important transportation port, financial center, and tourist destination. Economically, it depends on trade with other countries, manufacturing, and tourism. Malta has recently joined the European Union.

Monaco

Capital	Monaco
Land Area	0.75 sq mi; 1.95 sq km
Population	31,987
Ethnic Group(s)	French, Monégasque, Italian
Religion(s)	Roman Catholic
Government	constitutional monarchy
Currency	euro
Leading Exports	no information available
Language(s)	French (official), Italian, Monégasque, English

Monaco (MAHN uh koh) is located on the southeastern coast of France, bordering the Mediterranean Sea. In the late 1800s, Monaco was linked to France with a railroad. This event brought tourists and money to the small country. Since that time, Monaco has grown into a popular vacation destination for tourists seeking beautiful scenery, a pleasant climate, and shopping. The government is focused on developing other services and industries as well. Monaco has no income tax and low business taxes. However, the cost of living is high.

Introducing Western Europe

The Netherlands

Capitals	Amsterdam and The Hague
Land Area	13,082 sq mi; 33,883 sq km
Population	16.1 million
Ethnic Group(s)	Dutch, Southwest Asian, North African, Southeast Asian, South American, West Indian
Religion(s)	Roman Catholic, Protestant, Muslim
Government	constitutional monarchy
Currency	euro
Leading Exports	machinery and equipment, chemicals, fuels, foodstuffs
Language(s)	Dutch (official), Frisian

The Netherlands (NETH ur lundz) is located in northwest Europe between Belgium and Germany, bordering the North Sea. The country is also known by the name *Holland*. The Netherlands suffered through German invasion and occupation during World War II. Very active in international politics, the nation helped to form both NATO and the European Union. Stable relationships with other industrial countries help to keep its economy strong and growing. The Netherlands also serves as an important transportation center in Europe—particularly Rotterdam, on the Mans River.

Norway

Capital	Oslo
Land Area	118,865 sq mi; 307,860 sq km
Population	4.5 million
Ethnic Group(s)	Norwegian, Sami
Religion(s)	Protestant, Roman Catholic
Government	constitutional monarchy
Currency	Norwegian krone
Leading Exports	petroleum and petroleum products, machinery and equipment, metals, chemicals, ships, fish
Language(s)	Norwegian (official), Sami

Norway (NAWR way) is located in northern Europe west of Sweden. In 995, Norway's king converted to Christianity. He also ended two hundred years of Viking raids. In 1397, the nation became part of Denmark, and it remained so for more than four hundred years. The following two hundred years saw Norway gain independence, fall under Swedish rule, gain its independence again, fall under German rule, and regain its independence a third time, in 1945. In the 1960s, the discovery of oil and gas strengthened the Norwegian economy. Like Sweden, Norway has a mix of modern capitalism with many social welfare benefits, and has a very high standard of living. Norway has decided not to join the European Union.

A Sami man trains a reindeer to pull a sleigh.

Portugal

Capital	Lisbon
Land Area	35,502 sq mi; 91,951 sq km
Population	10.1 million
Ethnic Group(s)	Portuguese, African
Religion(s)	Roman Catholic, Protestant
Government	parliamentary democracy
Currency	euro
Leading Exports	clothing and footwear, machinery, chemicals, cork and paper products, hides
Language(s)	Portuguese (official)

Portugal (PAWR chuh gul) is located in southwestern Europe. It is west of Spain, bordered by the North Atlantic Ocean. Though Portugal is a fairly small country, it has played a major role in world history. From the 1400s to the 1600s, Portugal dominated the world sea trade. Portuguese explorers sailed the world, seeking wealth and colonies. They established colonies throughout the Americas and in Africa, some of which they ruled into the 1900s. Portugal became part of the European Union in 1986. Since then, the Portuguese economy has grown stronger, but a poor educational system is hindering greater growth.

San Marino

Capital	San Marino
Land Area	23.6 sq mi; 61.2 sq km
Population	27,730
Ethnic Group(s)	Sammarinese, Italian
Religion(s)	Roman Catholic
Government	independent republic
Currency	euro
Leading Exports	building stone, lime, wood, chestnuts, wheat, baked goods, hides, ceramics
Language(s)	Italian (official)

San Marino (sahn mah REE noh) is located in southern Europe, in the Italian Apennine Mountains. It is completely surrounded by the nation of Italy. San Marino is the third-smallest country in Europe and claims to be the world's oldest republic. It has remained independent since around A.D. 300. San Marino's political and social trends are similar to those of Italy. The tourist industry is extremely important to San Marino. Other industries include banking, clothing, electronics, ceramics, and cheese-making. San Marino enjoys a standard of living similar to the wealthiest areas of Italy.

Spain

Capital	Madrid
Land Area	192,873 sq mi; 499,542 sq km
Population	40.1 million
Ethnic Group(s)	Castilian Spanish, Catalan, Galician, Basque, Roma
Religion(s)	Roman Catholic
Government	parliamentary monarchy
Currency	euro
Leading Exports	machinery, motor vehicles, foodstuffs, other consumer goods
Language(s)	Spanish (official), Galician (official), Catalan (official), Basque (official)

Spain (spayn) is located in southwestern Europe between Portugal and France. It has coasts on the North Atlantic Ocean, the Mediterranean Sea, and the Bay of Biscay. Spain was a powerful world empire in the 1500s and 1600s. However, Spain's economy did not industrialize as quickly in later centuries as did other Western European countries such as Britain, Germany, and France. Spain was neutral during World War I and World War II but suffered through its own civil war in the 1930s. Spain joined the EU in 1986, and was among the first countries to begin using the euro currency. The country's economy is generally strong, though high unemployment continues to be a problem.

Introducing Western Europe

Sweden

Capital	Stockholm
Land Area	158,662 sq mi; 410,934 sq km
Population	8.9 million
Ethnic Group(s)	Swedish, Finnish, Sami
Religion(s)	Protestant, Roman Catholic, Muslim, Jewish, Buddhist
Government	constitutional monarchy
Currency	Swedish krona
Leading Exports	machinery, motor vehicles, paper products, pulp and wood, iron and steel products, chemicals
Language(s)	Swedish (official), Finnish, Sami

Sweden (SWEED un) is located in northern Europe between Norway and Finland, bordering the Baltic Sea and the Gulf of Bothnia. Sweden has a high standard of living, with a mixture of modern capitalism and broad social welfare benefits. The nation joined the EU in 1995 but has not accepted the euro as its own currency. Beginning in the 1990s, Sweden faced high unemployment and other economic problems. However, with a population of skilled workers, rich resources, and a modern transportation system, Sweden's economy is still relatively strong. Sweden is one of the world's leaders in equal rights for women.

Swedish soccer player Malin Moestroem in 2003

Switzerland

Capital	Bern
Land Area	15,355 sq mi; 39,770 sq km
Population	7.3 million
Ethnic Group(s)	German, French, Italian, Romansch
Religion(s)	Roman Catholic, Protestant
Government	federal republic
Currency	Swiss franc
Leading Exports	machinery, chemicals, metals, watches, agricultural products
Language(s)	French (official), German (official), Italian (official), Swiss German, Romansch

Switzerland (SWIT sur lund) is located between France and Italy. It is the source of all four of the region's major river systems: the Po, the Rhine, the Rhône, and the Inn-Danube. Politically, Switzerland is famous for its neutrality. Switzerland is also economically neutral and has so far remained outside the European Union. Switzerland does, however, participate in international organizations, including the UN. This small, landlocked Alpine country has one of the strongest market economies in Europe. It is a center of international finance.

United Kingdom

Capital	London
Land Area	93,278 sq mi; 241,590 sq km
Population	59.8 million
Ethnic Group(s)	English, Scottish, Irish, Welsh, Ulster, West Indian, South Asian
Religion(s)	Protestant, Roman Catholic, Muslim
Government	constitutional monarchy
Currency	pound sterling
Leading Exports	manufactured goods, fuels, chemicals, food, beverages, tobacco
Language(s)	English (official), Welsh (official), Scottish Gaelic, Irish Gaelic

The United Kingdom (yoo NYT id KING dum) is made up of several islands lying northwest of France, between the North Atlantic Ocean and the North Sea. In the 1800s, the United Kingdom was an expanding empire with great industrial and military strength. However, World War I and World War II seriously weakened the nation. In the following decades, the United Kingdom withdrew from its colonies around the world. It then rebuilt itself into a modern world power. The United Kingdom is a founding member of NATO and one of the five permanent members of the UN Security Council. It is also a member of the European Union, although the British have not accepted the euro.

Vatican City

Capital	Vatican City
Land Area	0.17 sq mi; 0.44 sq km
Population	900
Ethnic Group(s)	Italian, Swiss, Polish
Religion(s)	Roman Catholic
Government	ecclesiastical
Currency	euro
Leading Exports	none
Language(s)	Latin (official), Italian (official)

Vatican City (VAT ih kun SIH tee), also known as the Holy See, is an enclave of Rome. This means it is entirely surrounded by Italy's capital city. The Vatican is the world's smallest independent state. It is the home of the pope, who is the leader of the Roman Catholic Church. The pope is also the head of the Vatican City government. The Vatican's unique economy is supported by donations from Roman Catholics around the world. It also earns income from investments and tourism.

SOURCES: DK World Desk Reference Online; CIA World Factbook Online, 2002; *The World Almanac*, 2003

Assessment

Comprehension and Critical Thinking

1. Compare and Contrast Which countries in the region are the largest and the smallest?

2. Make Generalizations What are some characteristics that many of the region's countries share?

3. Infer Which countries do not have any exports? Why might this be so?

4. Categorize What kinds of exports do many of the countries of Western Europe rely on?

5. Make a Circle Graph The total population of Western Europe is about 392 million. Find the Western European country with the largest population. Make a circle graph that shows this country's population as a percent of the population of Western Europe as a whole.

Keeping Current

Access the **DK World Desk Reference Online** at **PHSchool.com** for up-to-date information about the 24 countries in this region.

Go Online
PHSchool.com
Web Code: lde-7400

Section 1

The United Kingdom
Democracy and Monarchy

Prepare to Read

Objectives

In this section you will

1. Examine the regions that make up the United Kingdom.
2. Learn about the United Kingdom's democratic heritage.
3. Find out how the United Kingdom combines democracy and monarchy.
4. Understand why trade is important to the United Kingdom.

Taking Notes

As you read this section, look for important events that have taken place in British history. Copy the table below, and write each event in the correct time period.

Events in British History			
1500s	1700s	1800s	1900s

Target Reading Skill

Use Context Clues When reading, you may come across a word that is used in an unfamiliar way. Look for clues in the context—the surrounding words, sentences, and paragraphs—to help you understand the meaning. Sometimes the context will define the word. In the first paragraph below, for example, you know the words *crown* and *jewels,* but may not know what the term *crown jewels* means. The context of the second paragraph helps explain this term.

Key Terms

- **Parliament** (PAHR luh munt) *n.* the lawmaking body of the United Kingdom
- **representative** (rep ruh ZEN tuh tiv) *n.* a person who represents, or speaks for, a group of people
- **constitution** (kahn stuh TOO shun) *n.* a set of laws that describes how a government works
- **constitutional monarchy** (kahn stuh TOO shuh nul MAHN ur kee) *n.* a government in which a monarch is the head of state but has limited powers

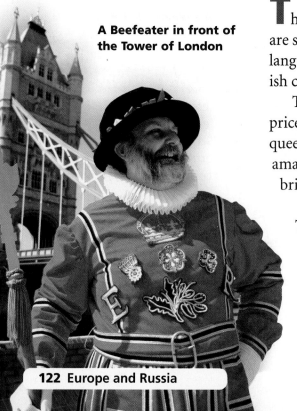

A Beefeater in front of the Tower of London

The line of tourists seems to go on forever. People in the line are speaking English, French, Arabic, and Japanese. In all of these languages, the tourists are talking about the same thing: the British crown jewels.

The jewels are kept under guard in the Tower of London. The priceless collection includes crowns worn by the kings and queens of England. After a long wait, the tourists finally reach the amazing jewels. Their eyes widen at the sight of huge diamonds, bright-red rubies, and cool-blue sapphires.

British history can be felt everywhere in and around the Tower of London. Near the Tower, rebellious nobles met their deaths on the executioner's block. Young King Edward V and his brother were most likely murdered in the Tower of London. The Tower is watched over by guards called Beefeaters. No one knows for sure where this name came from. But Beefeaters in their colorful red uniforms have guarded the Tower for hundreds of years.

Regions of the United Kingdom

You may have heard people use different names for the nation located on the British Isles: England, Great Britain, and the United Kingdom. Each name has a specific meaning.

England England is a region within the United Kingdom. Find England on the map below. About two thousand years ago, Romans ruled over present-day England. After the Roman Empire fell, many small kingdoms arose. Over time, one of these kingdoms, Wessex, grew stronger than the others. By conquering other kingdoms, Wessex unified England into a single nation by the 800s.

Great Britain England grew in power and strength. Soon, it began to exert power over its neighbors, including Wales and Scotland. Wales officially became part of the English nation in the 1500s. By the early 1700s, England and Scotland had joined together. Now all of the nations on the island of Great Britain were united. The name of the nation changed to Great Britain.

Hadrian's Wall, built in about A.D.122 by the Roman emperor Hadrian, marked the northern boundary of the Roman Empire. It still stands today in northern England.

Regions of the United Kingdom

KEY

- England
- Great Britain
- United Kingdom
- National border

0 miles 200
0 kilometers 200
Lambert Azimuthal Equal Area

Shetland Islands
Orkney Islands
Outer Hebrides
SCOTLAND
NORTHERN IRELAND
UNITED KINGDOM
North Sea
IRELAND
Isle of Man
Irish Sea
GREAT BRITAIN
WALES
ENGLAND
ATLANTIC OCEAN
Celtic Sea
Isle of Wight
English Channel

MAP MASTER™
Skills Activity

Regions The United Kingdom is a single nation made up of several smaller regions. **Identify** Which three regions do the islands called the Outer Hebrides belong to? **Compare and Contrast** How does the political structure of the United Kingdom compare to that of the United States?

Go Online
PHSchool.com Use Web Code ldp-7421 for step-by-step map skills practice.

United Kingdom

The United Kingdom has few mineral resources. Yet it has more energy resources—including coal, natural gas, and petroleum—than any other EU member. In the early 2000s, it was among the world's top ten oil producers. From about the mid-1970s on, the United Kingdom has produced enough fuel to export it to other countries. The United Kingdom also uses its energy resources to run the factories that produce manufactured goods, the country's most important export. Study the map and graphs to learn more about the United Kingdom's economy.

United Kingdom: Natural Resources

KEY
- Iron
- Tin
- Coal
- Peat
- Kaolin
- Salt
- Petroleum
- Natural gas
- Hydroelectric power
- National border
- National capital
- Other city

0 miles 200
0 kilometers 200
Lambert Azimuthal Equal Area

Leading Exports*

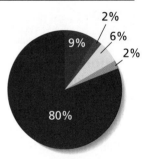

2% 9% 6% 2% 80%

Leading Imports*

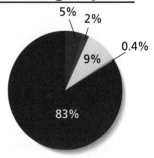

5% 2% 9% 0.4% 83%

- ■ Manufactured goods
- ■ Food, beverages, and tobacco
- ■ Raw materials
- Mineral fuels
- Other

*Note: Numbers may not equal 100% due to rounding.
SOURCE: U.K. Office for National Statistics, 2004

Fossil Fuel Production, 1972–2001

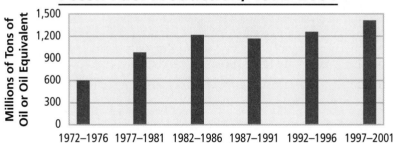

Millions of Tons of Oil or Oil Equivalent

1,500 / 1,200 / 900 / 600 / 300 / 0

1972–1976 1977–1981 1982–1986 1987–1991 1992–1996 1997–2001
Years

SOURCE: U.K. Office for National Statistics, 2002

Map and Chart Skills

1. **Locate** Where is the United Kingdom's petroleum located?
2. **Identify** What products make up the United Kingdom's largest import and export?
3. **Compare** How did the United Kingdom's fossil fuel production change from 1972 to 2001?

 Use Web Code **ldp-7431** for step-by-step **map skills** practice.

United Kingdom In 1801, Great Britain officially united with Ireland with a law called the Act of Union. The name of the nation changed to the United Kingdom of Great Britain and Ireland. In the 1920s, the southern part of Ireland became an independent nation. The rest of the island, Northern Ireland, has remained part of the United Kingdom. However, some Northern Irish groups seek to break away from Great Britain and join Ireland.

Today, the full name of this nation is the United Kingdom of Great Britain and Northern Ireland. Most people use the shortened form of the name, United Kingdom, or UK. Within the United Kingdom are four regions: England, Scotland, Wales, and Northern Ireland. Each region continues to have its own culture, traditions, and customs. The British government unifies them all.

Target Skill **Use Context Clues** How do the sentences in this paragraph explain what an *Act of Union* is?

✓ **Reading Check** **Which regions make up Great Britain?**

A Democratic Heritage

Today, the United Kingdom is headed by Queen Elizabeth II. As the country's monarch, she is a symbol of Britain's past and its customs. The United Kingdom also has a strong democratic government. The roots of British democracy go back many centuries.

The Magna Carta During the Middle Ages, kings needed large sums of money for major undertakings, such as going to war. If they did not have the money themselves, they asked the nobles to provide the funds. In the 1200s, the nobles used the influence their money gave them to limit the power of the king. In 1215, a group of nobles required King John to sign a document called the Magna Carta, or "Great Charter." The Magna Carta required the king to obey the laws of the land.

Links Across Time

The Magna Carta King John signed the Magna Carta in 1215 in a meadow called Runnymede, beside the River Thames in southeastern England. The Magna Carta holds an important place in history because it was the first written document that limited the power of a monarch. Hundreds of years later, British colonists in the Americas used the Magna Carta to support their fight for more rights. The document itself was written in Latin, which was the language of formal documents at that time. Four copies of the original charter still exist today in England, including the one shown at the right. Two are held in the British Library, while the other two are stored in the archives of the cathedrals at Lincoln and Salisbury.

Parliament In time, the group of nobles became known as the Parliament. **Parliament** is the legislature, or lawmaking body, of the United Kingdom. This word comes from the French word *parler* (PAHR lay), which means "to talk." Parliament is the place where officials discuss laws and other government business. Parliament changed over time. It later came to include common people as well as nobles. As it became more responsive to the needs of the people, it also gained more power. It helped decide the kinds of taxes paid by citizens. People elected from each region of the country served as representatives in the Parliament. A **representative** represents, or speaks for, a group of people.

The modern Parliament is made up of the House of Lords and the House of Commons. Members of the House of Lords are not elected. They are high-ranking clergy and judges or people who have distinguished themselves in public life. Their power has become limited over the years. In contrast, members of the House of Commons are elected. They govern the nation.

✓ **Reading Check** **What was the purpose of the Magna Carta?**

A Changing Monarchy

Today, the monarchy serves as an important symbol of Britain's past. It also helps to unify the British people. The British honor the monarchy in many ways. When the queen is in London, a royal flag is flown over her home at Buckingham (BUK ing um) Palace. A ceremony called the changing of the guard takes place there every day. Trumpets blare and guardsmen march back and forth at the palace gate.

A Constitutional Monarchy While Parliament gained power, the power of British monarchs lessened. They no longer make laws or collect taxes. The United Kingdom is now governed by a constitution. A **constitution** is a set of laws that describes how a government works. Some nations have one written document that serves as a constitution, such as the Constitution of the United States. The British constitution is different. It is not one written document. Instead, the British constitution is made up of laws passed by Parliament, important court decisions, and certain legal practices. Parliament can change it as necessary. One of the greatest strengths of the United Kingdom's government is its ability to adopt modern ideas while keeping old ideas that still work.

Parliament, Past and Present
Below, an illustration shows King Edward I before the Parliament in the late 1200s. At the bottom, Queen Elizabeth II attends a session of Parliament in 1995. **Compare** *Compare the two images. What traditions has Parliament kept throughout its history?*

The British government is a **constitutional monarchy,** or a government in which the power of kings and queens is limited. In a constitutional monarchy, kings and queens must obey the laws. And in the United Kingdom, the laws are made by Parliament, not by the monarch. This is very different from an absolute monarchy. An absolute monarch makes all the laws and has the power to ignore them as he or she chooses.

Devolution Until the late 1990s, Parliament made the laws for the entire nation. It even made specific laws for each of the country's regions—laws that affected only England, Scotland, Wales, or Northern Ireland. By the end of the 1990s, the national Parliament turned over some of its lawmaking powers to regional assemblies. Now, the Scottish Parliament makes certain laws that apply only to Scotland. The Welsh Assembly makes laws for Wales, and the Northern Ireland Assembly makes laws for Northern Ireland. Only England does not have a regional assembly. Its laws are still made by the national Parliament. The process of moving lawmaking power from the national level to the regional level is called devolution.

✓ **Reading Check** **What is devolution?**

Links Across The World

The Brightest Jewel Rare spices, silks, and other riches attracted the British East India Company to India in the 1600s. The company established trading outposts in India, with the goal of making huge profits. Over time, the company's goals changed. It gained great political power, and called for social change such as ending India's system of discrimination against people of lower class. In 1858, the British government took over the company, and officially turned India into a colony. Many people called India the "brightest jewel" in the British "crown" of colonies. The coat of arms shown here was a symbol of the British East India Company.

Regional Seats of Government
At the left, Queen Elizabeth II opens the Scottish Parliament in 1999—Scotland's first parliament in nearly 300 years. Northern Ireland's Assembly building is shown below. **Apply Information** *In what ways does allowing more power to regional lawmakers strengthen the United Kingdom's government?*

The Importance of Trade

As an island nation, the United Kingdom has limited natural resources. It must trade with other nations for resources. For that reason, trade has been important throughout the United Kingdom's history.

The British Empire In the 1500s, trade enabled the British to begin building a large empire. The British Empire grew to include colonies in British-ruled areas on six continents. Its empire was so vast that one could say in the 1800s, "The sun never sets on the British Empire." Recall that 13 of today's United States used to be British colonies. The American and other colonies provided British factories with raw materials. They also provided markets to sell the goods made in British factories. Its many colonies helped the United Kingdom become a world economic power.

But that changed in the 1900s. Fighting World War I and World War II weakened the United Kingdom. In the years after World War II, most of the colonies within the British Empire began seeking independence. The British Empire rapidly came to an end. It had turned over most of its colonies by the mid-1960s. The last colony, Hong Kong, was returned to China in 1997. However, the United Kingdom continues to trade with its former colonies.

A European Union Member The United Kingdom has many strong industries, or businesses. For example, it has good supplies of fossil fuels—especially oil from deposits beneath the North Sea. It also continues to export many manufactured goods, such as clothing and electronic products. However, the United Kingdom is not as strong a world power as it once was.

The United Kingdom no longer relies on its colonies to boost its economy. In 1973, the United Kingdom joined the European Union. As you have read, the EU is a group of nations that promotes trade and other forms of cooperation among its members.

The United Kingdom today is a leading member of the EU. Its experience in such areas as shipping and finance has strengthened the EU in global trade. In turn, easier access to European markets has helped replace the trade the United Kingdom lost when its empire broke apart. With new links to the resources and markets of other European countries, the British look forward to a bright economic future.

A woman paints figures by hand at a British company that exports tableware and gifts.

✓ **Reading Check** **In what ways did the United Kingdom rely on its colonies?**

Section 1 Assessment

Key Terms
Review the key terms at the beginning of this section. Use each term in a sentence that explains its meaning.

Target Reading Skill
Find the phrase *common people* on page 126. How do the other words in the same sentence explain its meaning?

Comprehension and Critical Thinking
1. (a) Explain What is the difference between the terms *Great Britain* and *United Kingdom*?

(b) Sequence List four events, in order, that led to the formation of the United Kingdom.

2. (a) Name What are the two houses of the British Parliament?

(b) Contrast How do the two houses of Parliament differ?

3. (a) Recall What kind of government does the United Kingdom have?

(b) Contrast How does the British constitution differ from that of the United States?

4. (a) Note What factor led the British to build a large empire?

(b) Draw Conclusions How did the United Kingdom remain strong after losing its colonies?

Writing Activity
Suppose that you are a British tour guide operator. You tell an American tourist that you are from three places: England, Great Britain, and the United Kingdom. Write a paragraph that explains to the tourist how this can be so.

For: An activity on the British Empire
Visit: PHSchool.com
Web Code: ldd-7401

France
Cultural Heritage and Diversity

Prepare to Read

Objectives

In this section you will
1. Find out why the French take pride in their traditional culture.
2. Learn about growing cultural diversity in France.

Taking Notes

As you read this section, look for details about French culture, including recent influences on it. Copy the chart below, and record your findings in it.

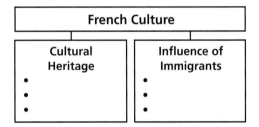

French Culture	
Cultural Heritage	**Influence of Immigrants**
•	•
•	•
•	•

Target Reading Skill

Use Context Clues
Context, the words and phrases surrounding a word, can help you understand a new word. In this example, the phrase in italics helps explain what Impressionism is: French Impressionist artists such as Claude Monet developed *new techniques to paint light and shadow.*

Key Term

• **philosophy** (fil LAHS uh fee) *n.* a system of ideas and beliefs

In 1998, the words "world champions" were projected onto France's Arc de Triomphe.

It's July of 1998 in Paris, France. Hundreds of thousands of people crowd onto the Champs Elysées (shawnz eh lee ZAY), one of the most fashionable streets in the world. The sidewalks are packed. Some people have even climbed to the tops of lampposts or newspaper stands for a better view. They're all here for a huge celebration. The French soccer team has just won the World Cup championship for the first time ever.

Fans are waving French flags. Others have their faces painted in the colors of the French flag—red, white, and blue. But in the crowd, many fans are waving the Algerian flag and chanting, "Zizou! Zizou!" They are calling for Zinedine Zidane, the midfielder who scored two of the goals in the winning game. Like many of the team's players, Zidane, of Algerian descent, is the son of immigrants.

This victory celebration is symbolic of a new France—a France that is fiercely proud of its culture and is increasingly diverse.

Pride in French Culture

French people generally take great pride in their culture—for good reason. Over centuries, the French have made many important contributions to art, religion, music, literature, and philosophy. A **philosophy** is a system of ideas and beliefs. Many French people are committed to preserving their traditional French culture.

The French Language Some people want to prevent the French language from changing too much. An organization called the French Academy determines which words are officially accepted as part of the French language. Since 1635, it has published dictionaries explaining the usage of these words. The Academy is one example of how the French strive to preserve their culture.

Enduring Philosophies Many important philosophies originated in France. Some of these philosophies had to do with government, and they had a great influence on many other nations. For example, the idea that government should be divided into three branches comes from a French philosopher named Baron de Montesquieu (MAHN tus kyoo). A Swiss philosopher living in France named Jean-Jacques Rousseau (zhahn zhahk roo SOH) developed the idea that no laws are binding unless the people have agreed to them. These ideas helped shape the United States Constitution.

Achievements in the Arts French painters are world-famous for their achievements. For example, Eugène Delacroix (ooh ZHEHN deh la KWAH) painted works full of intense emotion and rich color in the early 1800s. Impressionist artists such as Claude Monet (moh NAY) developed new techniques for painting light and shadow.

French composers have written beautiful works of classical music. Claude Debussy (deh boo SEE), for example, composed music in the late 1800s and early 1900s. His work was influenced by artists such as Monet. In turn, Debussy influenced other composers.

French literature is world-famous. For example, Alexandre Dumas (doo MAH) wrote novels in the 1800s. Even today, many of his novels are read by people around the world and have been made into movies.

French Cultural Milestones

1637 René Descartes publishes ▶ *Discourse on Method*, one of the world's most important works in philosophy.

1664 Molière, considered to be France's greatest comic playwright, writes his masterpiece, *Tartuffe*.

1751 Denis Diderot publishes an important encyclopedia of science and philosophy that reflects the ideals of the Scientific Revolution.

◀ **1790** Marie Louise Élisabeth Vigée-Lebrun, one of France's most successful woman painters, paints her self-portrait.

1830s A French artist and a French inventor together develop the first methods for making photographs.

1899 Claude Monet paints ▶ *The Water-Lily Pond*, an important Impressionist painting.

◀ **1908** Auguste Rodin, considered to be France's finest sculptor, creates *The Cathedral*.

1939 Film director Jean Renoir produces his masterpiece *The Rules of the Game*, which influences cinema around the world.

1957 Writer Albert Camus, who wrote about human emotion in the post–World War II world, wins the Nobel Prize in Literature.

■ Diagram Skills

The French have made major contributions to the world's art, literature, cinema, and philosophy. **Identify** Which event had an influence on cinema around the world? **Identify Causes** What earlier event in this diagram paved the way for this event?

The Eiffel Tower
Paris's Eiffel Tower was built in 1889 to celebrate the French Revolution. The 984-foot- (300-meter-) tall tower was the tallest structure in the world until 1930. **Infer** *What feelings about the French Revolution might this tower bring about in French people?*

Innovative Architecture French architects have created magnificent buildings. In the 1100s, a style of art and architecture called Gothic developed in and around Paris. Gothic architecture is characterized by high ceilings, thin walls, and the use of columns and arches. French architects built stunning Gothic-style medieval cathedrals, like the Cathedral of Notre Dame (noh truh DAHM). Built in the 1200s in Paris, Notre Dame is one of Europe's most famous cathedrals. It has a number of huge stained-glass windows, one of which is 42 feet (13 meters) in diameter.

In later years, French architects designed other important buildings. For example, work on the Louvre (LOO vruh) Museum was begun during the Renaissance. At first, the Louvre was a royal palace. Over time, many of France's monarchs added to the original building. As they collected great works of art, they housed them in different parts of the Louvre. By the late 1700s, monarchs no longer used the Louvre as a palace, and it became a national museum.

French architects today continue to design great buildings, such as the national library that opened in 1998. This library is made up of four glass skyscrapers surrounding an open square. Though the building is new and modern, the collection it holds is one of the oldest in the world.

Economics

The Department Store In 1852, a French merchant named Aristide Boucicaut (BOO sih koh) took over the Bon Marché, a fabric shop in Paris. By 1914, he had transformed it into the world's first single department store. The department store allowed people, mainly women, to choose from a variety of ready-made clothing and household items in one attractive store. Before this, people went to individuals who specialized in making or selling one type of product. The department store also introduced innovations such as advertising, fixed prices on goods, and a system of returns or exchanges. Department stores were also introduced in the late 1800s in the United States and England.

The Bon Marché, in an engraving made around 1880

New Styles in Fashion For centuries, many people looked to France for the latest styles. Russian aristocrats of the 1700s followed French fashion and used French manners. They even spoke French. Wealthy British and American women traveled to Paris in the 1800s to have their clothes made. Less wealthy women admired French fashions in magazines. They often had their local seamstresses make copies of French originals.

French fashion continued to set trends in the 1900s. For example, a French fashion designer named Christian Dior (dee AWR) created a "New Look" in 1947. His designs featured narrow shoulders and long, full skirts. His fashions became popular all over the world.

Paris continues to be one of the most important centers of the fashion industry. Each year, people come from countries around the world to see the latest fashions from French designers.

Fine Food French cooking has long been one of the most respected styles of cooking in the world. In about 1805, a French pastry chef named Marie-Antoine Carême (muh REE ahn TWAHN kuh REM) delighted the rich and powerful people of France with his desserts. Some of his cakes looked like buildings or monuments. His puddings looked like birds or flowers.

In 1833, Carême wrote a book on the art of French cooking. His book was similar to the dictionaries of the French Academy. It set strict standards of excellence for cooking. Today, many of the world's best chefs are trained in France.

✔ **Reading Check** Name two examples of the influence of French culture on the rest of the world.

DISCOVERY CHANNEL
SCHOOL Video
Learn about Napoleon Bonaparte.

France

Like most developed countries, France's economy is increasingly based on services. Agriculture, however, is still very important to the nation's economy. France is the leading agricultural exporter among EU nations. Agricultural products, mainly cereals such as wheat and corn, make up about 16 percent of France's total exports. Use the data on this page to learn more about France's land use and economy.

France: Farming and Land Use
KEY

- Livestock raising
- Commercial agriculture
- Forestry
- Mountain region
- Wetland
- —— National border
- ⊛ National capital
- • Other city
- Cereals
- Vineyards
- Root crops
- Cattle
- Market gardening

Export Partners

Export Destination	Percent of France's Exports
European Union	
Germany	15
Spain	10
United Kingdom	9
Italy	9
Belgium	7
United States	7
Other	43

SOURCE: *CIA World Factbook*

Labor Force by Occupation

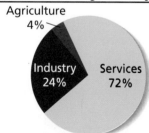

Agriculture 4%
Industry 24%
Services 72%

SOURCE: *CIA World Factbook*

Land Use

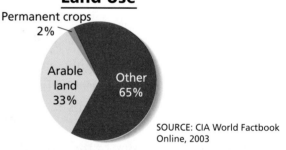

Permanent crops 2%
Arable land 33%
Other 65%

SOURCE: CIA World Factbook Online, 2003

Map and Chart Skills

1. **Note** How much of France's land can be used to grow crops? Where is this land located?

2. **Infer** Compare the percentage of France's arable land and cropland with the percentage of France's labor force in agriculture. From this information, what can you infer about how many laborers are needed to carry out modern agriculture?

3. **Transfer Information** What is the total percentage of France's exports to EU countries? What does this tell you about the importance of the EU to France's economy?

Use Web Code **Ide-7412** for **DK World Desk Reference Online.**

Diversity in France

Many French citizens believe French culture is both unique and valuable. Yet the cultures of other nations are influencing French culture more and more.

The French language, for example, has picked up words from other languages. French has borrowed words from English, such as *weekend, barbecue, laser,* and *cross-country.* French also includes words from languages such as Italian, Malaysian, Turkish, and Hindi. These words are a sign of France's ties with many other nations.

Cultural influences from other nations come from many different sources, such as film, television, and radio. Another source is immigration.

A History of Immigration Between 1850 and about 1940 France welcomed 7 million immigrants from European countries such as Poland, Italy, Spain, and Belgium. Because these immigrants came from cultures similar to that of France, they quickly and easily adopted French culture.

After World War II France had a shortage of workers. The French government began to encourage immigration to France. By the 1950s, the largest group of immigrants came from Algeria, a French colony in North Africa. In the past few decades, many immigrants have also arrived from Southeast Asia.

Influences on French Culture
At the top, Indian immigrants celebrate a Hindu festival. Above, a cable advertisement on a bus uses both French and English words.
Identify Effects *How might increasing immigration continue to affect the French language?*

A Political Protest
Muslim women protest a French law proposed in 2004 to ban students from wearing headscarves, Jewish caps, or other religious symbols in school. The women are holding a French flag. **Evaluate Information** *What point are the women making by displaying a French flag?*

Use Context Clues In the first paragraph, the contrast word *instead* gives you a clue to the meaning of the word *temporarily*.

Rising Tensions After World War II, Algerians and other immigrants helped rebuild France's economy. They took jobs that French employers found hard to fill. The French government assumed that these immigrants would work in France temporarily and then return home. Instead, many North African immigrants decided to make France their permanent home. Large numbers of immigrants along with their families moved to France in the 1970s, a time when the French economy was weak. Tension began to build between native-born French citizens and recent immigrants.

Some native French people had questions about the immigrants. Would they take jobs away from people already in France? Would the immigrants adopt French culture, or would they try to change it? Unlike earlier European immigrants, these recent immigrants often came from very different cultures. As they thought about these questions, some French people felt threatened by the immigrants. In the 1970s, the French government began to limit immigration.

In November 2005, discouraged immigrants in several French cities began to riot. Immigrants faced economic disadvantages and claimed that the French government and people had treated them unfairly. To combat the violence, the French government imposed temporary security measures, such as curfews and police raids, in affected areas. French leaders also promised to fight discrimination and improve opportunities for France's immigrants.

Immigrants' Influences Today the debate over immigration continues. Immigrants from Algeria, Morocco, and Tunisia bring African and Arab cultures with them. Their food, dress, and music are quite different from those of traditional French culture. The same is true of immigrants from Asia and other regions. The influence of all these groups can be seen especially in the big cities. In Paris and in many other large cities in France, it is common to hear people speaking languages other than French. Every year, there are more and more restaurants and stores that sell foreign food.

France has always been a diverse society. But unlike in the past, recent immigrants have arrived from countries with very different cultures from that of France. France and its people are making adjustments. Many French people were shocked when a politician who promoted an anti-immigrant message won significant popular support in the 2002 presidential election. But most people have come to value the benefits of a diverse population.

An African immigrant selling fresh fish

✓ **Reading Check** How are France's immigrants today different from those of the past?

Section 2 Assessment

Key Terms
Review the key terms at the beginning of this section. Use each term in a sentence that explains its meaning.

 **Target Reading Skill**
Find the word *aristocrat* on page 133. What clues in that paragraph helped you figure out its meaning?

Comprehension and Critical Thinking
1. (a) List Name two French cultural contributions to the arts.

(b) Explain What were Montesquieu's and Rousseau's philosophies about government?
(c) Synthesize How did these philosophies influence the United States?
2. (a) Recall Why did the French government encourage immigration following World War II?
(b) Summarize Why did tensions arise between native-born French citizens and immigrants to France in the 1970s?
(c) Identify Effects When immigrants move to a new country, how do they change a country for better or worse?

Writing Activity
Suppose that you are a television reporter covering a story on French culture. You interview an elderly woman for your report. What questions might you ask her to determine how French culture has changed and how it has stayed the same over the past few decades?

> **Writing Tip** Use the blue headings in this section to help you decide on topics. Reread the text under the headings to get ideas for your questions.

Sweden

A Welfare State

Prepare to Read

Objectives

In this section you will

1. Learn about Sweden's welfare state.
2. Find out how Sweden became a welfare state.
3. Examine possible solutions to Sweden's economic problems.

Taking Notes

As you read this section, look for details about Sweden's welfare state. Copy the table below and record your findings in it.

Sweden's Welfare State	
Benefits	Economic Challenges
•	•
•	•
•	•

Target Reading Skill

Use Context Clues
Remember that a word that looks familiar to you may have a different meaning in the context of the text you are reading. For example, you have probably heard of the word *welfare*. As you read the text under the red heading A Welfare State, you will learn that the word has a different meaning than the one you have thought of. The last sentence of the first paragraph under A Welfare State makes that difference clear.

Key Terms

• **welfare state** (WEL fayr stayt) *n.* a country in which many services and benefits are paid for by the government
• **national debt** (NASH uh nul det) *n.* the amount of money a government owes

A baby being examined by a doctor in Sweden

A young Swedish couple is expecting a new baby any day now. Excited, they decorate the baby's room and talk about how they will raise her. They even joke about where she will go to college and what career she might choose when she grows up.

Like all new parents, they have many hopes and plans for their baby. They have concerns, too—concerns about her health and well-being. But they feel confident about certain things. For example, both parents will have paid time off from work to care for the baby. The baby will also receive excellent health care, child care, and schooling—all for free or at a very low cost. To understand why the government provides these services, you need to understand the nature of Sweden's society.

A Welfare State

Sweden is a welfare state. In a **welfare state,** the government provides many services and benefits either for free or for a very low cost. These services and benefits include medical care, paid time off from work, and child care. A welfare system means something very different in Sweden than it does in the United States. The American welfare system helps people who are in great need—people who cannot afford medical care or food. The Swedish system helps everyone.

A Cradle-to-Grave System Sweden has a "cradle-to-grave" welfare system. That means that the system provides basic services for all people at every stage of life. When a child is born, the government pays for parents to stay home from work for at least 12 months. The state then provides child care at a reduced cost, so that parents can work or continue their education. The government pays the costs of schooling, including books and lunches for all students. College education is also paid for every student, through a combination of grants and loans. And every Swedish citizen has access to free or inexpensive health care.

As part of the government benefits program, all workers receive five weeks paid vacation. Most workers generally take their vacation at the same time during the summer. That is because in the summer, the nights in this far-northern country are very short. It is daylight for most of the day.

Swedish people take more paid sick days than the workers of any other European nation. Some of the money for this leave comes from the government. And when workers retire, they receive a monthly payment from the government. This payment generally equals more than half of the pay they received when they were working.

Daily Life in Sweden
Sweden's government funds this day care center (below) and senior citizen community center (bottom left). Both are located in Stockholm, Sweden's capital. **Summarize** *What other benefits do Swedes receive from the government?*

Sweden

Sweden is located far to the north, with about a fifth of its land within the Arctic Circle. Because of its great length from north to south, its climate varies greatly. The northern interior receives heavy snowfall and is cold for months, while in the southern regions temperatures are moderate, and the coastal waters do not freeze. The country is heavily forested, especially in the northern part of the country. Study the map and the charts to learn how Sweden's geography shapes the lives of its people.

Sweden: Natural Vegetation
KEY

- Deciduous forest
- Mixed forest
- Coniferous forest
- Highland (vegetation varying with elevation)
- Tundra
- National border
- ⊛ National capital
- • Other city

0 miles 300
0 kilometers 300
Lambert Azimuthal Equal Area

Largest Cities

City	Population (2005)
Stockholm	🧍🧍🧍🧍🧍🧍🧍
Göteborg	🧍🧍🧍🧍🧍
Malmö	🧍🧍🧍
Uppsala	🧍🧍
Linköping	🧍🧍

SOURCE: Statistics Sweden

🧍 This figure represents 100,000 people.

Sweden's Weather

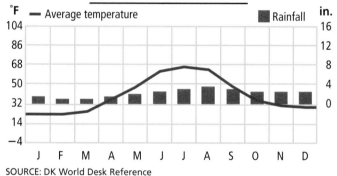

— Average temperature   ■ Rainfall

SOURCE: DK World Desk Reference

Urban and Rural Population

83% Urban   **17% Rural**

SOURCE: United Nations Population Division

Map and Chart Skills

1. **Locate** Where are Sweden's five largest cities located?

2. **Contrast** How is the vegetation of that area different from that of the regions with no large cities?

3. **Synthesize Information** What factors might explain the location of the majority of Sweden's population?

Use Web Code **lde-7413** for **DK World Desk Reference Online.**

High Taxes Swedish people believe that welfare benefits are very important. They are willing to pay the highest taxes in Europe in order to have these benefits. Swedes pay as much as 60 percent of their income in taxes. Food is taxed at 12 percent. Clothing and other goods are taxed at 25 percent. But in exchange for these high taxes, all Swedes have financial security. Whether they are rich or poor, they know that their children will get a good education. Medical costs are low. Rents are affordable.

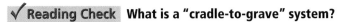

✓ **Reading Check** **What is a "cradle-to-grave" system?**

Building a Welfare State

As it has been for hundreds of years, Sweden is a monarchy. Yet the government has changed greatly throughout Sweden's history.

Sweden's History The history of Sweden begins with the Vikings—an early sailing people from Scandinavia who colonized many parts of Europe. Beginning in about the 900s, Sweden was ruled by a series of kingdoms. In the 1600s, Sweden emerged as a great power in northern Europe. From its capital city, Stockholm, Sweden ruled a thriving empire. However, the country's strength declined in the 1700s after Sweden lost a war with Russia. Sweden remained neutral in both world wars.

Like the monarchy in the United Kingdom, Sweden's monarchy changed over time. The monarch slowly gave more and more power to the people, represented in a parliament. And political parties arose to represent the people and bring about change in government. Today Sweden is a constitutional monarchy. The monarch is the ceremonial leader, but parliament makes the laws.

A 2002 photo shows the current Swedish monarch, King Carl Gustaf XVI, with other members of the royal family.

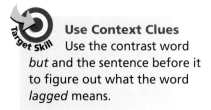

Use Context Clues Use the contrast word *but* and the sentence before it to figure out what the word *lagged* means.

Meeting Economic Challenges Economic problems led to the rise of Sweden's modern welfare state. By the late 1800s, industry had grown in the United States and most of Europe. But Sweden lagged far behind. There were few factories or railroad lines or even good roads. Farming methods had not changed much since the Middle Ages. Many people were very poor. By the end of the 1800s, about 1.5 million Swedes had left the country in search of a better life. Most of them settled in the midwestern states of the United States, such as Minnesota and Wisconsin.

In 1932, a political party called the Social Democrats came to power. The Social Democrats promised a better life for Swedes. Over the next few decades, the party made Sweden into a welfare state. At the same time, Sweden became an industrial country, and its economy grew stronger. Today the Social Democrats are still the country's largest political party.

✓ **Reading Check** Which political party created Sweden's welfare state?

Problems and Solutions

Sweden's welfare state has served as a model for government throughout Europe. Still, the system has its problems. Everyone in Sweden receives benefits, but the government has faced challenges in providing those benefits.

Facing Challenges For decades, Sweden was able to offer its citizens generous benefits. But things changed in the 1980s. People bought fewer items because of the high taxes on groceries, clothing, and other goods. Thus, there was less spending to boost the economy. Sweden's economic growth stalled. The government had to borrow money to continue paying for the benefits provided under the welfare system. Soon, the **national debt**, or the amount of money their government owed, began to grow.

The government increased taxes and cut spending in the 1990s to control the debt. Eventually, the Swedish government no longer had to borrow money to fund welfare benefits. In fact, every year since 1998, the government has had a budget surplus, or more money than is needed to pay for benefits. However, as its population ages, Sweden will need more money to care for its people.

■ Chart Skills

Sales tax is a tax on goods and services. This chart shows the rate, or percent, of sales tax in various Western European countries and two American states. **Compare** How does Sweden's sales tax compare to those of the other European countries shown? To the states shown? **Generalize** Do you think governments with very low taxes generally provide many or few social services? Why do you think so?

Sales Tax Rates in Western Europe and the United States

Country or State	Standard Rate (%)
France	19.6
Germany	16.0
Sweden	25.0
United Kingdom	17.5
United States: Florida	6.0
United States: California	7.25

SOURCE: The Economist Intelligence Unit Limited; Federation of Tax Administrators (www.taxadmin.org), California State Board of Equalization

A Graying Population Sweden has 1.5 million retired people out of a population of about 9 million. This means that about one out of six people is retired. That is the highest proportion of retired people in the world. Sweden's aging population presents many challenges for the nation. Elderly people often need increased health care and medicines.

Yet an aging population presents an even greater problem. As you have read, Swedes receive many benefits. The money for these benefits comes from the paychecks of Swedish workers, who pay high taxes on their salaries. In an aging population, there are fewer workers, because so many people are retired. As a result, there is less tax money to pay for benefits.

Over time, the money received from taxes may not be enough to pay for the extra care needed by an elderly population. Raising taxes even higher to cover the high costs of benefits has been proposed, but it is not a popular idea. The government is trying to save money now to pay for this care in the future. However, if Sweden does not stick to its budget reforms, money for welfare benefits could run out.

Government Solutions Sweden's government is working to solve these problems. The government reformed its own budget process through new rules, such as balanced budget requirements, surplus goals, and spending limits. In addition, the government tried to reduce benefits in the 1990s. It reduced the payments for sickness benefits and required workers to save more of their own money for retirement. But the reduction in benefits angered Swedish voters, who voted against their leaders in two major elections.

Links to

Science

Sun at Midnight It is midnight in northern Sweden, and some friends are playing volleyball outside. How is this so? From about March 20 to September 23 in the most northern arctic regions, the sun can be seen on the horizon 24 hours a day. This is because the northern hemisphere is tilted directly toward the sun at this time. In northern Sweden, the sun never sets for a few days around June 21. The Swedes celebrate this time as Midsummer's Eve, with dancing (below), food, and music.

12:05 AM

A woman assembles parts at a car factory in Göteborg, Sweden.

Business Solutions Another solution would be for businesses to earn more, giving more money to the government in the form of taxes. One way for businesses to grow is to take better advantage of Sweden's natural resources. Sweden has high-grade iron ore and produces enough steel for itself and for export. Hydroelectric turbines run by Sweden's fast rivers and many waterfalls produce half of Sweden's electricity. Sweden's vast forests support the timber industry, which supplies Sweden's needs as well as those of other countries.

Even with these ample resources, Swedish companies have had trouble competing with firms in other countries. Most Swedish products are of high quality. But the Swedes have not been able to make them as quickly and cheaply as other countries. Some companies have found a solution to this problem. Swedish automakers, for example, have followed the example of American companies. Using the methods of American auto factories, the Swedes can now make a car in about 40 hours. It used to take them about 100 hours.

Improving the economy means changing the ways that things are done in Sweden. Because the welfare system is very important to Swedes, they are working to find better ways of paying for it. That is one challenge facing Sweden today.

✓ **Reading Check** What natural resources could help the Swedish economy?

 Section 3 Assessment

Key Terms
Review the key terms at the beginning of this section. Use each term in a sentence that explains its meaning.

Target Reading Skill
Find the word *vast* in the first paragraph on this page. How does its context explain its meaning?

Comprehension and Critical Thinking
1. (a) Describe What benefits do Swedish citizens receive?

(b) Identify Frame of Reference Why are some Swedes willing to pay such high taxes?

2. (a) Explain Why did many Swedes leave their country in the late 1800s?

(b) Identify Effects What effect did industrialization have on Sweden's economy?

3. (a) Explain Why did the Swedish economy stall in the late 1980s?

(b) Apply Information How did the government and businesses work together to solve Sweden's economic problems?

Writing Activity
Consider that in the United States, most people pay 20 to 30 percent of their income in taxes, compared to about 60 percent in Sweden. What lessons do you think the two countries might learn from each other? Write a paragraph summarizing your thoughts.

For: An activity on the Vikings
Visit: PHSchool.com
Web Code: ldd-7403

Prepare to Read

Objectives

In this section you will

1. Discover that there is another country within Italy called Vatican City.
2. Understand why there are divisions between northern and southern Italy.

Taking Notes

As you read this section, look for ways that life is similar and different in northern and southern Italy. Copy the Venn diagram below and record your findings in it.

Life in Italy

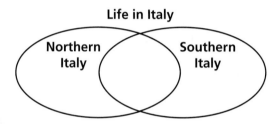

Northern Italy   Southern Italy

Target Reading Skill

Use Context Clues To make sure you have correctly determined the meaning of an unfamiliar word by looking at its context, look at the word itself for clues. For example, examine the word *guidance* in the first paragraph below. The sentence in which the word appears tells you that it has something to do with the leader. To double check, look at the word itself. What verb sounds like *guidance*?

Key Terms

- **basilica** (buh SIL ih kuh) *n.* a Roman Catholic church that has special, high status because of its age or history
- **manufacturing** (man yoo FAK chur ing) *n.* the process of turning raw materials into finished products
- **land reform** (land ree FAWRM) *n.* the process of dividing large properties into smaller ones

Can you solve this riddle? A magazine photographer spent about a year exploring a certain country, yet the country is so tiny that he was able to walk around it in 40 minutes. Its population is only about 1,000. But about one billion people look to its leader for guidance. What is the country?

The tiny country is called Vatican City (VAT ih kun SIH tee). It is the world headquarters of the Roman Catholic Church. The pope is its leader. Every day, Roman Catholics all over the world look to him for leadership. Politically, Vatican City is not part of Italy. Yet it holds an important place in the culture of all Italians.

St. Peter's Basilica rises above Vatican City.

Vatican City

Vatican City is also known as the Vatican. It is a country within a country. Located within Rome, the capital of Italy, the Vatican is an independent city-state. The Vatican has its own banks and its own money, although you can also use euros there. It is a member of the United Nations. It also has its own police force, radio station, newspaper, and fire department.

Vatican City symbolizes the Roman Catholic Church that unites most Italians. Every day, Catholics and non-Catholics stream into this little country. Most visitors come to see St. Peter's Basilica. A **basilica** is a Roman Catholic church that has a special, high status because of its age or history. The Vatican's palace and art museums are also popular attractions. These museums have priceless collections of religious art, as well as artwork from ancient Greece and Rome.

The Sistine (SIS teen) Chapel, located inside the Vatican, contains many famous paintings, sculptures, and other works of art. Tourists crowd into this chapel, but there is nearly perfect silence inside. No one is allowed to speak above a whisper. Everyone leans back to see the religious scenes painted on the ceiling. The artist Michelangelo painted the ceiling in the 1500s. It is the most famous ceiling in the world.

✓ **Reading Check** What is the Vatican?

Use Context Clues
If you do not know what *priceless* means, look in the surrounding words and phrases for context clues.

A View Inside St. Peter's
Tourists gaze in awe at the art decorating St. Peter's Basilica, including these sculptures by the Italian Renaissance artist Bernini. **Apply Information** *How was the Vatican influenced by the Renaissance?*

NC VNA FIDES   MVNDO REFVLG

Italy

Historically, Italy's location on the Mediterranean Sea made it an important agricultural center and a crossroads of world trade. Today, Italy's economy is shifting toward services, and its main trade partners are other EU members. The "two Italies"—northern and southern—continue to have unequal economies. Use the data on this page to learn more about the economy of Italy.

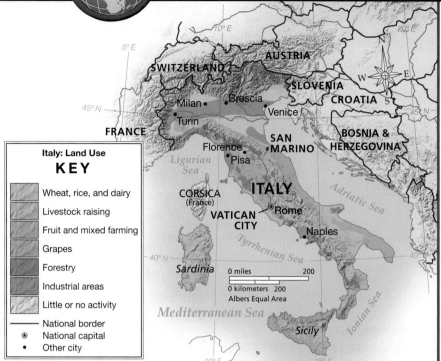

Italy: Land Use
KEY

Wheat, rice, and dairy
Livestock raising
Fruit and mixed farming
Grapes
Forestry
Industrial areas
Little or no activity
— National border
⊛ National capital
• Other city

Economic Output per Person, 2001

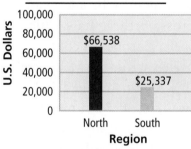

U.S. Dollars

$66,538 — North
$25,337 — South

Region

SOURCES: The European Commission;
The World Bank Group

Structure of Italy's Economy

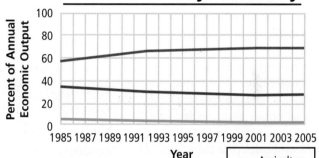

Percent of Annual Economic Output

Year

SOURCE: *The World Bank Group, CIA World Factbook*

— Agriculture
— Industry
— Services

Trade, 2001

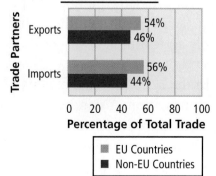

Trade Partners

Exports 54% / 46%
Imports 56% / 44%

Percentage of Total Trade

■ EU Countries
■ Non-EU Countries

SOURCE: Italy in Figures

Map and Chart Skills

1. **Identify** Where is most of Italy's industry?
2. **Compare and Contrast** How does northern Italy's economic output per person compare to that of southern Italy?
3. **Predict** What changes might southern Italy need to make to its economy in order to catch up with the economy of northern Italy?

Use Web Code **Ide-7414**
for **DK World Desk Reference Online.**

Learn about life
in ancient Rome.

Divisions Between North and South

Roman Catholicism, with its base in the Vatican, unites about one billion people around the world. It also unites most Italians. Not every Italian is a Catholic, but Italy's history is closely tied to the history of Catholicism. Other things also bring Italians together. Most people living in Italy are ethnic Italians. There are few ethnic minorities. Strong family ties are common among Italians. Even a love of soccer unites many Italians.

Despite these things that many Italians have in common, there are many differences among Italians. Some of the major differences are regional. Italians in the north and Italians in the south live, work, and even practice Roman Catholicism in different ways.

A Divided History For hundreds of years, there was no single, unified Italy. What we now call Italy was once the center of the Roman Empire. Around 2,000 years ago, the Roman Empire stretched across Europe and into northern Africa. When the Roman Empire broke up, Italy itself was divided into many separate city-states, territories, and small kingdoms. The people in these areas had different governments and spoke different languages.

Over time, a regional pattern emerged. Invaders came by land from the north. They swept across northern Italy, which retained close ties with the rest of Western Europe. In contrast, invaders from the Byzantine Empire traveled across the Mediterranean Sea to conquer southern Italy. This region retained links to other Mediterranean countries but was cut off from much of Western Europe.

The two regions also developed differently in terms of government and economy. In northern Italy, city-states became bustling cities. In modern times, this region became a center of industry. In contrast, in southern Italy, feudal kingdoms dominated, with large numbers of peasants working the land. As a result, southern Italy has always been heavily agricultural.

Italy Unites In the late 1800s, the regions of Italy were united into one nation. A standard form of the Italian language was introduced to help unify the people. After hundreds of years of a divided history, it was not always easy for Italians to identify themselves with this new nation. Even today, there are strong differences between life in the north and in the south.

Links Across Time

The Risorgimento: "Rising Again" The Risorgimento was a movement in the 1800s that inspired the Italian people to unite as one nation. Poets and philosophers used words and ideas to create a sense of nationalism. Today, Italian school children learn about and celebrate the movement. Cities have streets and squares that bear the names of many of the Risorgimento's heroes. Giuseppe Garibaldi (right) was one of the Risorgimento's leaders and is today considered an Italian patriot.

Life in the North Milan (mih LAN) is typical of northern Italy. Abundant minerals, fast rivers, and a well-developed economy have brought wealth to the region. Many international businesses are located there. Northern Italy is much more prosperous than southern Italy.

The cities of Milan, Turin, and Genoa are home to most of Italy's manufacturing industries. **Manufacturing** is the process of turning raw materials into finished products. Milan's factories produce cars, planes, leather goods, and plastics.

Milan has a more stylish side, too. Every season, people interested in fashion crowd into Milan to see the new collections from clothing designers. Milan is now second only to Paris as a fashion capital.

Like many European cities, Milan is a mix of the old and the new. In a 400-year-old palace, you can see one of the oldest public libraries in Europe. Millions of dollars have been spent to keep it in good condition. Less than a mile away, you can drive past modern steel and glass office buildings.

Cars being assembled at the Ferrari factory in Maranello, Italy

Life in the South Southern Italy is very different from Milan. Southern Italy is mostly agricultural. Fertile areas near the coast receive enough rainfall to grow abundant crops. Olives, tomatoes, fruits, and other crops grow there. Inland, farmers have difficulty making a living because of the thin soil and dry climate.

Making Cheese
These men use traditional methods to make cheese. **Contrast** *How does this work differ from that performed by the men in the photo at the top of this page?*

Locorotondo (loh koh roh TOHN doh) is a small town located in the southernmost part of Italy. It is on the "heel" of the Italian "boot." Most people in Locorotondo make a living by farming. They grow wheat, olives, and fruits there. Fishing is also an important business for people there.

Most people in southern Italy follow a more traditional way of life. Many people in southern Italy talk about northern Italy as if it were another country. There are fewer large cities in southern Italy. The high fashions of Milan and the busy city of Turin seem very far away.

Religion in the Two Italies The Roman Catholic Church provides a focus particularly for southern Italians. Today, in the small towns of the south, life is organized around the larger family of the Church and the smaller family in the home. In the north, these ties may not be as strong.

Many religious events are celebrated in the streets of southern towns. Every year, the Feast of Corpus Christi, a Catholic religious festival, takes place several weeks after Easter. In this festival, women hang their wedding clothes over their balconies and place flowers on them. Additional displays are set up on the streets around town. People walk together around the town, from church to church and from display to display.

Economics and the Two Italies After World War II, Italy's economy boomed. Because most of its large cities and industrial centers are located in the north, northern Italy boomed, too. Meanwhile, the agriculture-based economy of southern Italy failed to thrive. Southern Italians moved to the north in large numbers to find jobs.

Italy's government took measures to help the south catch up with the north. First, it introduced land reform. **Land reform** is a process of dividing large properties into smaller ones. Governments sponsor land reform so that more people can own land. Italy's government hoped that land reform would increase agricultural production. The government also modernized the southern region by building roads and new irrigation systems.

A Coastal Scene
The town of Positano clings to a steep cliff on the edge of the ocean in southern Italy. **Analyze Images** *What evidence do you see in the photo of the importance of religion to southern Italians?*

These measures increased agricultural output in the south. Still, southern Italy today lags behind northern Italy. Unemployment in southern Italy is higher than elsewhere in the country. And many southern Italians still move north, particularly to the cities of Rome and Milan. There, they seek jobs and a better standard of living.

Politics and the Two Italies Northern and southern Italy are so different that some Italians have urged northern Italy to become a separate country. Throughout the 1990s, a party called the Northern League called for northern Italy to secede, or leave the rest of Italy to form its own country. In 1996, the party won 10 percent of the vote in a national election.

However, in recent elections, the Northern League has not done so well. For most Italians, no matter how much they differ, they will never lose their strong Italian identity. Religion and family will probably keep the people of Italy unified for many years to come.

✔ **Reading Check** Why do some Northern Italians support the Northern League?

Links to Art

Futurism Italian Futurism was an art movement in the early 1900s inspired by the speed and energy of modern life. As their name suggests, Futurists believed that art should look to the future rather than remain tied to traditions from the past. Beauty, they said, lies in modern machinery—factories, cars, planes, or even machine guns. Boccioni's 1913 sculpture *Unique Forms of Continuity in Space* shows a human figure in motion. More than just a person walking, the piece gives an idea of energy and movement. It even suggests how currents of air might rush around a body moving quickly through space.

Section 4 Assessment

Key Terms
Review the key terms listed at the beginning of this section. Use each term in a sentence that explains its meaning.

Target Reading Skill
Use context clues to explain the meaning of the word *secede* in the second paragraph on this page.

Comprehension and Critical Thinking
1. (a) Locate Where is Vatican City?
(b) Summarize How does the Vatican operate as a city-state?

(c) Synthesize Information How does the Roman Catholic religion unite Italians?
2. (a) List Name three differences between life in northern Italy and life in southern Italy.
(b) Sequence How did regional differences emerge in Italy over time?
(c) Make Generalizations Do you think Italy's government should continue to introduce reforms to make northern Italy and southern Italy equal? Explain why or why not.

Writing Activity
Write a letter as if you are an Italian writing to a relative about life in either northern or southern Italy. Write details about your life, including what you do for fun, what kinds of work your parents do, and so on.

Writing Tip Be sure to include a greeting, a closing, and a signature in your letter. Also decide on the age, gender, and personality of the person writing the letter.

Skills for Life

Using Visual Information to Write a Paragraph

Jerry had to write a report on Rome's Vatican City. He was surprised to discover that Vatican City is a country. He had thought that it was only a religious center in Italy. To write his report, Jerry looked at different charts, graphs, maps, and diagrams. He found that the Vatican has been a country since 1929. From a chart, Jerry learned that the Vatican is about 109 acres (44 hectares) in area. Looking at a diagram, he saw that it is surrounded by a wall with gates that can be locked at night. Its population is fewer than a thousand people. The number of tourists who visit the Vatican each day is far greater than the number of its residents.

St. Peter's Basilica

Information can be presented as pictures, as numbers, or as text. When you translate the meaning of visual information into words, you are transferring information from one medium into another. Jerry transferred visual information from charts, graphs, and diagrams into a written report.

Learn the Skill

Use these steps to transfer visual information into a paragraph.

1. **Identify the topic of the chart, diagram, or graph by reading the title.** Then look at it to get a general idea of its purpose.

2. **Identify the key pieces of information.** Read headings and other key pieces of information carefully. The headings are usually set off in some way. If you are using a chart or a table, look for similarities and differences among the types of information in the columns.

3. **Analyze the meaning of the information.** Write down several conclusions that can be drawn from the information you have put together.

4. **Rewrite the key pieces of information and your conclusions in a clear paragraph.**

Practice the Skill

Use the steps in Learn the Skill to translate the information in the table into a paragraph.

ITALY: POPULATION STATISTICS		
	1990	2006 (Estimated)
Population	57,664,405	58,133,509
Birth Rate	10 births per 1,000 population	9 births per 1,000 population
Death Rate	9 deaths per 1,000 population	10 deaths per 1,000 population
Fertility Rate	1.4 children born per woman	1.3 children born per woman
Life Expectancy	74, male; 81, female	77, male; 83, female

1 What is the title of the table? What does it tell you about the subject of the table?

2 What are the important headings in the table? Do they indicate key pieces of information? Note the information that is compared and contrasted in the table. How are all the statistics shown on this table related? In what ways are the two sets of numbers similar and different? Which categories have changed over time? Why do you think they have changed?

3 Analyze the meaning of the facts you have learned. What conclusions can you draw? For example, how might the change in the birth rate have affected Italy's population? How might the change in the death rate have affected Italy's population? Is the population getting older or younger? In what ways might the changes in Italy's population affect life in Italy in the future? Consider jobs, school, family life, health care, and so on.

4 Write a paragraph that contains the major pieces of information you have learned. Include the conclusions you have drawn.

Italian Workforce by Occupation

1990: 5%, 37%, 58%
2003: 5%, 32%, 63%

■ Services ■ Industry ■ Agriculture

Apply the Skill

Compare the circle graphs. Then use the steps above to write a short paragraph. Include key facts from the graphs, explaining what has changed from 1990 to 2003. Note that agriculture has remained the same. Why do you think that is so? Look at the two graphs and draw some conclusions about how these changes might have affected the country.

Germany
A Unified Nation

Prepare to Read

Objectives

In this section you will
1. Learn about Germany's past.
2. Find out how Germany became reunited.

Taking Notes

As you read this section, look for the events that caused Germany to be divided and later reunited. Copy the flowchart below and record your findings in it.

1918: Germany loses World War I.

↓ ↓ ↓

1933:

↓ ↓ ↓

Target Reading Skill

Use Context Clues When you first encounter an unfamiliar word, jot down some ideas about its meaning. As you read and reread the paragraphs that provide its context, adjust the word's definition until you are certain of it. For example, find the word *desperate* in the first paragraph on the next page. You may need to read several paragraphs before you can be certain of its meaning.

Key Terms

- **Holocaust** (HAHL uh kawst) *n.* the mass murder of six million Jews
- **reunification** (ree yoo nih fih KAY shun) *n.* the process of becoming unified again
- **standard of living** (STAN durd uv LIV ing) *n.* the level of comfort in terms of the goods and services that people have

A guard stands watch while East Berlin workmen add blocks to the Berlin Wall in October, 1961.

In 1961, Conrad Schumann, a 19-year-old policeman, stood guard at a barbed-wire fence in East Berlin. His job was to shoot anyone who tried to get across the fence. East Berlin was part of communist East Germany. The fence was built to prevent East Berliners from escaping to West Berlin, where they could reach democratic West Germany.

To Schumann, the fence was a terrible thing. He could see the buildings of West Berlin on the other side. They seemed very beautiful. On television, he had seen a program from West Berlin that showed people dancing to Western music and speaking their views freely. In East Germany, the government did not approve of Western music and free speech. The stores had few interesting things to buy.

Schumann thought about all these things. Then he made a decision and jumped over the barbed wire. A moment later, he was on the other side—in the freedom of the West. Just a few days after Schumann jumped to freedom, a concrete wall replaced the barbed-wire fence. The Berlin Wall separated families and friends. On one side of it, communism ruled. On the other side, the people did. What were the effects of a divided Germany?

Germany's Past

To understand the importance of the Berlin Wall, you need to understand part of Germany's past. Germany lost World War I in 1918. The German government had to pay billions of dollars as punishment for attacking other countries. In the early 1920s, the German economy collapsed. Prices soared. Germans became desperate.

Hitler and World War II When World War I began, Adolf Hitler (AD awlf HIT lur) was a 25-year-old Austrian soldier in the German army. When Germany lost the war, he promised himself that Germany would never suffer such a defeat again. Hitler became deeply involved in politics. In speech after speech, he promised to make Germany great again. By 1933, this former soldier had become dictator of Germany.

Hitler blamed Germany's economic problems on Jews. He spread hateful theories about Jews, Roma, and other groups in Germany. He claimed that they were inferior to other Germans. He claimed that Germans were a superior ethnic group—and that they should rule Europe.

Adolf Hitler salutes a crowd of people in 1934.

Divided Berlin

KEY
— Berlin Wall
— City border
✈ Airport

0 miles 10
0 kilometers 10
Transverse Mercator

EAST GERMANY

Berlin

WEST GERMANY

East Berlin

Tegel Airport
Reichstag
Brandenburg Gate

Havel River

Gatow Airport

Tempelhof Airport

West Berlin

Spree River

Schönefeld Airport

N
W E
S

MAP MASTER Skills Activity

Location Though Berlin was divided into eastern and western halves, the entire city itself lay within the country of East Germany. **Locate** Which half of the city contained three airports? **Identify Point of View** How might Germans living in West Berlin have felt being surrounded by a communist nation?

Go Online
PHSchool.com Use Web Code **ldp-7415** for step-by-step map skills practice.

Germany

Germany has a long, complex history. At the time of the Roman Empire, various Germanic tribes lived all across Central Europe and into Scandinavia. Present-day Germany developed in the late 1800s out of a patchwork of kingdoms and small states. Just a few decades later, the country dramatically altered its history by fighting a global war. Use the data on this page to learn about modern Germany's history.

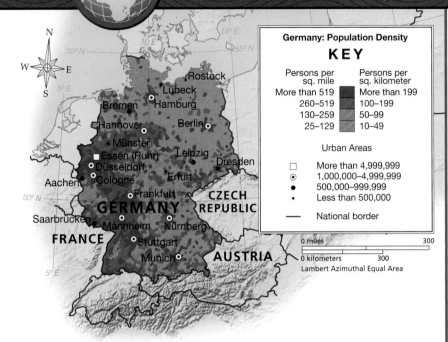

Germany Since 1914

1914–1918 Germany is defeated in World War I; loses land, colonies, and wealth.

1933 Adolf Hitler and Nazi Party take political control.

1939–1945 Germany fights in World War II; is defeated by Allies.

1961 Berlin Wall is built.

1990 East Germany and West Germany reunite.

| 1910 | 1920 | 1940 | 1960 | 1980 | 2000 |

1920s Germany faces severe economic challenges.

1935 Nuremberg Laws legalize the persecution of Jews.

1949 Germany divides into communist East Germany and democratic West Germany.

1989 Berlin Wall falls.

2002 Germany adopts euro as its currency.

A World War I gas mask

SOURCE: DK World Desk Reference

German Capital Cities

Years	German Region	Region's Capital
1871–1918	German Empire	Berlin
1919–1949	Germany	Berlin
1949–1990	East Germany	East Berlin
1949–1990	West Germany	Bonn
1990–1999	Germany	Bonn
1999–present	Germany	Berlin

SOURCE: Encyclopedia Britannica Online

Map and Chart Skills

1. **Note** What was the capital of West Germany from 1949 to 1990?

2. **Explain** Why did Germany have two different capitals during the years 1949–1990?

3. **Predict** How might the population density of eastern Germany change as long as Berlin remains the capital?

Use Web Code **Ide-7415** for **DK World Desk Reference Online.**

Many people did not believe Hitler's ideas. But Hitler was deadly serious. He ordered attacks on neighboring countries and forced them to submit to German rule. His actions led to the start of World War II in 1939. Great Britain, the Soviet Union, and finally the United States joined other nations to stop the Germans.

By the end of the war, Europe was in ruins. People around the world learned that the Germans had forced countless Jews, Roma, Slavs, and others into brutal concentration camps. Millions of people were murdered in these camps. The majority of them were Jews. This horrible mass murder of six million Jews is called the **Holocaust** (HAH luh kawst).

A Divided Capital At the end of the war, the victors divided up Germany. The Americans, British, and French joined their sections together to create the Federal Republic of Germany. This democratic country was also known as West Germany. The Soviet Union created a communist system in the German Democratic Republic, or East Germany.

The city of Berlin was in East Germany. But the western half of the city, called West Berlin, became part of democratic West Germany. The western half of Berlin was turned into an island of democracy in the middle of communism. The Berlin Wall separated the two halves of Berlin. It also stood as a symbol of a divided world.

Berlin had once been the capital of all of Germany. But now Germany was divided. The city of Bonn became the new capital of West Germany. East Berlin was the capital of East Germany.

Citizen Heroes

Raoul Wallenberg
Raoul Wallenberg (rah OOL WAHL un burg) came from a wealthy Swedish family of bankers and diplomats. Wallenberg studied architecture in the United States. But in 1944, with World War II raging, he persuaded the Swedish government to send him to Hungary as a diplomat. In Hungary, Wallenberg used Sweden's status as a neutral nation to create "safe houses" for Hungarian Jews. Wallenberg's safe houses sheltered several thousand Hungarian Jews and ultimately saved their lives. Wallenberg's efforts put his own life at great risk. In 1945, he was mistakenly arrested as a spy by Soviet troops in Hungary. Wallenberg died in a Soviet prison.

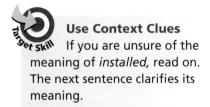

Use Context Clues If you are unsure of the meaning of *installed,* read on. The next sentence clarifies its meaning.

The Cold War During the Cold War, the United States and Western Europe became partners. These countries had democratic governments and were opposed to communism. Eastern European countries had communist governments that had been installed by the Soviet Union. Soviet troops stayed in Eastern Europe to make sure that these countries remained communist.

Think about the effects of the Cold War on European countries. Recall that these countries are small and close together. Cold War borders separated families and friends. Even some who had managed to escape to the West suffered. They could no longer see the relatives they had left behind.

East Germans led far different lives from West Germans. The communist government required people to obey without asking questions. It even encouraged people to spy on family members and neighbors. Children were taught to respect only those things that promoted communism. Western movies, music, and magazines were seen as harmful influences.

While Eastern German border guards look on, a protestor hammers against the Berlin Wall in November, 1989.

The Communists Weaken In time, communist rule started to change. The East German economy fell far behind the West German economy. The average West German had a much more comfortable life than the average East German had. Many East Germans wanted to go to the West, but the East German government did not let them.

In the late 1980s, changes in the Soviet Union weakened the East German government. It became clear that the Soviets would no longer use force to protect communism in Eastern Europe. Fear of the Soviets had helped keep the East German government in power. Now this fear was gone, and the people were ready for change.

Some East Germans began to escape to West Germany by way of Hungary, Czechoslovakia, and Poland. Others began protesting in the streets. To stop the protests, the East German government softened its rules. It announced that under certain conditions, East Germans could visit West Germany.

The East German Government Falls Many people misunderstood the announcement. They thought that the government was opening the Berlin Wall permanently. On November 9, 1989, huge crowds of people demanded to cross into West Berlin. The border guards let them.

Thousands of East Berliners crossed into West Berlin that night. People climbed on top of the wall. They danced and celebrated their new freedom. They also began to destroy the wall, taking it apart piece by piece. The hated wall that had separated them for so long was now gone.

The destruction of the Berlin Wall was the beginning of the end for the East German government. People continued protesting against the government. They wanted more democracy. They wanted Germany to be united again. Less than a year later, the governments of East Germany and West Germany united. Germany had become a single country again.

✓ **Reading Check** **How was Germany divided after World War II?**

Germany Reunited

Most Germans were thrilled about the fall of the Berlin Wall. Despite having been separate countries for about 50 years, the cultures of East Germany and West Germany had remained similar in many ways. People in both East Germany and West Germany spoke the same language and ate the same foods. They knew the same German composers, writers, and painters. Still, **reunification** (ree yoo nih fih KAY shun), or the process of becoming unified again, would not be easy.

Changing East Germany The East German economy was very weak. Germans in the west had to spend huge amounts of money to improve the economy in the east. The government sold the state-owned factories of East Germany to private companies. They modernized factories and businesses. They cleaned up toxic waste sites. They began producing more consumer goods, such as televisions and cars. This process was very expensive.

East Germans had some concerns about life after communism. For example, in communist East Germany, people had had guaranteed jobs. There were no such guarantees under the democratic system of West Germany. Even today, there are many more people in the east without jobs than there are in the west. Even so, Germans in the east now enjoy a much better standard of living than they did under communism. A **standard of living** is the level of comfort in terms of the goods and services that people have.

Discovery CHANNEL
SCHOOL Video
Learn about the history of the Berlin Wall.

The German flag flies in front of the Reichstag, Germany's parliament building.

Moving Forward When Germany reunited, the German legislature decided Berlin would be the nation's capital once more. By 1999, most government offices had been moved back to Berlin from Bonn.

The cost of moving the capital was enormous. It led to budget cuts and the elimination of many public-service jobs. Still, Germans believed that the move benefited the "new Germany." Berlin's central location, they said, would aid reunification by linking Germans in the east with Germans in the west.

Reunification has been a huge undertaking. It has been difficult and expensive to merge two countries into one unified nation. Even so, Germany remains strong. Despite the high cost of reunification, Germany still has one of the world's strongest economies. It is also a powerful member of the European Union. As the European Union adds new members from Eastern Europe, Germany's central location will be to its advantage. Finally, because Germany was divided for only about 50 years, its people remember their shared history and culture. They will build on this common heritage as they move forward.

✓ **Reading Check** Why was Berlin chosen as the reunified nation's capital?

 Section 5 Assessment

Key Terms
Review the key terms listed at the beginning of this section. Use each term in a sentence that explains its meaning.

 Target Reading Skill
Find the word *elimination* at the top of this page. How do the surrounding phrases help explain it?

Comprehension and Critical Thinking
1. (a) **Explain** What was Germany's punishment for its role in World War I?

(b) **Identify Effects** How did that punishment lead to the rise of Adolf Hitler and the beginning of World War II?
(c) **Sequence** Describe the events that led to the division of Germany.
2. (a) **Recall** How did most Germans feel about the fall of the Berlin Wall?
(b) **Sequence** Describe the events that led to the reunification of Germany.
(c) **Identify Effects** How has the reunification of Germany affected life in the former East Germany?

Writing Activity
Write a journal entry from the point of view of an East Berliner. Describe the night the Berlin Wall was torn down. How did you feel? Whom and what did you want to see?

Writing Tip Before you write, decide what your age will be. If you are a young East Berliner, write as if you have never lived without the wall. If you are older, write as if you have experienced life both with and without the wall.

◆ Chapter Summary

Section 1: The United Kingdom

- There are four regions within the United Kingdom: England, Scotland, Wales, and Northern Ireland.
- The Magna Carta and Parliament played important roles in the development of British democracy.
- The United Kingdom is a constitutional monarchy.
- Trade is important to the United Kingdom because it is an island with limited natural resources.

Section 2: France

- France has made important contributions to art, philosophy, architecture, fashion, and cooking.
- France is becoming more culturally diverse.

Boccioni's *Unique Forms of Continuity in Space* (1913)

Section 3: Sweden

- Sweden is a welfare state that provides many services to its citizens.
- Sweden became an industrialized country in the early 1900s.
- The Swedish government faces challenges as it tries to continue providing benefits to everyone.

Section 4: Italy

- Vatican City is an important city-state within Rome, Italy.
- Many Italians have close ties to the Roman Catholic Church.
- Life in northern Italy differs in many ways from life in southern Italy.

Section 5: Germany

- The Berlin Wall divided communist East Germany from democratic West Germany.
- After the fall of the Berlin Wall, the governments of East and West Germany reunited.

◆ Key Terms

Complete each sentence with a key term from the list.

Parliament

standard of living

land reform

philosophy

national debt

reunification

welfare state

constitutional monarchy

1. A _____ is a system of ideas or beliefs.
2. _____ is the lawmaking body of the United Kingdom.
3. A _____ is the level of comfort in terms of the goods and services that people have.
4. A _____ is a government in which a monarch is the head of state but has limited powers.
5. The process of dividing large properties into smaller ones is called _____.
6. In a _____, the government provides many services and benefits for free or at a low cost.
7. _____ is the amount of money a government owes.
8. The process of becoming unified again is called _____.

◆ Comprehension and Critical Thinking

9. (a) Explain What is the role of the British monarch?
(b) Draw Conclusions Why does Britain remain a monarchy even though the monarch now has little power?
(c) Predict Do you think the United Kingdom will continue to have a monarch in the future? Explain why or why not.

10. (a) Explain What is the French Academy?
(b) Infer Why do foreign words enter the French language even though the French Academy tries to limit them?

11. (a) Explain What benefits does Sweden's welfare system provide?
(b) Summarize What challenges does Sweden face today?
(c) Predict How might Sweden solve some of its economic challenges?

12. (a) Identify What is the political status of Vatican City?
(b) List Which things do most Italians have in common?
(c) Compare and Contrast How is life in northern Italy different from life in southern Italy?

13. (a) Recall How was Germany divided?
(b) Explain Why was Germany reunified?
(c) Summarize What challenges has reunification brought to Germany?

14. (a) List Name two things that the East German government did not allow.
(b) Compare and Contrast Compare personal freedom in East Germany and West Germany during the Cold War.

◆ Skills Practice

In the Skills for Life activity in this chapter, you learned how to use visual information to write a paragraph. Review the steps you followed to learn this skill. Then turn to the Country Profile on page 156. Use the data on this page to write a paragraph titled A History of Germany Since World War I.

◆ Writing Activity: Government

You read about Germany's division after World War II. Recall that some Italians today are in favor of dividing Italy. Write a paragraph comparing Germany's situation after World War II with Italy's situation today.

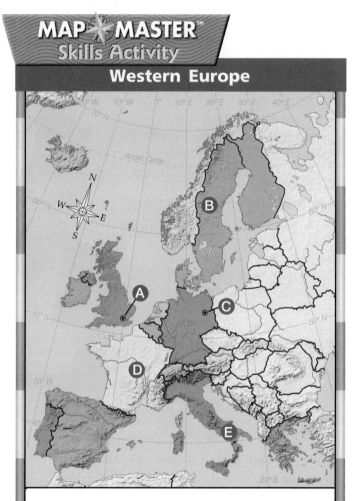

MAP MASTER™ Skills Activity

Western Europe

Place Location For each place listed below, write the letter from the map that shows its location.
1. France
2. London
3. Sweden
4. Italy
5. Berlin

Go Online
PHSchool.com Use Web Code ldp-7455 for an **interactive map.**

Standardized Test Prep

Test-Taking Tips

Some questions on standardized tests ask you to analyze a point of view. Read the passage below. Then follow the tips to answer the sample question.

On November 9, 1989, crowds began to tear down the Berlin Wall, block by block. People helped each other over the wall to the other side. Some-one watching from a window nearby said, "Today they are happy. But will they still be cheering when they realize that they no longer have the promise of either a job or food to eat?"

Choose the letter that best answers the question.

Who might have made this statement?

A an old East German who wants to have his son visit from West Germany

B a young East German who dreams of finding a job in West Germany

C an East German communist with a job running a state business

D a West German whose parents live in East Germany

Think It Through

The person who made this statement is not happy that the wall is coming down. He or she wonders whether the people tearing it down will still be cheering about it in the future. Who would not be happy about the wall coming down? You can eliminate A and D because both people have families that will be reunited with the wall torn down. You can also rule out B because that person will now be able to go to West Germany to look for work. The correct answer is C.

> **TIP** Use good reasoning to help you choose an answer that makes sense.

> **TIP** Be sure that you understand the question: Who might have said the words that begin, *Today they are happy. But will they still be cheering . . .?*

Practice Questions

Use the tips above and other tips in this book to help you answer the following questions.

1. What historical document first limited the power of the British king?
   A the Magna Carta
   B Parliament
   C the British constitution
   D the Northern League

2. Which style of architecture began in the region of Paris hundreds of years ago?
   A Renaissance
   B French Academic
   C Gothic
   D classical

3. What happened when the Roman Empire broke up?
   A The nation of Italy was formed.
   B It broke into a number of kingdoms, city-states, and territories.
   C Italy became part of the United Kingdom.
   D The Italian language became standardized.

4. When was Germany divided into two countries?
   A at the end of the Cold War
   B at the end of World War I
   C during the Cold War
   D at the end of World War II

Go Online
PHSchool.com

Use Web Code **lda-7405** for a **Chapter 4 self-test.**

Chapter

5

Eastern Europe and Russia

Chapter Preview

This chapter focuses on Poland, new Balkan nations, Ukraine, and Russia.

Country Databank

The Country Databank provides data and descriptions of Russia and each of the countries in Eastern Europe.

Section 1
Poland
Preserving Tradition Amidst Change

Section 2
New Balkan Nations
A Region Tries to Rebuild

Section 3
Ukraine
Independence and Beyond

Section 4
Russia
A Huge Country Takes a New Path

 **Target Reading Skill**

Comparing and Contrasting In this chapter you will focus on comparison and contrast to help you sort out and analyze information.

▶ Harvesting lavender on a hillside in Croatia

MAP★MASTER™
Skills Activity

ARCTIC OCEAN
East Siberian Sea

Barents Sea

RUSSIA

⊛ Moscow

See Inset

Black Sea

Sea of Okhotsk

R U S S I A

N

W E

S

Caspian Sea

Arabian Sea

Tropic of Cancer

Bay of Bengal

KEY

—— National border

⊛ National capital

0 miles 1,500

0 kilometers 1,500

Lambert Azimuthal Equal Area

Inset:

Tallinn ⊛ ESTONIA

Riga ⊛ LATVIA

RUSSIA LITHUANIA

Vilnius ⊛

⊛ Minsk

BELARUS

POLAND

Warsaw ⊛

RUSSIA

⊛ Kiev

Prague ⊛ CZECH REPUBLIC UKRAINE

Bratislava ⊛ SLOVAKIA MOLDOVA

SLOVENIA ⊛ Budapest ⊛ Chișinău

Ljubljana ⊛ HUNGARY

⊛ Zagreb ROMANIA

CROATIA ⊛ Belgrade Bucharest ⊛

Sarajevo ⊛ *Black Sea*

BOSNIA & ⊛ SERBIA

HERZEGOVINA MONT.

Podgorica ⊛ BULGARIA

Skopje ⊛ Sofia ⊛

Tiranë ⊛ MACEDONIA

ALBANIA

0 miles 500

0 kilometers 500

Regions For many years following World War II, the Soviet Union dominated many of the countries of Eastern Europe. **Identify** Which countries border Russia? **Analyze Information** How did the size and location of these countries make them more open to Soviet domination?

Go Online
PHSchool.com Use Web Code **ldp-7511** for step-by-step **map skills practice.**

Guide for Reading

This section provides an introduction to Russia and the 20 countries of Eastern Europe.

- Look at the map on the previous page and then read the paragraphs to learn about each nation.
- Analyze the data to compare the countries.
- What characteristics do most of these countries share?
- What are some key differences among the countries?

Viewing the Video Overview

View the World Studies Video Overview to learn more about each of the countries. As you watch, answer these questions:

- What are the major land regions in Eastern Europe?
- How is the terrain both different from and similar to that in Western Europe?

Explore the geography of Eastern Europe and Russia.

Albania

Capital	Tirana
Land Area	10,578 sq mi; 27,398 sq km
Population	3.5 million
Ethnic Group(s)	Albanian, Greek
Religion(s)	Muslim, Eastern Orthodox, Roman Catholic
Government	emerging democracy
Currency	lek
Leading Exports	textiles and footwear, asphalt, metals and metallic ores, crude oil, vegetables, fruits, tobacco
Language(s)	Albanian (official), Greek

Albania (al BAY nee uh) is located in southeastern Europe on the Adriatic and Ionian Seas. It is bordered by Serbia, Montenegro, Macedonia, and Greece. Albania became a communist state during World War II. In the early 1990s, the country tried to establish democracy. But government instability, high unemployment rates, and violence have prevented Albania from achieving that goal. Economically, the country is poor and struggling. Today, the country depends on aid from other countries to survive. However, the Albanians are slowly creating an open-market economy.

Belarus

Capital	Minsk
Land Area	80,154 sq mi; 207,600 sq km
Population	10.3 million
Ethnic Group(s)	Belarusian, Russian, Polish, Ukrainian
Religion(s)	Eastern Orthodox, Roman Catholic, Protestant, Muslim, Jewish
Government	republic
Currency	Belarusian ruble
Leading Exports	machinery and equipment, mineral products, chemicals, textiles, foodstuffs, metals
Language(s)	Belarusian (official), Russian (official)

Belarus (bay luh ROOS) is located between Poland and Russia. It was a Soviet republic for seven decades until its independence in 1991. Unlike many other former Soviet republics, Belarus has remained politically close to Russia. Russia also supplies Belarus with resources, as the country has few natural resources of its own. Belarus does have the potential, however, to develop its agriculture and forestry industries. Belarus faces major health and environmental problems caused by the 1986 Chernobyl explosion in neighboring Ukraine.

Bosnia and Herzegovina

Capital	Sarajevo
Land Area	19,741 sq mi; 51,129 sq km
Population	4.0 million
Ethnic Group(s)	Serb, Bosniak, Croat
Religion(s)	Muslim, Eastern Orthodox, Roman Catholic, Protestant
Government	emerging federal democratic republic
Currency	marka
Leading Exports	miscellaneous manufactured goods, raw materials
Language(s)	Serbo-Croat (official)

Bosnia and Herzegovina (BAHZ nee uh and hurt suh goh VEE nuh) is located on the Adriatic Sea in southeastern Europe, bordered by Croatia, Serbia, and Montenegro. Bosnia and Herzegovina declared independence from Yugoslavia in 1992. However, conflict among Serbs, Bosniaks, and Croats drew the country immediately into civil war. Peace was reached in 1995 with the help of NATO. Today, Bosnia and Herzegovina is struggling to recover from the years of war. Because of its natural resources, it has the potential to develop a thriving economy.

Bulgaria

Capital	Sofía
Land Area	42,683 sq mi; 110,550 sq km
Population	7.6 million
Ethnic Group(s)	Bulgarian, Southwest Asian, Roma, Macedonian, Armenian, Tartar, Circassian
Religion(s)	Eastern Orthodox, Muslim, Roman Catholic, Jewish
Government	parliamentary democracy
Currency	lev
Leading Exports	clothing, footwear, iron and steel, machinery and equipment, fuels
Language(s)	Bulgarian (official), Turkish, Macedonian, Romany

Bulgaria (bul GEHR ee uh) is located in southeastern Europe between Romania and Greece, bordering the Black Sea. The first Bulgarian state was created in the 600s when a central Asian Turkic tribe merged with the Slavic people of the region. Bulgaria was ruled by the Ottoman Empire for hundreds of years. The country regained its independence in 1878 but fell under communist rule after World War II. In 1990 the first open elections were held. Since then, the country has continued to develop a democratic political system with a free-market economy. Bulgaria is a member of NATO and became an EU member in 2007.

Croatia

Capital	Zagreb
Land Area	21,781 sq mi; 56,414 sq km
Population	4.4 million
Ethnic Group(s)	Croat, Serb, Bosniak, Hungarian, Slovene, Czech, Albanian, Montenegrin, Roma
Religion(s)	Roman Catholic, Eastern Orthodox, Muslim
Government	presidential-parliamentary democracy
Currency	kuna
Leading Exports	transport equipment, textiles, chemicals, foodstuffs, fuels
Language(s)	Croation (official)

Croatia (kroh AY shuh) is located in southeastern Europe between Slovenia and Bosnia and Herzegovina. It borders the Adriatic Sea. Croatia was formerly part of the nation called Yugoslavia. Croatia declared its independence in 1991, but Serbian armies remained and fought on Croatian land for several years afterward. Economically, the country is struggling to recover from costly war damage and a high unemployment rate. The EU has spent over $1 billion in aid to help Croatia rebuild. The nation has rich fishing resources in the Adriatic Sea.

Introducing Eastern Europe and Russia

Czech Republic

Capital	Prague
Land Area	29,836 sq mi; 78,276 sq km
Population	10.3 million
Ethnic Group(s)	Czech, Moravian, Slovak, Polish, German, Silesian
Religion(s)	Roman Catholic, Protestant, Eastern Orthodox
Government	parliamentary democracy
Currency	Czech koruna
Leading Exports	machinery and transportation equipment, intermediate manufactured goods, chemicals, raw materials, fuel
Language(s)	Czech (official), Slovak, Hungarian

The Czech Republic (chek rih PUB lik) is a landlocked nation surrounded by Germany, Slovakia, Austria, and Poland. In 1918, the Slovaks joined with the Czechs to form Czechoslovakia. Czechoslovakia fell under Soviet rule after World War II but gained back its freedom in 1989. In 1993, the Czechs and the Slovaks peacefully separated into two nations, the Czech Republic and Slovakia. The Czech Republic has become one of the most stable and successful countries of those dominated by the Soviet Union during the Cold War. It has strong industries, mineral resources, and a thriving tourist industry. The Czech Republic has become a member of NATO and the EU.

Estonia

Capital	Tallinn
Land Area	16,684 sq mi; 43,211 sq km
Population	1.4 million
Ethnic Group(s)	Estonian, Russian, Ukrainian, Belarusian, Finnish
Religion(s)	Protestant, Eastern Orthodox, Jewish
Government	parliamentary republic
Currency	kroon
Leading Exports	machinery and equipment, wood products, textiles, food products, metals, chemical products
Language(s)	Estonian (official), Russian

Estonia (es TOH nee uh) borders the Baltic Sea, Latvia, and Russia. It is actually a small peninsula, and includes more than 1500 small islands. For centuries, foreign powers controlled the region. But in 1918, Estonia gained its independence. Like several other eastern European states, it was taken over by the Soviet Union in 1940 and regained its independence in 1991. Since then, Estonia has adopted political and economic ideas from Western Europe. Its three major trading partners are Finland, Sweden, and Germany. The country has joined the EU and NATO.

A hawk moth in Viidumae Nature Reserve, Estonia

Hungary

Capital	Budapest
Land Area	35,652 sq mi; 92,340 sq km
Population	10.1 million
Ethnic Group(s)	Hungarian, Roma, German, Serb, Slovak, Romanian
Religion(s)	Roman Catholic, Protestant
Government	parliamentary democracy
Currency	forint
Leading Exports	machinery and equipment, other manufactured goods, food products, raw materials, fuels and electricity
Language(s)	Hungarian (official)

Hungary (HUNG guh ree) is landlocked among Austria, Romania, and five other countries in central Europe. For hundreds of years the nation was part of the Austro-Hungarian Empire. After World War II, the country came under communist rule. In the late 1960s, Hungary took some steps away from a government-controlled economy. But real reforms came in 1990 with the first open elections and a free-market economy. Since then, Hungary has had strong economic growth, and has become a member of both NATO and the EU. Hungary's capital, Budapest, has long been a cultural center of the region.

Latvia

Capital	Riga
Land Area	24,552 sq mi; 63,589 sq km
Population	2.4 million
Ethnic Group(s)	Latvian, Russian, Belarusian, Ukrainian, Polish, Lithuanian
Religion(s)	Protestant, Roman Catholic, Eastern Orthodox
Government	parliamentary democracy
Currency	lat
Leading Exports	wood and wood products, machinery and equipment, metals, textiles, foodstuffs
Language(s)	Latvian (official), Russian

Located between Estonia and Lithuania, Latvia (LAT vee uh) sits on the eastern coast of the Baltic Sea. The entire country lies on a flat, low plain. Its climate is temperate, with cool summers and cold winters. Between World War I and World War II, Latvia enjoyed a period of independence, but in 1940 it was taken over by the Soviet Union. Along with many other Soviet republics, it declared its independence in 1991. Since then it has adopted many of the political and economic ideas of Western Europe. After a Russian economic crisis in 1998, Latvia further decreased is dependence on Russia. It has joined the EU and NATO.

Lithuania

Capital	Vilnius
Land Area	25,174 sq mi; 65,200 sq km
Population	3.6 million
Ethnic Group(s)	Lithuanian, Russian, Polish, Belarusian
Religion(s)	Roman Catholic, Protestant, Russian Orthodox, Muslim, Jewish
Government	parliamentary democracy
Currency	litas
Leading Exports	mineral products, textiles and clothing, machinery and equipment, chemicals, wood and wood products, foodstuffs
Language(s)	Lithuanian (official), Russian

Lithuania (lith oo AY nee uh) is located between Latvia and Poland and borders the Baltic Sea. It was an independent state before World War II, but the Soviet Union claimed it in 1940. Lithuania was the first Soviet republic to declare independence in 1990. Since independence, the Lithuanians have taken steps toward establishing a free-market economy and privatizing businesses. Most of Lithuania's income is from services and agriculture. However, it has few natural resources and is one of the poorer nations in the region. Lithuania has joined the EU and NATO.

Introducing Eastern Europe and Russia

Macedonia

Capital	Skopje
Land Area	9,597 sq mi; 24,856 sq km
Population	2.1 million
Ethnic Group(s)	Macedonian, Albanian, Southwest Asian, Serb, Roma
Religion(s)	Eastern Orthodox, Muslim
Government	emerging democracy
Currency	Macedonian denar
Leading Exports	food, beverages, tobacco, miscellaneous manufactured goods, iron and steel
Language(s)	Macedonian (official), Albanian (official), Serbo-Croat

Macedonia (mas uh DOH nee uh) is located in southeastern Europe north of Greece. It gained its independence from Yugoslavia in 1991. Macedonia is the poorest of the countries that used to make up Yugoslavia. The nation has a weak economy, and one third of its labor force is unemployed. Macedonia faces ethnic conflict and government instability. It has also faced political conflict with its neighbor, Greece. Because Macedonia is the name of a region in northern Greece, Greece opposed the country's choice of name. However, a treaty signed in 1995 settled the dispute.

Moldova

Capital	Chisinau
Land Area	12,885 sq mi; 33,371 sq km
Population	4.4 million
Ethnic Group(s)	Moldovan, Ukrainian, Russian, Bulgarian, Gagauz
Religion(s)	Eastern Orthodox, Jewish
Government	republic
Currency	Moldovan leu
Leading Exports	foodstuffs, textiles and footwear, machinery
Language(s)	Moldovan (official), Romanian, Russian

Moldova (mohl DOH vuh) is located between Romania and Ukraine. Before World War II, Moldova was ruled by Romania. It became part of the Soviet Union after World War II and gained its independence in 1991. With few minerals and energy sources, Moldova's economy is based mostly on farming. One of the poorest nations in Europe, it recently saw an improvement in its economy due to some free-market reforms. However, in 2001 Moldova became the first former Soviet state to elect a communist president. Consequently, fewer free-market reforms are expected in the future.

Montenegro

Capital	Podgorica
Land Area	5,333 sq mi; 13,812 sq km
Population	620,145
Ethnic Group(s)	Montenegrins, Serbs, Albanians
Religion(s)	Eastern Orthodox, Muslim, Roman Catholic
Government	republic
Currency	euro
Leading Exports	foodstuffs
Language(s)	Serbian (official)

Montenegro (mahnt uh NEE groh) is located in southeastern Europe. It borders Bosnia and Herzegovina, Serbia, Croatia, Albania, and the Adriatic Sea. Montenegro was once part of Yugoslavia. It experienced years of ethnic conflict after Yugoslavia broke up in the 1990s. In 2003, it formed a partnership with Serbia, another part of the former Yugoslavia. However, in 2006, Montenegrins voted to become an independent country. After years of war and political instability, the Republic of Montenegro is focused on rebuilding its troubled economy. Promising industries include tourism, metal processing, and textiles.

Poland

Capital	Warsaw
Land Area	117,554 sq mi; 304,465 sq km
Population	38.6 million
Ethnic Group(s)	Polish, German, Ukrainian, Belarusian
Religion(s)	Roman Catholic, Eastern Orthodox
Government	republic
Currency	zloty
Leading Exports	machinery and transport equipment, intermediate manufactured goods, miscellaneous manufactured goods, food and live animals
Language(s)	Polish (official)

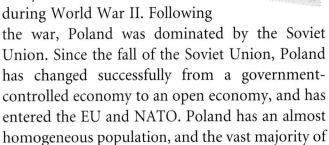

Polish postage stamps

Poland (POH lund) is located in central Europe between Germany and Ukraine. Poland was taken over by Germany and the Soviet Union during World War II. Following the war, Poland was dominated by the Soviet Union. Since the fall of the Soviet Union, Poland has changed successfully from a government-controlled economy to an open economy, and has entered the EU and NATO. Poland has an almost homogeneous population, and the vast majority of Poles are Roman Catholic.

Romania

Capital	Bucharest
Land Area	88,934 sq mi; 230,340 sq km
Population	22.3 million
Ethnic Group(s)	Romanian, Hungarian, Roma, Ukrainian, German, Russian
Religion(s)	Eastern Orthodox, Protestant, Roman Catholic
Government	republic
Currency	Romanian leu
Leading Exports	textiles and footwear, metals and metal products, machinery and equipment, minerals and fuels
Language(s)	Romanian (official), Hungarian, German, Romany

Romania (roh MAY nee uh) is located in southeastern Europe between Ukraine and Bulgaria, bordering the Black Sea. Following World War II, Romania was occupied by the Soviet Union. It became a communist republic in 1947. A single harsh dictator ruled Romania from 1965 to 1989. In the late 1990s, the country became a limited democracy. Today, the country still struggles with widespread poverty and government instability. Romania is carrying out political and economic reforms required for it to join the European Union. It joined the EU in 2007.

Russian Federation

Capital	Moscow
Land Area	6,592,100 sq mi; 16,995,800 sq km
Population	145 million
Ethnic Group(s)	Russian, Tatar, Ukrainian, Chuvash, Bashkir, Belarusian, Moldavian
Religion(s)	Russian Orthodox, Muslim, Jewish
Government	federation
Currency	Russian ruble
Leading Exports	petroleum and petroleum products, natural gas, wood and wood products, metals, chemicals
Language(s)	Russian (official), Tatar, Ukrainian, Chuvash, and others

Russia (RUSH uh), the world's largest country, is located in northern Asia between Ukraine and China, bordering the Arctic and North Pacific Oceans. The region west of the Ural Mountains is considered part of Europe. Throughout most of its history, Russia was ruled by royal families. The last royal dynasty was overthrown in 1917. The world's first communist government, the Soviet Union, was formed after World War I and ruled for decades. In 1991, the USSR split into 15 independent nations. Russia is by far the largest, with most of the former Soviet Union's area and population.

Introducing Eastern Europe and Russia

Serbia

Capital	Belgrade
Land Area	34,116 sq mi; 88,361 sq km
Population	9.4 million
Ethnic Group(s)	Serb, Albanian, Hungarian, Bozniak, Roma
Religion(s)	Eastern Orthodox, Muslim, Roman Catholic
Government	republic
Currency	dinar
Leading Exports	foodstuffs and live animals, manufactured goods, raw materials
Language(s)	Serbian (official)

Serbia (SUR bee uh) is a diverse country in southeastern Europe with about 40 different ethnic groups. It was once part of Yugoslavia and experienced years of civil war after Yugoslavia broke up. Serbia's violence against ethnic Albanians in Kosovo caused NATO troops to invade the region in 1999 to restore peace. In 2003, Serbia formed a partnership with Montenegro, another part of the former Yugoslavia. However, in 2006, Montenegro voted to become independent. The Republic of Serbia is now focused on rebuilding its economy and recovering from years of war.

Slovakia

Capital	Bratislava
Land Area	18,842 sq mi; 48,800 sq km
Population	5.4 million
Ethnic Group(s)	Slovak, Hungarian, Roma, Czech, Moravian, Silesian, Ruthenian, Ukrainian, German, Polish
Religion(s)	Roman Catholic, Protestant, Eastern Orthodox
Government	parliamentary democracy
Currency	Slovak koruna
Leading Exports	machinery and transport equipment, manufactured goods, chemicals
Language(s)	Slovak (official), Hungarian, Czech

Slovakia (sloh VAH kee uh) is located in Central Europe between the Czech Republic and Ukraine. In 1918, the Slovaks joined with the Czechs to form Czechoslovakia. Czechoslovakia fell under Soviet domination after World War II but gained back its freedom in 1989. In 1993, the Slovaks and the Czechs peacefully separated into two democratic nations, Slovakia and the Czech Republic. Slovakia has a stable economy and has joined the EU and NATO.

An Eastern Orthodox Church in Montenegro

Slovenia

Capital	Ljubljana
Land Area	7,780 sq mi; 20,151 sq km
Population	1.9 million
Ethnic Group(s)	Slovene, Croat, Serb, Bosniak, Yugoslav, Hungarian
Religion(s)	Roman Catholic, Protestant, Muslim
Government	parliamentary democratic republic
Currency	tolar
Leading Exports	manufactured goods, machinery and transport equipment, chemicals, food
Language(s)	Slovene (official), Serbo-Croat

Slovenia (sloh VEE nee uh) is located in Central Europe between Austria and Croatia, bordering the Adriatic Sea. The Slovene lands were once part of Austria and the Holy Roman Empire. In the mid-1900s, they became part of Yugoslavia. Since independence in 1991, Slovenia has become a stable democracy with a strong economy and a good relationship with Western Europe. Slovenia has joined the EU and NATO. The country has Eastern Europe's highest standard of living.

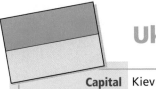

Ukraine

Capital	Kiev
Land Area	233,090 sq mi; 603,700 sq km
Population	48.4 million
Ethnic Group(s)	Ukrainian, Russian, Belarusian, Moldovan, Crimea Tartar, Bulgarian, Hungarian, Romanian, Polish
Religion(s)	Eastern Orthodox, Jewish
Government	republic
Currency	hryvnia
Leading Exports	ferrous and nonferrous metals, fuel and petroleum products, machinery and transport equipment, food products
Language(s)	Ukrainian (official), Russian, Tartar

Ukraine (yoo KRAYN) is located between Poland and Russia, bordering the Black Sea. During the 900s and 1000s, Ukraine was the center of the largest and most powerful state in Europe. However, since that time, the region has suffered invasions, occupations, and rebellions. Millions of Ukrainians died under Soviet occupation in the 1920s and 1930s and millions more during World War II. Although Ukraine gained independence from the Soviet Union in 1991, many of its leaders have been slow to encourage political or economic reforms.

SOURCES: CIA World Factbook Online; DK World Desk Reference Online; *The World Almanac,* 2003

Assessment

Comprehension and Critical Thinking

1. Compare and Contrast Compare the physical size and the population of Ukraine to those of Macedonia.

2. Make Generalizations Identify the six countries that were once part of Yugoslavia. What are some characteristics that they share?

3. Categorize Which religions do most people in the region practice?

4. Draw Conclusions The governments of some of these countries are listed as "emerging," or developing democracies. Read about these countries' histories. Why might it be difficult for them to establish democratic governments?

5. Make a Bar Graph Create a bar graph that shows the populations of the countries in the region.

Keeping Current

Access the **DK World Desk Reference Online** at **PHSchool.com** for up-to-date information about the 20 countries in this region.

Web Code: lde-7500

Poland
Preserving Tradition Amidst Change

Prepare to Read

Objectives

In this section you will
1. Find out about Polish traditions.
2. Learn about economic changes that have taken place in Poland since the collapse of communism.
3. Understand the future challenges that Poland faces.

Taking Notes

As you read, create an outline of this section. The outline below has been started for you.

> I. Tradition in Poland
>   A. Catholicism
>   B.
>   1.
>   2.
> II.

🎯 Target Reading Skill

Compare and Contrast When you compare, you look for the similarities between things. When you contrast, you look at the differences. Comparing and contrasting can help you sort out and analyze information. As you read this section, look for similarities and differences in Polish life during and after Soviet domination.

Key Terms

- **shrine** (shryn) *n.* a holy place
- **capitalism** (KAP ut ul iz um) *n.* an economic system in which businesses are privately owned
- **entrepreneur** (ahn truh pruh NOOR) *n.* a person who develops original ideas in order to start new businesses

Dancers at a traditional festival in Mazuka, Poland

In June of 2003, Polish citizens celebrated an event that could not possibly have occurred just two decades earlier. Poland had voted to join the European Union. It was an exciting event for a nation that at one time did not even appear on maps of Europe.

Poland has had a difficult history. In medieval times, it was the largest state in Europe. But by the late 1700s, it had been divided up among its stronger neighbors. For the next two hundred years, Polish territory changed hands many times. Controlled at different times by Russia, Germany, and Austria, Poland became free again at the end of World War I. But after World War II, the Polish government fell under the influence of the Soviet Union. For several decades, Poles lived under a harsh communist government. Poles regained their freedom when that government fell in 1989. Poland then began a long process of reform and rebuilding.

Tradition in Poland

Poland has experienced great change in its long history. Borders have shifted. Rulers have come and gone. Economic systems have changed. But many parts of Polish life have remained the same.

Catholicism in Poland Catholicism has been at the center of Polish tradition for centuries. The communist government tried to discourage Catholicism, but it could not change the devotion many Poles have for the Roman Catholic Church.

Today, about 90 percent of Poles are Catholic. Poles have their own way of observing Catholic holidays and their own way of prayer. Polish Catholics felt tremendous pride in 1978, when a Pole was selected as pope of the Catholic Church. Pope John Paul II quickly became the most widely traveled Catholic leader in history. He also made the world more aware of Poland and its struggle under communism.

In 1979, the pope visited Poland. About one million joyful and enthusiastic Poles gathered to see him. Mothers held babies over their heads for the pope's blessing. The crowd sang hymns and threw flowers toward the stage on which he sat. For most of these people, the pope stood for traditional Poland.

Orthodoxy in Poland However, not all Poles are Catholic. A minority of Poles are Polish Orthodox. An example of Polish Orthodox religious life can be seen in northeastern Poland, near the forest of Bialowieza (byah woh VYEH zhah). Not far from the forest is the holy hill of Grabarka, with an Orthodox church at the top. In mid-August, visitors climb this hill to visit the church. Each visitor plants a cross in the earth. Among the trees on the hillside are hundreds of crosses. Some are as tall as trees, and others as tiny as flowers. You can see such Orthodox shrines, or holy places, all over Poland.

Judaism in Poland A small minority of Poles are Jewish. Today, Poland's Jewish population numbers only in the thousands. However, more than 3 million Jews used to live in Poland. During the Holocaust, about 85 percent of Polish Jews were killed by the German government.

Polish Religious Traditions
Roman Catholic Pope John Paul II, at the top, waves to crowds in his hometown of Wadowice (vah duh VEET seh). Above, Eastern Orthodox worshipers take part in a festival in Bialowieza. **Apply Information** *What role does religion play in the lives of most Poles?*

Poland

A few powerful people had run Poland's communist government. In contrast, as a republic, Poland has a three-branch form of government similar to that of the United States. Poland's economy has also changed. Under communism, the government took control of most privately owned businesses and industries. Poland's republic has encouraged the development of small businesses, as well as foreign trade. Study the map and charts to learn more about Poland's government.

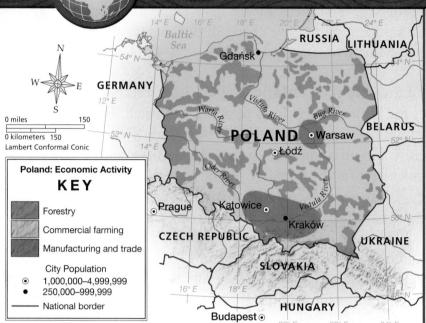

Poland: Economic Activity

KEY

Forestry

Commercial farming

Manufacturing and trade

City Population
- ⊙ 1,000,000–4,999,999
- • 250,000–999,999
- — National border

Employment by Sector and Ownership

1989

Sector	Privately Owned	Government Owned
Agriculture	79%	21%
Industry	15%	85%
Construction	27%	73%
Transport	6%	94%
Trade	8%	92%

2001

Sector	Privately Owned	Government Owned
Agriculture	99%	1%
Industry	77%	23%
Construction	94%	6%
Transport	48%	52%
Trade	98%	2%

SOURCES: Glowny Urzad Statystyczny (GUS), Rocznik Statystyczny

Poland's Government

Executive Branch	Legislative Branch	Judicial Branch
President Elected by the people for a five-year term	**National Assembly** Made up of two houses, the Sejm and the Senate	**Supreme Court** Judges appointed by the president for life
Prime Minister Appointed by the president, and confirmed by the Sejm	**Sejm** Includes 460 members, who are elected to four-year terms	**Constitutional Tribunal** Judges appointed by the Sejm for nine-year terms
Council of Ministers Appointed by the President, and approved by the Sejm	**Senate** Includes 100 members, who are elected to four-year terms	SOURCE: CIA World Factbook Online, 2003

Map and Chart Skills

1. **Locate** Around which Polish cities are the manufacturing industries and trade centered?
2. **Compare** How did the percentage of people employed in privately owned industries change from 1989 to 2001?
3. **Apply Information** How does Poland's government compare to that of the United States?

 Use Web Code **ldp-7521** for **DK World Desk Reference Online**.

The Polish Language The language of the Poles has stood the test of time. In the past, some foreign rulers banned the use of Polish in schools and in the government. Although the communists did not ban Polish, they did force Polish schoolchildren to learn Russian, the official language of the Soviet Union.

Today, Polish is spoken by the majority of the population. The Polish language is a cultural tie that unites Poles, giving them pride in their unique heritage. As a Slavic language, it also links the nation to other Slavic nations in Eastern Europe.

Learn about life for Jews in Poland.

✓ **Reading Check** **What religion do most Poles belong to?**

Great Economic Changes

Communism ended in Poland in 1989. After that, Poland underwent rapid change. The greatest of these changes occurred in Poland's economy.

Capitalism Poland has been very successful in making the change from communism to capitalism. **Capitalism** is an economic system in which businesses are privately owned. Most former communist countries made this change gradually. Poland changed almost overnight. On January 1, 1990, Polish leaders made a number of changes. They ended the government's control over prices. They also froze taxes and wages. A year later, Poland set up a stock market. Although these were dramatic changes, they helped Poland successfully make the difficult transition to capitalism.

Links to

Government

Poland's Solidarity Movement In the 1980s, a radical group formed in Poland. This was a labor union—a group of people seeking workers' rights—called Solidarity. This group was radical because it was the first independent labor union to form in a Soviet-dominated country. Solidarity was formed to protest rising food prices. It organized strikes and demonstrations such as the 1987 march shown in the photo at the left. Solidarity's first leader was an electrician named Lech Walesa. Under Walesa, Solidarity began openly criticizing the communist government, and helped bring about its downfall. Lech Walesa served as president of Poland from 1990 to 1995. Solidarity is still a political party in Poland today.

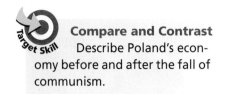

Compare and Contrast Describe Poland's economy before and after the fall of communism.

Foreign Investment With the collapse of the communist government, many foreigners began to invest their money in Poland. By 2001, Poland had brought in more foreign investment than had any other Central European country. Foreign investment has greatly strengthened the Polish economy.

Privatization A growth in the number of private businesses has also helped Poland's economy. With the end of communist rule, Poles were free to find new ways of making money. Small businesses soon blossomed in Poland's cities. At first, traders set up booths on the streets. They sold everything they could find, from American blue jeans to old Soviet army uniforms.

Slowly but surely, some traders earned enough money to take over stores that the government had once owned. Now, more than two million businesses are run by entrepreneurs (ahn truh pruh NOORZ). An **entrepreneur** is a person who develops original ideas in order to start new businesses.

Polish industries have also been slowly privatized over the last few years. Poland's most important private industries are food, energy, and mining.

Consumer Goods Poles now have access to more consumer goods than they did under communism. Only half of the homes in Poland had televisions in 1989. Now, almost every home has one. On the streets of cities such as Warsaw, Poland's capital, many people use mobile phones and wear the latest fashions. For these people, the new way of life is good.

Chart Skills

Life expectancy and per capita GDP, or the economic output per person, are two factors used to measure a country's standard of living. **Compare** Which Eastern European country has the highest standard of living? **Infer** Why do you think the standard of living is higher in Germany than in the other countries in this chart?

Standard of Living Comparison for Selected European Countries

Country	Per Capita GDP	Life Expectancy	
		Male	Female
Bulgaria	$6,600	68.3	75.6
Czech Republic	$15,300	71.7	78.9
Hungary	$13,300	67.8	76.8
Poland	$9,500	69.8	78.3
Slovenia	$18,000	71.7	79.6
Germany (Western Europe)	$26,600	75.5	81.6

Changes in Farm Life Unlike many businesses, most farms under communism had remained privately owned. Still, the change to a capitalist economy was harder on farmers than on most other Poles. Under communism, the government always bought produce and meat from farmers, providing them with a reliable income. The government also made sure that prices for farm produce stayed high. After communism, prices dropped, and sales were no longer guaranteed. Farmers learned to be innovative, or creative, to survive.

Some farmers now take on part-time jobs to make extra money. Others invite paying guests from the city to stay on their farms for rural vacations. Some farmers produce organic vegetables, fruits, and meats, which they can sell at higher prices than other farmers' products.

Farmers who cannot find other sources of income often struggle to make a living. Most farms in Poland are small. Many farmers only own about 5 to 12 acres (2 to 5 hectares) of land, which may not produce enough money to live on.

A Polish husband and wife use a draft horse to plow a field in Bialowieza.

✓ **Reading Check** Why did farmers have a steady income under communism?

Future Challenges

Poland has made the change from communism to capitalism with speed and success. It has the strength to compete with other nations as part of the EU. However, the Polish people still face many challenges.

Kraków—A Cultural Treasure Kraków is Poland's third-largest city. It is also a cultural center with historic architecture, an excellent university, and a marketplace that has existed since the 1200s. **Infer** *How have cities such as Kraków changed since the fall of communism in Poland?*

Pollution During the communist era, coal-mining and steel production in southern Poland caused terrible pollution. This pollution destroyed much of the forests in southern Poland and increased rates of diseases, such as cancer.

After the communists left power, Polish leaders began to repair some of the damage to the environment. Old polluting factories were closed. Other factories invested in equipment to reduce pollution. The use of unleaded gasoline reduced the pollutants coming from cars. By 2003, Poland had reduced many forms of pollution by 50 percent.

Unemployment Poland faces other challenges, such as a high unemployment rate. Under communism, people were guaranteed jobs. In the current capitalist system, there is no such guarantee. Many Poles emigrate to other places in Europe to find work. In fact, about one out three Poles today lives outside of Poland. Other Poles hope that membership in the EU will bring more long-term investment into Poland, creating more jobs.

Poles will have to find ways to deal with such challenges, but they are ready to do whatever is needed. For the first time in many years, their future is in their own hands.

✓ **Reading Check** How did Poland reduce its air pollution?

Bringing Back the Forests
People on a tree farm plant young trees. Once the trees have grown larger, they will be transplanted to regions that were deforested during the communist years. **Conclude** *How can renewed forests strengthen Poland's economy?*

Section 1 Assessment

Key Terms
Review the key terms at the beginning of this section. Use each term in a sentence that explains its meaning.

Target Reading Skill
How is farm life in Poland the same as and different from the way it was under communism?

Comprehension and Critical Thinking
1. (a) Identify What parts of Polish life did not change under communism?

(b) Analyze Information Why did the communist government force Polish schoolchildren to learn Russian?

2. (a) Explain What measures did Poland's leaders take to convert the economy to capitalism?

(b) Identify Point of View How might many Polish farmers view the transition to capitalism?

3. (a) Recall What major challenges does Poland still face?

(b) Predict What further changes might membership in the EU bring to Poland?

Writing Activity
Suppose you are a journalist in Poland today. You interview two Poles—a young entrepreneur in Warsaw and an elderly farmer in the countryside. Write a dialogue that gives their views on how capitalism has changed the country.

> **Writing Tip** Be sure to use appropriate language for each of the two people. Also, consider what is important to people of different ages before you begin writing.

Section 2
New Balkan Nations
A Region Tries to Rebuild

Prepare to Read

Objectives

In this section you will
1. Identify the groups of people who live in the Balkans.
2. Understand how Yugoslavia was created and how it broke up.
3. Identify issues that these Balkan nations face in the future.

Taking Notes

As you read this section, look for important events in the history of these six Balkan nations. Copy the timeline below and record the events in the proper places on it.

```
├─────────┼─────────┼─────────┤
1918
```

Target Reading Skill

Make Comparisons Comparing two or more situations enables you to see how they are alike. This section is about six countries with similar situations. As you read this section, compare the six nations by considering their histories, economies, cultures, and challenges.

Key Terms

- **civil war** (sih vul wawr) *n.* a war between groups of people within the same nation
- **secede** (sih SEED) *v.* to leave a group, especially a political group or a nation
- **embargo** (em BAHR goh) *n.* a ban on trade
- **economic sanctions** (ek uh NAHM ik SANGK shunz) *n.* actions to limit trade with nations that have violated international laws

In January 1984, the people of the city of Sarajevo (sa ruh YAY voh) were filled with anticipation. They had proudly won the right to host the 1984 Winter Olympics. To prepare for the games, they had built new hotels and restaurants. They had carved ski-racing trails into the mountains and built ski lifts. New bobsled runs and an elegant skating complex awaited the athletes. A shiny new Olympic Village waited to welcome athletes and visitors to the Games.

Ten years later, most of these facilities lay in ruins. So did much of Sarajevo. How could this have happened? The answer is **civil war,** or a war between groups of people within the same nation. Civil war broke up the nation of Yugoslavia and shattered the grand city.

Scenes of Sarajevo's Olympic Village before and after the war

New Balkan Nations

Ethnic diversity is one of the most enduring characteristics of the Balkans. In ancient times, the region was occupied by different tribes who often fought among themselves. The arrival of Christianity and then Islam brought more diversity and more ethnic and political differences to the region. Political unrest still continues in modern times. The Balkans occupy an area slightly smaller than the state of Texas. As you study the map and the table, think about what challenges great diversity might present to a small region.

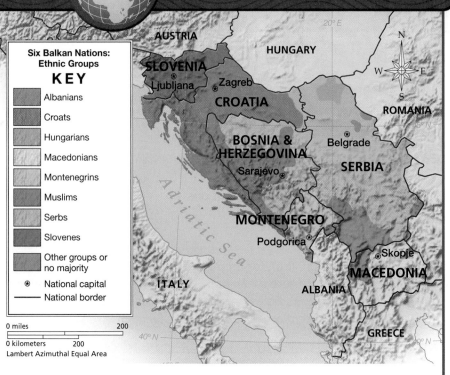

Six Balkan Nations: Ethnic Groups

KEY

- Albanians
- Croats
- Hungarians
- Macedonians
- Montenegrins
- Muslims
- Serbs
- Slovenes
- Other groups or no majority
- ⊛ National capital
- — National border

0 miles   200
0 kilometers   200
Lambert Azimuthal Equal Area

Peoples of the Former Yugoslavia

Ethnic Group	Population (millions)	Main Homeland(s)	Language	Main Religion
Croats	4.7	Croatia, Bosnia & Herz.	Croatian, Serbian	Roman Catholicism
Serbs	7.5	Bosnia & Herz., Serbia, Montenegro	Serbian, Croatian, Bosnian	Orthodox Christian
Slovenes	1.6	Slovenia	Slovenian	Roman Catholicism
Bosniaks	2.7	Bosnia & Herz.	Bosnian, Croatian, Serbian	Islam
Montenegrins	0.6	Montenegro, Serbia	Serbian	Orthodox Christian
Macedonians	1.3	Macedonia	Macedonian	Macedonian Orthodox
Albanians	2.3	Montenegro, Serbia, Macedonia	Albanian	Islam
Hungarians	0.3	Serbia	Hungarian	Roman Catholicism
Turks	0.8	Serbia, Macedonia	Turkish	Islam
Roma	0.05	Serbia, Macedonia	Roma	Various Beliefs

SOURCE: *CIA World Factbook*

Map and Chart Skills

1. **Identify** Which ethnic group lives in Slovenia?

2. **Analyze Information** Which religions do most people in the region practice? What language is spoken by the most people?

3. **Apply Information** How do the data help explain today's political unrest in the region?

Use Web Code **Idp-7512** for **DK World Desk Reference Online.**

Land of Many Peoples

The Balkan Peninsula—also known as the Balkans—is located in southeastern Europe. The Balkans include Serbia, Montenegro, Bosnia and Herzegovina, Macedonia, Croatia, Slovenia, Albania, Romania, Bulgaria, Greece, and European Turkey. This section discusses the first six of these countries, which used to make up the nation of Yugoslavia.

Different ethnic groups in these Balkan countries speak similar languages. The Serbs and Montenegrins (mahnt uh NEE grinz) speak Serbian, Croats (KROH atz) speak Croatian, and Bosniaks speak Bosnian. The Serbian, Croatian, and Bosnian languages are as close as American English and British English. Although these Slavic languages are similar, the Serbian language has a different alphabet than Croatian and Bosnian. Slovenes and Macedonians (mas uh DOH nee unz) speak related Slavic languages.

Although these groups speak related languages, there are important cultural differences among them. Religion may be the most important difference, since it separates groups that speak the same language. Most Serbs, Montenegrins, and Macedonians are Orthodox Christians. Croats and Slovenes are mainly Roman Catholic. Bosniaks are mainly Muslim.

In these six countries, there are also groups that speak non-Slavic languages. These groups include Albanians, Hungarians, Roma, and Turks. The Albanians and Turks are mainly Muslim. The Hungarians are mostly Roman Catholic. The Roma have their own unique customs and religious beliefs.

✔ **Reading Check** **What are the largest ethnic groups in the Balkans?**

Faces of the Balkans
Both of the photos above show children of various ethnic groups. The upper photo is from Macedonia, while the lower photo is from Croatia. **Apply Information** *Though these children all live on the Balkan Peninsula, what cultural differences might there be among them?*

The Creation of Yugoslavia

For hundreds of years, the Ottoman Empire, based in Turkey, ruled much of the Balkans. Beginning in the late 1800s, several kingdoms within the empire attempted to form their own states. Sometimes they were supported in their efforts by Russia or western nations, who hoped to gain influence in the region. But none of these groups was successful until World War I ended, and the Ottoman Empire broke up.

A New Nation Is Formed Yugoslavia was the first new Balkan nation to emerge from the old Ottoman Empire. Formed in 1918, the new nation joined together many ethnic and religious groups. From the beginning, these groups disagreed about how the government should be structured.

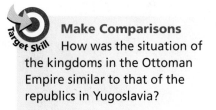

Make Comparisons
How was the situation of the kingdoms in the Ottoman Empire similar to that of the republics in Yugoslavia?

Though one nation, Yugoslavia was divided into smaller units called republics. These republics included Serbia, Montenegro, Croatia, Bosnia and Herzegovina, Slovenia, and Macedonia. In each of those republics, one ethnic group held the majority. Yugoslavia's largest republic was Serbia, peopled by Serbs. This republic held the most power, and ran the national government. Other republics, in which Serbs were not the majority, did not always support the government. Resentment against the government grew, along with ethnic conflict among peoples.

The Communist Era During World War II, Germany and Italy occupied Yugoslavia. Josip Broz Tito led the Yugoslav fight against Germany. When the war ended in 1945, Tito became head of the government and changed Yugoslavia into a communist state. Yugoslavia became a firm ally and trade partner of the Soviet Union.

At first, Tito modeled his government after that of the Soviet Union. After a few years, however, he wanted to develop his own government and economic policies. For example, he wanted to maintain trading relations with Western countries in order to strengthen Yugoslavia's economy. This put him in conflict with the Soviet dictator, Joseph Stalin, who broke many ties with Yugoslavia in 1948.

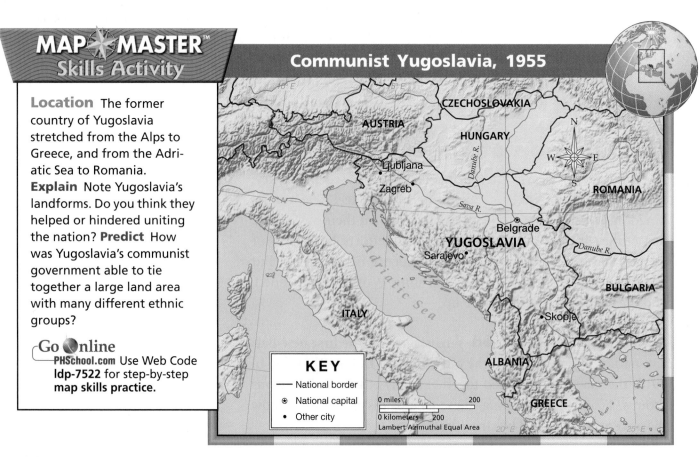

MAP MASTER™ Skills Activity

Communist Yugoslavia, 1955

Location The former country of Yugoslavia stretched from the Alps to Greece, and from the Adriatic Sea to Romania. **Explain** Note Yugoslavia's landforms. Do you think they helped or hindered uniting the nation? **Predict** How was Yugoslavia's communist government able to tie together a large land area with many different ethnic groups?

Go Online
PHSchool.com Use Web Code ldp-7522 for step-by-step map skills practice.

KEY
— National border
⊛ National capital
• Other city

0 miles 200
0 kilometers 200
Lambert Azimuthal Equal Area

Tito continued to rule Yugoslavia according to communist principles, but he also had good relations with anti-communist nations. For several years, the economy under Tito grew strongly. Tito's strong government also unified Yugoslavia by reducing tensions among ethnic groups. During Tito's time, people began to identify themselves as citizens of a united Yugoslavia.

Yugoslavia Begins to Splinter After Tito's death in 1980, politicians from various ethnic groups struggled for power. They encouraged their followers to once again identify strongly with their own ethnic group. People began to think of themselves less and less as citizens of Yugoslavia.

✓ Reading Check What event caused Yugoslavia to splinter?

Yugoslavia Breaks Up

Yugoslavia's problems continued to worsen through the 1980s. In 1989, communism began to crumble in Eastern Europe. Yugoslavia had an unstable government and economy. Many people blamed the Serbs, who still held most of the power in the government. Some republics wanted to govern themselves. In some cases, political change happened almost peacefully. In others, bitter civil wars erupted.

Slovenia and Croatia In 1990, Slovenes and Croats began to pull away from Yugoslavia. That year, the leaders of Slovenia issued a new constitution in which they said they had the right to secede from, or leave, the state of Yugoslavia. Meanwhile, the Yugoslav army threatened to take territory from the republic of Croatia. This alarmed Slovenes and Croats, but also strengthened their desire for independence.

A Croat was elected the new president of Yugoslavia in May 1991. However, Serbia refused to accept the new president. This was the last straw for Slovenia and Croatia. Both republics declared their independence. Serb forces briefly tried to prevent Slovenia from seceding. But soon Serbia recognized the country's independence.

In contrast, war erupted in Croatia. The Serbs attacked Croatian cities. They used terror to drive out the people. This led the United Nations to become involved. In an effort to restore peace, the UN sent peacekeepers to the area and imposed an embargo against Yugoslavia. An embargo is a ban on trade. But peace could not be reached until conflict in neighboring Bosnia and Herzegovina was settled.

Learn about the rebuilding of Kosovo.

Bosnia and Herzegovina Tensions among different ethnic groups led to a long and bitter war in Bosnia and Herzegovina, beginning in 1992. People on all sides were mistreated by their enemies. Many people were killed. Some were forced to move away from where they had lived peacefully for years, simply because they were Serbs or Croats.

As you have read, during the war much of Sarajevo, the capital of Bosnia and Herzegovina, was destroyed. Homes and schools were bombed. People were shot as they tried to go about their daily business. Serb armies cut Sarajevo off from the rest of the world. People ran out of food and other necessities.

In 1993, the United Nations began sending troops and supplies to the city. In 1995, NATO forces joined the fighting. Finally, peace talks took place. In 1995, the United States played a key role in getting the Serbs, Croats, and Bosniaks to sign a peace treaty in Dayton, Ohio.

Serbia: Crisis in Kosovo Conflict also broke out in the Serbian province of Kosovo. The population of Kosovo is about 90 percent Albanian. In the old Yugoslavia, Albanians in Kosovo were autonomous, or able to make many decisions for themselves. That situation changed dramatically.

In 1989, Yugoslavian President Slobodan Milosevic (SLOH boh dawn mih LOH suh vich) wanted to increase Serbia's power. He took away Kosovo's freedoms. Tensions between Serbs and Albanians in Kosovo increased, and many Albanians began rebelling against Serbian rule. In the late 1990s, Milosevic tried to end the uprising. Serb forces attacked Albanians in Kosovo. They destroyed homes and villages, forcing thousands of Albanians to become refugees.

These attacks prompted western nations to ask NATO to intervene. A peace agreement was signed in June 1999. Serb forces withdrew from Kosovo, and NATO troops took their place to keep the peace. Many of the Albanian refugees returned to Kosovo.

Peace Rally in Sarajevo
Before war broke out in 1992, people in Bosnia and Herzegovina held a peace rally. Some of them displayed a picture of Tito. **Infer** *Why might people have used images of Tito to support their drive for peace?*

Macedonia Macedonia declared its independence from Yugoslavia in 1991. From the beginning, ethnic conflict was a problem in the new country. Tensions existed between ethnic Macedonians and ethnic Albanians, who make up a large minority of the population.

Albanians began demanding a number of reforms. The call for reform erupted into violence in 2001. Clashes between ethnic Albanians and the Macedonian military lasted seven months. This prompted fears of another war in the Balkans. A peace agreement was reached after the involvement of NATO.

Soon, Macedonia adopted a new constitution. It made Albanian an official language of the nation. It increased Albanians' access to government jobs. Most important, it removed language in the constitution that had made Albanians second-class citizens.

Ethnic Albanians in Macedonia demand more rights in 2004.

✓ **Reading Check** **To which ethnic group do most of the people of Kosovo belong?**

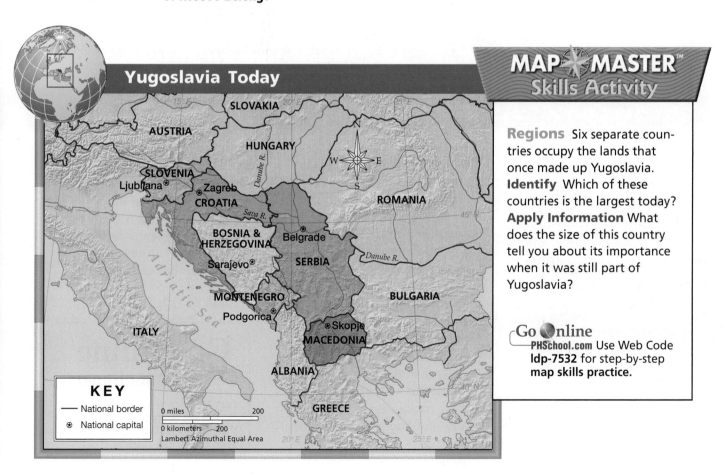

Yugoslavia Today

SLOVAKIA
AUSTRIA
HUNGARY
SLOVENIA
Ljubljana ⊛
⊛ Zagreb
CROATIA
Danube R.
Sava R.
ROMANIA
BOSNIA & HERZEGOVINA
⊛ Belgrade
Sarajevo ⊛
SERBIA
Danube R.
Adriatic Sea
MONTENEGRO
Podgorica ⊛
BULGARIA
ITALY
⊛ Skopje
MACEDONIA
ALBANIA
GREECE

KEY
— National border
⊛ National capital

0 miles 200
0 kilometers 200
Lambert Azimuthal Equal Area

MAP★MASTER™
Skills Activity

Regions Six separate countries occupy the lands that once made up Yugoslavia. **Identify** Which of these countries is the largest today? **Apply Information** What does the size of this country tell you about its importance when it was still part of Yugoslavia?

Go Online
PHSchool.com Use Web Code **ldp-7532** for step-by-step map skills practice.

Business has picked up at markets like this one in Slovenia.

The Region's Future

Although several republics in the region gained independence, trouble did not end. The United States and Europe held Slobodan Milosevic responsible for the violence that had occurred in the region. To show their disapproval, they placed economic sanctions on Yugoslavia. **Economic sanctions** are actions to limit trade with nations that have violated international laws.

In 2000, Yugoslavia held new presidential elections. Milosevic was defeated and then arrested by the new government. He was put on trial for war crimes by the court of the United Nations, but he died in 2006, before the trial ended. With Milosevic out of power, the United States and European nations lifted sanctions against Yugoslavia.

In 2003, the two remaining republics of Yugoslavia—Serbia and Montenegro—decided to no longer call themselves Yugoslavia. They became known as the country of Serbia and Montenegro. In 2006, however, the people of Montenegro voted to become independent of Serbia. And many people in Kosovo would like to become independent of Serbia as well.

The destruction that occurred in the 1990s has left the region with deep economic problems. These countries will have to overcome a history of ethnic conflict to move toward peace.

✔ **Reading Check** What problems face people of the Balkans today?

 Section 2 Assessment

Key Terms

Review the key terms at the beginning of this section. Use each term in a sentence that explains its meaning.

 Target Reading Skill

Compare the histories of these six nations.

Comprehension and Critical Thinking

1. (a) List Which six Balkan nations used to make up the country of Yugoslavia?
(b) Contrast What differences exist among the people of these nations today?

2. (a) Note Which foreign power ruled the Balkans for hundreds of years?
(b) Sequence When was Yugoslavia created? When did its government turn to communism?
(c) Synthesize Information How did the collapse of communism affect Yugoslavia?
3. (a) Identify Who did the United States and European nations hold responsible for the violence in the Balkans?
(b) Identify Effects How did these nations show their disapproval of Yugoslavia's president?

Writing Activity

Choose one of the Balkan nations discussed in this section. What do you think is the most important challenge facing this nation in the future? Write a paragraph that explains why.

For: An activity on the Dayton peace accord
Visit: PHSchool.com
Web Code: ldd-7502

Section 3

Ukraine
Independence and Beyond

Prepare to Read

Objectives

In this section you will

1. Understand how Ukraine's history has been shaped by foreign rule.
2. Explain the major issues that Ukrainians have faced since independence.
3. Describe life in Ukraine today.

Taking Notes

As you read this section, look for ways in which the natural resources of Ukraine have shaped its history. Copy the flowchart below and record your findings in it.

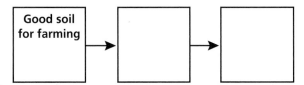

Target Reading Skill

Compare and Contrast One way to understand a nation's history is to compare and contrast different times in its history. When you compare, you look at similarities between things. When you contrast, you look at differences. As you read this section, compare and contrast life in Ukraine before and after independence.

Key Terms

- **chernozem** (CHEHR nuh zem) *n.* rich, black soil
- **collective** (kuh LEK tiv) *n.* a huge government-controlled farm

How many people, linked hand-to-hand, would it take to cover 300 miles (483 kilometers)? The people of Ukraine can tell you, because they did it in 1990. It took about 500,000 Ukrainians to make a human chain that long. It stretched from Kiev, Ukraine's capital, to the city of L'viv (luh VEEF). The chain was a symbol of protest against the Soviet Union's control of Ukraine. It also showed that Ukrainians know how to work together to solve their problems. Today, the people of Ukraine are enjoying their independence and are working hard for a better future.

Ukrainians form a human chain.

Ukraine

When Ukraine became independent in 1991, it faced economic hardship. The Soviet Union had controlled Ukraine's economy. Ukraine's new leaders had no experience with capitalism, and the country had no free markets for its products. After a slow, painful transition, Ukraine's economy began to strengthen. Still, Ukraine's economy relies heavily on Russia as a trade partner. Study the map and graphs to learn more about Ukraine's economy today.

Ukraine: Agricultural Products and Land Use

KEY

Forestry	—— National border
Livestock raising	⊛ National capital
Commercial farming	• Other city

Wheat   Root crops   Sunflowers

Vineyards   Cattle   Sheep   Hogs

0 miles   200
0 kilometers   200
Lambert Azimuthal Equal Area

Leading Export Partners

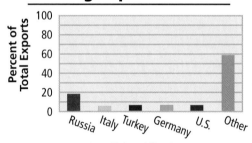

SOURCE: *CIA World Factbook*

Leading Import Partners

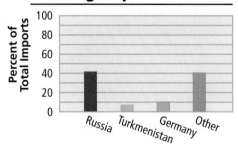

SOURCE: *CIA World Factbook*

Structure of the Economy, 2005

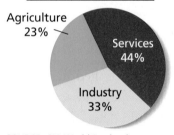

Agriculture 23%

Services 44%

Industry 33%

SOURCE: *CIA World Factbook*

Map and Chart Skills

1. **Locate** In what regions of Ukraine is land used for forestry?
2. **Synthesize Information** In 2005, what percentage of Ukraine's economy did agriculture make up? How much of Ukraine's land is used for this purpose?
3. **Make Inferences** Why do you think Ukraine exchanges more exports and imports with Russia than with its other trade partners?

Use Web Code **Idp-7513** for **DK World Desk Reference Online.**

A History of Occupation

For hundreds of years, Ukraine was ruled by its more powerful neighbors. You can see how this happened if you look at Ukraine's location on the map on page 165. This huge land lies between Russia and the other nations of Europe. In fact, the name Ukraine means "borderland." Look at the political map of Eastern Europe and Russia at the beginning of this chapter. Notice that to the west of Ukraine are Poland, Slovakia, and Hungary. To the east of Ukraine is Russia. The map makes it easy to see why Ukraine has been open to invasion by its neighbors.

Location has been only part of the problem. The other problem has been Ukraine's vast natural resources. These resources have attracted invaders. At one time or another, Poland, Czechoslovakia, and Romania have occupied areas of Ukraine. During World War II, the German army invaded Ukraine to gain access to its natural resources. Russia has been the most difficult neighbor of all, however. Russia, and later the Soviet Union, ruled Ukraine between the late 1700s and 1991.

Supplying the Soviets Under Soviet rule, Ukrainian industries grew. In time, factories in Ukraine were making nearly 20 percent of the Soviet Union's goods. Ukraine produced much of the equipment for the Soviet armed forces. And Ukrainian mines supplied much of the iron ore, coal, and other minerals for Soviet industries.

The Soviets used other Ukrainian resources as well. Ships used Ukraine's ports on the Black Sea to bring goods into and out of the Soviet Union. Several of Ukraine's rivers reach like highways into other countries. The Soviets made use of these rivers to ship goods.

Because Ukraine was one of Europe's largest grain-producing regions, it became known as the breadbasket of Europe. Why is Ukraine's farmland so productive? More than half of the country is covered by a rich, black soil called **chernozem** (CHEHR nuh zem). When the Soviet Union took control of Ukraine in 1922, Ukrainian farmers were forced to supply the rest of the Soviet Union with food. By the end of the 1980s, they were producing one fourth of the grain and meat consumed by the Soviet Union.

Ukraine Under Foreign Rule

1854 An illustration shows the port of Odessa when Ukraine was part of the Russian Empire.

1941 Ukrainian villagers report to soldiers of the German forces that occupied Ukraine during World War II.

1947 Farmers work on a collective farm during the Soviet rule of Ukraine.

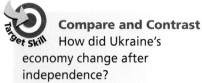
Compare and Contrast
How did Ukraine's economy change after independence?

Collectives Bring Starvation To produce all of this grain and meat, Soviet rulers took land away from farmers and created huge government-controlled farms called **collectives.** Most farmers were forced to become workers on these collectives. Other farmers were sent to cities to work in the new factories. All the crops from the collectives went to the government. The people who worked the land were allowed to keep very little of the food they grew. As a result, millions of Ukrainians died of hunger in the 1930s. Over the years, however, life improved on the farms.

✓ **Reading Check** For what purpose did the Soviets use Ukraine's ports and rivers?

Odessa—A Thriving Seaport
In the 1800s and 1900s, huge quantities of grain were shipped from Odessa to Russia and later the Soviet Union. Today, the city is a major port and a center of Ukrainian industry. **Compare and Contrast** Compare this photo with the illustration of Odessa on page 191. What similarities and differences do you see?

Independence Brings Challenges

In 1991, Ukraine won its independence from the Soviet Union. After centuries of foreign rule, the new country now had to decide many important issues for itself.

Building an Independent Economy One of the first issues Ukrainians had to decide was how to build up their economy. Like people in other former Soviet republics, Ukrainians had to learn how to start new businesses. They also needed to learn how to make consumer goods and keep prices under control. Finally, they had to improve their agricultural production by breaking up the inefficient collective farm system put in place by the Soviets.

Choosing a Language Ukrainians also had to restore their culture. Under Soviet rule, the official language of Ukraine was Russian. Books and newspapers were published only in Russian, and schools used Russian textbooks. As a result, many Ukrainians speak only Russian, especially in the cities and in the eastern part of the nation. Russian is also the language of ethnic Russians, who make up about one fifth of the population. The Ukrainian language is widely spoken only in rural areas and in the western part of the nation.

A Ukrainian Classroom
Elementary school students sit in class on their first day of school.
Analyze Images *Besides language, what other cultural traditions are important to Ukrainians?*

With independence, Ukrainian was made the official language. Many of the people of Ukraine believe that speaking Ukrainian could tie the country together and free Ukraine from its Soviet past. Elementary and secondary schools have begun using Ukrainian, though Russian is also still used in high schools. Most Ukrainians are pleased about the change. One teacher said, "Language is the anchor of our independence."

Learn about the after-effects of Chernobyl.

Recovering From Chernobyl Ukraine is still recovering from a terrible event that occurred during the Soviet period. It became one of the most difficult issues Ukraine has had to face since it gained independence.

Under Soviet rule, Ukrainians built five nuclear power plants. These supply about one third of the country's electricity. The Chernobyl (chehr NOH bul) nuclear plant is located 65 miles (105 kilometers) from the city of Kiev. In 1986, an explosion caused by carelessness rocked the Chernobyl plant. Radioactive materials filled the air. Some people died within days or weeks. Others developed serious health problems that killed them slowly or left them suffering. More than 100,000 people had to be moved out of the area. It was no longer safe to live there. In later years, traces of the dangerous materials released at Chernobyl were found all over the world.

Even today, much of Ukraine's soil and water are still poisoned. More than 32,000 square miles of farmland are contaminated. Some towns and farms remain abandoned. With the help of other nations, the Ukrainians are cleaning up the dangerous materials around Chernobyl, but it may take as long as a hundred years to repair the damage.

✓ **Reading Check** What are the far-reaching effects of Chernobyl?

Links to
Science

Creating Nuclear Power
Nuclear power is produced from a metal called uranium. When uranium is put through a process called nuclear fission, heat is released. The heat can be used to turn water into steam. The steam can be used to power large machines called generators, which produce electricity. When nuclear power is made, radioactive waste is produced. The waste must be carefully stored, because radioactive materials are dangerous to people. If the process of making nuclear power is not tightly controlled, too much heat can destroy the reactor and the entire building that contains it, as happened at Chernobyl. Then radioactive materials can escape into the air. The photo at the right shows a town near Chernobyl after the explosion.

Life in Ukraine

Independence has brought changes to life in Ukraine. For example, the Kreshchatik (kresh CHAH tik), the main street in Kiev, is often jammed with people. Along this street are many parks, stores, and restaurants. People sell ice cream and pyrohy (pih ROH hee), dumplings filled with vegetables, cheese, or fruit. Newsstands are filled with magazines and newspapers, many of which have been published only since independence. At local markets, farmers sell cheese or produce from their own farms.

Other Ukrainian cities are also alive with the new spirit of freedom. East of Kiev is the city of Kharkiv. Located near huge reserves of iron ore and coal, it is the busiest industrial center in the nation. But Kharkiv is not all work. It is also a vibrant cultural area, where people can attend plays or concerts.

Ukraine is in the early stages of an exciting time in its history. The people have always wanted freedom, and now they have it in their grasp. They know that independence is not easy. But with the land's great resources and the people's ability to work together, the Ukrainians have the ability to make independence succeed.

Vendors sell souvenirs in front of a Roman Catholic church in Kiev.

✓ **Reading Check** What is Ukraine's busiest industrial center?

Section 3 Assessment

Key Terms
Review the key terms at the beginning of this section. Use each term in a sentence that explains its meaning.

Target Reading Skill
Describe education in Ukraine before and after independence.

Comprehension and Critical Thinking
1. (a) Identify Who controlled Ukraine until 1991?
(b) Find the Main Idea What uses were made of Ukraine's resources?

(c) Predict Now that Ukraine is not supplying another country with its resources, how might that affect its economy?
2. (a) Explain What issues faced Ukraine after independence?
(b) Identify Point of View How might ethnic Russians have reacted when Ukrainian was made the official language?
3. (a) Describe What changes has independence brought to Ukrainian life?
(b) Contrast How was life different in Ukraine before independence?

Writing Activity
Suppose you are a newspaper writer in Ukraine in 1991. Write a short article that describes the views of the people as they start life in an independent country. Be sure to include the views of both Ukrainians and ethnic Russians.

For: An activity on Chernobyl
Visit: PHSchool.com
Web Code: ldd-7503

Skills for Life
Identifying Frame of Reference

Before Poland joined the European Union, Poles strongly debated the subject. According to 48-year-old Polish farmer Lech Lebedzki, ". . . both of my hands were raised, ready to vote for [it]. . . ." But after hearing that as part of the EU Polish farmers would not receive as much support from the government, he changed his mind. "It's a stab in the back. . . . I will vote against it."

Lebedzki's job as a farmer gave him a certain frame of reference, which influenced his view on EU membership. When you identify a person's frame of reference, you can better understand the influences that shaped his or her position. Writers, for example, may leave information out of an article on purpose to give a stronger argument for their point of view. They may only present one side of the story. Understanding a writer's frame of reference can help you decide whether the writer is a reliable source.

A Polish farmer

Learn the Skill

To identify frame of reference, use the following steps:

1 **Determine the issue.** Read through the passage quickly. What is the main idea?

2 **Look carefully at who the writer is.** What qualifications, if any, does he or she bring to the topic of the passage?

3 **Identify the position taken by the writer.** Look for direct statements of the writer's position. Look also for any emotional language that may give clues to the writer's views. What is the tone, or overall feeling, of the passage? Think about why the writer feels he or she has to write.

4 **Note how the writer's frame of reference may have influenced his or her position on the issue.** Look for connections between who the writer is, the language he or she uses, and the writer's stated position.

5 **Draw a conclusion identifying the writer's position and his or her frame of reference.** Decide whether the writer is giving a reliable picture of the situation.

Practice the Skill

Use the steps in Learn the Skill to identify frame of reference in the passage at the right.

1 Read through the passage to identify the issue. What main idea does the writer develop in the passage?

2 Look at who the writer is. What qualifications does the writer have that enables her to write the article? Does she have any experience that helps her write the article?

3 What is the writer's position? What is the tone of the passage? Can you find any emotional language in the passage?

4 How might the writer's age affect her viewpoint? Why might her opinion be different from the one expressed by the Polish farmer at the beginning of the previous page?

5 Write a short paragraph explaining the writer's frame of reference.

Over the months Poland's youth gradually became aware that the issue [of joining the EU] was important to us, because it is we, not our parents, who are going to spend much of our lives in the enlarged EU. Through referenda [votes] and debates in our high schools and universities, we demanded that our voice be heard by those who were longer in the tooth [older]—even though our opinions had no legal value.

—*Joanna Margueritte, a young Polish woman*

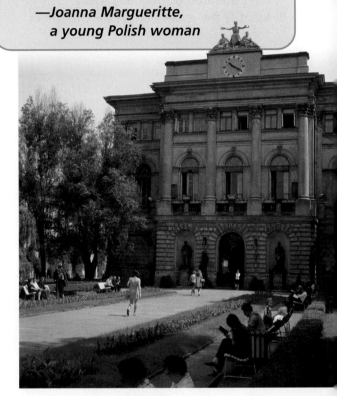

The University of Warsaw

Agricultural production in Poland is now lower than it's been in any time in the last 50 years. . . . The reason is that the European Union and America and other countries have turned Poland into a dumping ground for overproduction. If we are not treated as equals, if the European Union tries to exploit us . . . we will start a propaganda war and make sure that Poles vote No in the referendum. . . .

—*Andrzej Lepper, leader of the Self Defence Alliance, a Polish political party*

Apply the Skill

Read the passage at the left. Use the steps above to identify the frame of reference of the writer. Then compare this writer's views with those of the writer at the top of this page. How does the tone differ? How would you compare the writers' purposes? Which of these writers do you think is presenting a more reliable picture of the situation?

Prepare to Read

Objectives

In this section you will
1. Investigate the changes that capitalism has brought to Russia.
2. Understand the cultural traditions that have endured throughout Russia.
3. Identify the issues that create challenges for Russians.

Taking Notes

As you read the section, look for details about the changes in Russia since the fall of Soviet communism. Copy the flowchart below and write each detail under the correct heading.

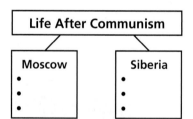

Target Reading Skill

Identify Contrasts When you contrast two regions, you examine how they are different. In this section you will read about two regions in Russia—Moscow and Siberia. As you read, list the differences between these two regions and ways people live in them.

Key Terms

- **investor** (in VES tur) *n.* someone who spends money on improving a business in the hope of making more money
- **inflation** (in FLAY shun) *n.* an increase in the general level of prices when the amount of goods and services remains the same.

Open-air markets like this one in Perm are a more common sight since the fall of communism.

In 1991, Yura and Tanya Tabak lived in a tiny one-bedroom apartment in Moscow. Soviet communism had ended. Yura had more freedom to pursue his interest in religious studies. Yet life was difficult for the couple. Their wallpaper was peeling off the walls, and their plumbing didn't always work.

In 2002, the Tabaks had a large, bright apartment filled with goods such as a new television. They had even sent their daughter abroad to study. Yura said, "Sometimes I wake up in the morning and want to pinch myself. . . . Are these things really available to us?"

Yet like many Russians, the Tabaks fear what would happen if one of them were to become ill. Medical care used to be free. Now it is expensive and hard to get. Corruption in business and government is widespread, and the economy is unstable. In Russia, many things have changed—but life is still difficult for most Russians.

Emerging Capitalism

When the Soviet Union dissolved in 1991, the new Russian Federation—the world's largest country—had to find a new identity for itself. The nation had no experience of democracy, or any laws that supported it. Russian leaders often fought for power within the new government. The new country also struggled to make the transition from communism to a free-market economy.

Explore life in Moscow.

Moscow, Russia's Capital Moscow is the capital of Russia and the center of its economic activities. It has a population of more than 9 million people. When the Soviet Union first collapsed, business in Moscow boomed. Investors came from many different countries to make money in Moscow. An **investor** is someone who spends money on improving a business in the hope of making more money if the business succeeds.

Some investors became very wealthy. When the first American fast-food chain in Russia opened in Moscow, people lined up in the streets to eat there. The restaurant served 30,000 people on the first day. Ikea, a Swedish furniture store, opened a 250-store mall in Moscow. Russian investors opened 24-hour supermarkets and high-tech companies.

Economic success has not come equally to all Russians. Some Russians have become wealthy because they have influence within the government. For example, a former Soviet official started Russia's largest oil and gas company, Gazprom (GAHS prahm), which is hugely profitable. Other Russians have gained their wealth through corruption.

Investment in Moscow Russia's biggest department store (at the left), built over a hundred years ago in a traditional style, bustles with people and new stores. The modern International Business Center (above) was built in 2001.
Analyze Images *Describe the scene in the department store. Would the scene have been different during Soviet times?*

Widespread Corruption Average Russians have been working hard since the collapse of the Soviet government. Many have opened small businesses or factories. Like the Tabaks, more Russians today can afford to fix up their apartments, buy expensive goods, and travel abroad. Yet most Russians still face challenges in their daily lives. Salaries are still low for Russian workers. About 25 percent of all Russians live in poverty.

Corruption is one reason that many Russians have not been able to improve their situations. Criminal gangs often force honest people who own businesses to pay them money. The Russians who own or work in these businesses therefore cannot keep all the money they earn. Laws meant to protect people are often not enforced.

Economic and Health Problems Average Russians also suffer when the economy does not thrive. In the 1990s, large numbers of Russians lost their life savings when banks failed and inflation rose to high levels. **Inflation** is an increase in the general level of prices at a time when the amount of goods and services remains the same. The economy slowly recovered. But some Russians are still working to regain the money they lost years ago.

Finally, as you have read, Russians have major concerns about health care. Life expectancy in Russia is very low for a developed country—just 62 years for men. Hospitals often contain outdated equipment. In some hospitals, patients have to bring their own sheets. Russia's wealthy people can afford better care, but ordinary Russians cannot.

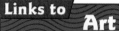

Links to
Art

Moscow's "Underground Palaces" When work on Moscow's subway began in the 1930s, its planners wanted to build more than a comfortable, useful mode of transportation. They also wanted to surround the subway riders with beauty. Architects created palace-like subway stations using more than 20 kinds of marble and other different colored stones. The Kievskaya station, shown below, includes domed ceilings hand-painted by famous artists. Others contain stained-glass windows, murals, and statues. Light reflects off of the colored walls of many stations, filling the halls and brightening the day of many passengers.

Russia

As the world's largest country in area, Russia spreads across nearly 180° of latitude. Because of its vast size, the country is divided into eleven separate time zones. While the climate varies from place to place, the summers are generally mild and the winters chilly to bitterly cold. Russia is home to many different landforms, from arctic deserts and tundra to forests, plains, and mountains. Study the map and tables to learn more about Russia's geography.

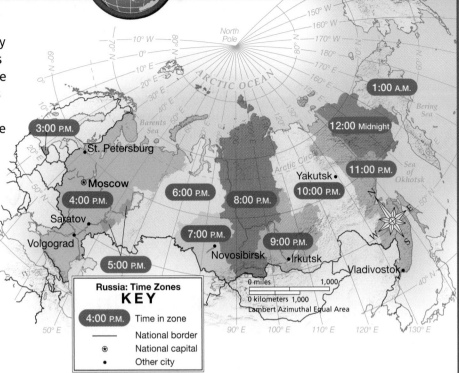

Russia: Time Zones
KEY

4:00 P.M.	Time in zone
———	National border
⊛	National capital
•	Other city

0 miles 1,000
0 kilometers 1,000
Lambert Azimuthal Equal Area

European Railroads by Length

Country	Total Mileage
Russia	▦▦▦▦▦▦▦▦▦▦▦▦
Germany	▦▦▦▦▦
France	▦▦▦▦
Italy	▦▦
Spain	▦▦
Romania	▦▦

This symbol represents 5,000 miles of railroad track.

SOURCE: *DK World Desk Reference*, 2002

World's Largest Countries

Country	Land Area
Russia	6,562,110 sq mi; 16,995,790 sq km
China	3,600,944 sq mi; 9,326,406 sq km
Canada	3,560,234 sq mi; 9,220,968 sq km
United States	3,536,292 sq mi; 9,158,958 sq km
Brazil	3,265,074 sq mi; 8,456,506 sq km

SOURCE: *The World Almanac*, 2004

Map and Chart Skills

1. **Identify** What time is it in Yakutsk when it is noon in Moscow?

2. **Compare** How does Russia's land area compare to that of the United States?

3. **Analyze Information** Why do you think there are so many more miles of railroad track in Russia than in other European countries?

Use Web Code **ldp-7514** for **DK World Desk Reference Online.**

Changes in Siberia Siberia is a region with rich reserves of coal, gold, iron, oil, and natural gas. During the Soviet years, the government built factories, set up mining operations, and built the Trans-Siberian railroad to carry out materials. Although much of Siberia is rural, large cities developed there over time. In fact, four of the ten largest Russian cities are located in Siberia. The city of Novosibirsk (NOH vuh sih BIHRSK) has a population of more than 1.3 million people. Outside of the cities, much of Siberia is agricultural.

Under the Soviet communist system, factory workers and miners were guaranteed jobs, and farmers were guaranteed certain prices for their crops. Now Siberians worry about losing their jobs or their farms. On the other hand, Siberians are able to buy their own homes and make their own decisions.

√ **Reading Check** Why are Siberians worried about jobs?

Cultural Traditions Continue

The collapse of Soviet communism brought major changes to the lives of many Russians. But traditional Russian ways endure.

Life in Moscow As it was in Soviet times, Moscow is still the cultural center of the nation. Art, theater, and dance thrive there. The Bolshoi (BOHL shoy) Ballet is based in Moscow. Dancers from this famous Russian school of ballet have performed around the world. And traveling performers, such as folk dancers from northern Russia, come to Moscow.

On Moscow's streets street vendors sell traditional Russian crafts next to vendors selling electronic goods from China. On very cold winter days, some people in Moscow go to the parks to celebrate an old tradition: picnicking in the snow.

Target Skill **Identify Contrasts** What are two ways that life has changed for Siberians since the fall of Soviet communism?

Russian Teenagers Teenagers walk across the square in front of St. Basil's Cathedral in Moscow. **Generalize** *How might teenagers' lives have been the same and different before and after the fall of Soviet communism?*

Life in Rural Siberian Villages Much of Siberia's vast expanse is rural. Few people live in these areas, where change comes slowly. Many homes have no running water. Water has to be hauled from wells. Sometimes the wells freeze in the winter. Then people have to drink and cook with melted snow.

Despite problems like these, Siberians have adapted to life in their frigid climate. Farmers work overtime to harvest crops before the frost. Before winter comes, they start collecting nuts and honey. In winter, some families hang huge pieces of meat from their porches. Temperatures in winter are so cold that the meat freezes solid and does not spoil.

During winter, women wearing many layers of clothing leave their log houses to fetch firewood. Inside the log houses, large stoves are used for both cooking and heating. When the nights become bitterly cold, the family may spread a straw mat on top of the still-warm stove and sleep there to stay warm.

✓ **Reading Check** What are some cultural traditions in Moscow?

A Nenets mother and child in a reindeer-skin tent in Siberia

Uniting a Vast Nation

Russia is a vast country, covering more than 6 million square miles (17 million square kilometers). Russia has more than 144 million people. The majority of these people are ethnic Russians. However, the nation also includes many different ethnic groups who speak different languages and practice different religions. How can a country with so much land, so many different ethnic groups, and a struggling economy stay united?

War in Chechnya You have read that some Russian republics populated by ethnic minorities have grown tired of Russian rule. One such republic, located in southwestern Russia, is called Chechnya (CHECH nee uh). The people who live in this oil-rich republic are mainly Muslims. In 1991, Chechnya declared its independence from Russia. To prevent the republic from seceding, Russia sent troops into the Chechen capital. For several years during the 1990s, Russian and Chechen troops fought bitterly over the status of the republic. Tens of thousands of people were killed in the struggle. Hundreds of thousands were forced to flee their homes. Although Chechnya remains part of Russia today, conflict still goes on there.

Chechen refugees make a temporary home in a train car.

Economic Problems Remain In the early 2000s, Russia's economy shows signs of strengthening. Yet serious economic problems remain. Even one of the country's most important assets—its natural resources—presents problems. For example, Russia has enormous deposits of oil, natural gas, and metals. But Russia depends too heavily on sales of these materials, rather than on creating new jobs. If world prices are low, then Russia's economy suffers.

Corruption is still a problem throughout the country. Laws are still not usually enforced. And banks have never fully recovered from the failures in the 1990s. For these reasons, many Russians distrust the government.

However, Russia is still a powerful nation with many important assets. Besides its natural resources, it has a talented workforce of scientists and engineers. If the country can continue to improve its economy and resolve some of its ethnic tensions, its future should be bright.

✓ **Reading Check** Why is Russia's dependence on its natural resources a problem?

The Russian Dacha
Country homes called *dachas*, like the one below, were first built by Peter the Great and given to wealthy nobles. In Soviet times, they were usually given to Communist Party officials. **Infer** *Do you think average Russians are able to buy dachas today? Explain why or why not.*

Section 4 Assessment

Key Terms
Review the key terms at the beginning of this section. Use each term in a sentence that explains its meaning.

Target Reading Skill
Contrast the situation in Chechnya before and after the fall of the Soviet Union.

Comprehension and Critical Thinking
1. (a) **Explain** Why have average Russians had difficulty running their own businesses?

(b) **Draw Conclusions** How has the change to a free-market economy both helped and harmed ordinary Russians?
2. (a) **Describe** What cultural traditions have endured throughout Russia?
(b) **Contrast** How does life in rural Siberia differ from life in Moscow?
3. (a) **Recall** Which Russian republic declared its independence in 1991?
(b) **Infer** Why did Russia go to war to prevent that republic from seceding?

Writing Activity
Do you live in a city, a small town, or the countryside? Write a paragraph comparing your life with the lives of Russians in one of the places described in this section.

Writing Tip Before you begin, list details about Russian life in the place you have chosen. For each detail, record a detail about your own life that relates to that topic.

Review and Assessment

Poland

◆ Chapter Summary

Section 1: Poland
- Despite years of foreign rule, cultural traditions and language have endured in Polish life.
- In 1990, Poland's communist-based economy shifted to capitalism.
- Poland must still overcome environmental problems and unemployment.

Section 2: New Balkan Nations
- The Balkans is a diverse region of many ethnic groups, religions, and languages.
- Yugoslavia had a troubled history of ethnic conflict from its beginning.
- The countries created upon the breakup of Yugoslavia hope to overcome a history of ethnic conflict and move towards peace.

Section 3: Ukraine
- Ukraine has a long history of occupation by foreign powers.
- Since independence from the Soviet Union, Ukraine has had to face economic and environmental challenges.
- Life in Ukraine is changing as the country embraces its independence.

Section 4: Russia
- Since the fall of the Soviet government, the transition to capitalism has brought some benefits, but also many economic challenges.
- Many cultural traditions have endured throughout Russia.
- Russia's huge size, ethnic diversity, and economic problems have presented challenges to preserving national unity.

◆ Key Terms

Each of the statements below contains a key term from the chapter. If the statement is true, write *true*. If it is false, replace the term to make it true.

1. In the Eastern Orthodox religion, a shrine is a holy place where visitors often plant crosses.

2. An investor is a person who spends money to make more money.

3. Slovenia and Croatia seceded from Yugoslavia in 1991.

4. Capitalism is an economic system in which the government owns the businesses.

5. More than half of Ukraine is covered with a thick, black soil called collectives.

6. After Yugoslavia broke apart, entrepreneurs erupted in Bosnia and Herzegovina.

Review and Assessment (continued)

◆ Comprehension and Critical Thinking

7. (a) Identify What religion do most Poles belong to?
(b) Synthesize Information How has religious belief strengthened the pride Poles feel for their country?

8. (a) Name What group of people in Poland has found it hardest to manage the transition to capitalism?
(b) Analyze Information In what ways did communism help Polish farmers?
(c) Identify Effects What are Polish farmers doing to make extra money?

9. (a) List Which six Balkan nations share a Slavic heritage?
(b) Contrast Discuss the differences among the peoples of these nations.
(c) Summarize How did these differences lead to the breakup of Yugoslavia?

10. (a) Recall What problems are faced by all the nations created by Yugoslavia's breakup?
(b) Identify Cause and Effect Why were UN and NATO forces sent to the Balkans several times?

11. (a) Note What are the natural resources of Ukraine?
(b) Identify the Main Idea How have these resources affected Ukraine's history?

12. (a) Describe What changes did the transition to capitalism bring to Russia?
(b) Evaluate Information How has capitalism both helped and hurt average Russians?

◆ Skills Practice

Identifying Frame of Reference In the Skills for Life activity in this chapter, you learned how to identify frame of reference. Review the steps you followed to learn this skill. Then reread the quotation by Vaclav Havel on page 95. Identify the writer's tone and qualifications for his position. Then use this information to write a paragraph that explains his frame of reference.

◆ Writing Activity: Science

Suppose you are a writer for a science magazine. Your assignment is to write an article about environmental problems in Eastern Europe. Write a short article about the causes and effects of pollution in Poland, or of the Chernobyl accident in Ukraine.

MAP☆MASTER™
Skills Activity

Eastern Europe

Place Location For each place listed below, write the letter from the map that shows its location.

1. Ukraine
2. Kiev
3. Sarajevo
4. Bosnia and Herzegovina
5. Serbia

Go Online
PHSchool.com Use Web Code **ldp-7524** for an **interactive map.**

Standardized Test Prep

Test-Taking Tips

Some questions on standardized tests ask you to analyze graphic organizers. Study the table below. Then follow the tips to answer the sample question.

Six Balkan Nations: Ethnic Groups	
Macedonia	Macedonian (64%) Albanian (25%)
Croatia	Croat (90%) Serb (5%)
Bosnia and Herzegovina	Bosniak (48%) Serb (37%)
Serbia	Serb (66%) Albanian (17%)
Montenegro	Montenegrin (43%) Serb (32%)
Slovenia	Slovene (83%) Croat (2%)

TIP Use what you know about history and geography to help you answer the question.

What is the subject of this chart?

A major ethnic groups of countries that make up Eastern Europe

B major ethnic groups of countries that made up the former Soviet Union

C major ethnic groups of countries that were formed after Yugoslavia broke up

D major ethnic groups of countries that were formed at the end of World War II

TIP Try to answer the question before you look at the answer choices.

Think It Through Each of the names in bold print is a country; to the right of each country is its ethnic makeup. You can eliminate A and B. Eastern Europe includes more than these six countries, and the Soviet Union did not include these countries. You may not know which countries were formed after World War II, but you have probably heard most of these six countries mentioned in reference to Yugoslavia. The answer is C.

Practice Questions

Use the tips above and other tips in this book to help you answer the following questions.

1. Which of the following is NOT an important Polish tradition?

   A communism **B** Polish Orthodoxy

   C Roman Catholicism **D** the Polish language

2. In which country is the republic of Kosovo located?

   A Macedonia

   B Croatia

   C Bosnia and Herzegovina

   D Serbia

3. What led to the growth of towns and cities in Siberia?

   A the collapse of Soviet communism

   B the Trans-Siberian Railroad

   C the transition to capitalism

   D migration from Europe

Use the table below to answer Question 4. Choose the letter of the best answer to the question.

Ukrainian Resources	
Resource	**Use by Soviet Union**
Farmland	Grain, meat
Minerals	Iron ore, coal for industries
	Shipping of goods to and from Soviet Union

4. Which answer would best fit in the blank space on the table?

   A Collectives **B** Seaports and rivers

   C Mines **D** Factories

Use Web Code lda-7504 for a **Chapter 5 self-test.**

Projects

Create your own projects to learn more about Europe and Russia. At the beginning of this book, you were introduced to the **Guiding Questions** for studying the chapters and the special features. You can also find answers to these questions by doing projects on your own or with a group. Use the questions to find topics you want to explore further. Then try the projects described on this page or create your own.

1 **Geography** What are the main physical features of Europe and Russia?

2 **History** How have Europe and Russia been affected by their history?

3 **Culture** How have the people of Europe and Russia been shaped by their cultures?

4 **Government** What types of government have existed in Europe and Russia?

5 **Economics** How have Russian and European economies developed into what they are today?

Project
CREATE A DISPLAY

Folklore Corner
Create a library of folk and fairy tales from countries throughout Europe. As you read about a country in this book, find a traditional tale from that country. Think about how the stories reflect the country's culture. With your classmates, build a Folklore Corner in your classroom. Create a display of books of folk tales. Include objects, drawings, and photographs that represent the culture in these tales. Label each tale with its country of origin.

Project
WRITE A PROPOSAL

Olympic Cities
Plan an Olympic season in a European city. As you read this book, keep track of cities that you find interesting. Research them at the library or on the Internet. After you have gathered your information, choose a city that you think would be a good host of either the summer or winter Olympics. Write a proposal to Olympic officials, explaining what the city has to offer to the Olympics. Include maps or pictures of your city with your proposal.

Table of Contents

The World: Political

ARCTIC OCEAN

RUSSIA

ALASKA (U.S.)

GREENLAND (Denmark)

Reykjavík

CANADA

NORTH AMERICA

Ottawa

UNITED STATES

Washington, D.C.

ATLANTIC OCEAN

MEXICO

Tropic of Cancer

HAWAII (U.S)

Mexico City

CENTRAL AMERICA AND THE CARIBBEAN
For detail, see map North and South America: Political.

CAPE VERDE

Praia

20° N

Caracas

MARSHALL ISLANDS
Majuro

KIRIBATI

NAURU
Tarawa

PALMYRA ATOLL (U.S.)

Equator

GALÁPAGOS ISLANDS (Ecuador)

Quito

VENEZUELA Georgetown
Bogotá Paramaribo
COLOMBIA GUYANA SURINAME
FRENCH GUIANA (France)

ECUADOR

SOUTH AMERICA

BRAZIL

TUVALU
Funafuti

SOLOMON ISLANDS
Honiara

VANUATU
Port-Vila FIJI
Suva

SAMOA
Apia AMERICAN SAMOA (U.S.)

Nuku'alofa TONGA

NIUE (New Zealand)

COOK ISLANDS (New Zealand)

FRENCH POLYNESIA (France)

PITCAIRN ISLANDS (U.K.)

PACIFIC OCEAN

PERU

Lima

La Paz
BOLIVIA
Sucre

Brasília

PARAGUAY
Asunción

NEW CALEDONIA (France)

Tropic of Capricorn

CHILE

ARGENTINA

URUGUAY
Montevideo

Santiago

Buenos Aires

NEW ZEALAND

Wellington

FALKLAND ISLANDS (U.K.)

SOUTH GEORGIA & SOUTH SANDWICH ISLANDS (U.K.)

SOUTHERN OCEAN

Antarctic Circle

ANTARCTICA

0 miles 2,000

0 kilometers 2,000

Robinson

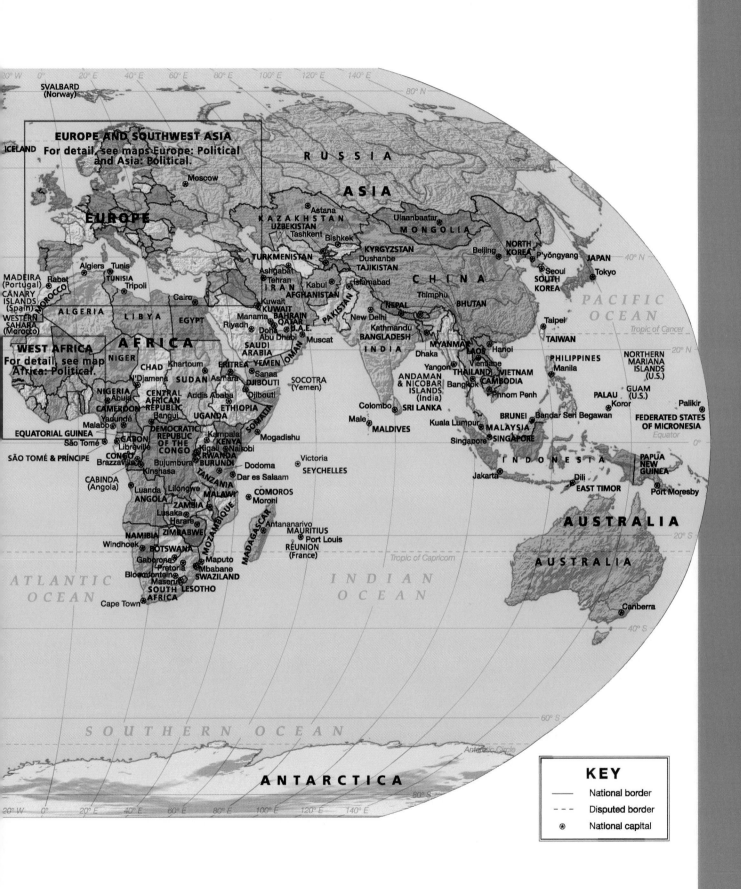

SVALBARD
(Norway)

ICELAND

EUROPE AND SOUTHWEST ASIA
For detail, see maps Europe: Political
and Asia: Political.

RUSSIA

Moscow

ASIA

EUROPE

⊛ Astana
KAZAKHSTAN
UZBEKISTAN
Tashkent Bishkek

Ulaanbaatar ⊛
MONGOLIA

NORTH
KOREA
Beijing ⊛   P'yŏngyang   JAPAN
Seoul ⊛   Tokyo ⊛
SOUTH
KOREA

MADEIRA
(Portugal) Rabat
CANARY
ISLANDS
(Spain)

Algiers Tunis
TUNISIA
Tripoli

TURKMENISTAN
Ashgabat
Tehran
IRAN   Kabul
Kuwait   Islamabad
AFGHANISTAN
KYRGYZSTAN
Dushanbe
TAJIKISTAN

CHINA

Thimphu   BHUTAN

NEPAL
New Delhi
Kathmandu

Taipei
TAIWAN

PACIFIC
OCEAN

Tropic of Cancer

WESTERN
SAHARA
(Morocco)

MOROCCO

ALGERIA

LIBYA   EGYPT

Cairo

Manama BAHRAIN
Riyadh   Doha U.A.E.
Abu Dhabi Muscat
SAUDI
ARABIA   OMAN

BANGLADESH
Dhaka
MYANMAR
Yangon

Hanoi
LAOS
Vientiane

PHILIPPINES
Manila

NORTHERN
MARIANA
ISLANDS
(U.S.)

20° N

WEST AFRICA
For detail, see map
Africa: Political.

NIGER
CHAD   Khartoum
N'Djamena   SUDAN
NIGERIA   CENTRAL
Abuja   AFRICAN
CAMEROON   REPUBLIC
Yaoundé   Bangui

AFRICA

ERITREA YEMEN
Asmara Sanaa
DJIBOUTI
Addis Ababa Djibouti
ETHIOPIA

INDIA

SOCOTRA
(Yemen)

THAILAND VIETNAM
Bangkok CAMBODIA
Phnom Penh

ANDAMAN
& NICOBAR
ISLANDS
(India)

Colombo
SRI LANKA

BRUNEI
Bandar Seri Begawan

PALAU
Koror

GUAM
(U.S.)

Palikir

FEDERATED STATES
OF MICRONESIA

EQUATORIAL GUINEA
São Tomé

UGANDA
DEMOCRATIC
REPUBLIC
OF THE
CONGO
Kampala
Kigali KENYA
Nairobi
RWANDA

SOMALIA

Male
MALDIVES

Kuala Lumpur
MALAYSIA
Singapore SINGAPORE

INDONESIA

Equator   0°

SÃO TOMÉ & PRÍNCIPE

GABON
Libreville
CONGO
Brazzaville
Kinshasa

BURUNDI
Bujumbura   Dodoma

Mogadishu

Victoria
SEYCHELLES

Jakarta

Dili
EAST TIMOR

PAPUA
NEW
GUINEA

Port Moresby

CABINDA
(Angola)

Luanda Lilongwe
ANGOLA   MALAWI

TANZANIA
Dar es Salaam

COMOROS
Moroni

AUSTRALIA

20° S

NAMIBIA
Windhoek

ZAMBIA
Lusaka
Harare
ZIMBABWE
BOTSWANA

MOZAMBIQUE

MADAGASCAR
Antananarivo
MAURITIUS
Port Louis
RÉUNION
(France)

AUSTRALIA

ATLANTIC
OCEAN

Gaborone
Pretoria
Bloemfontein Mbabane
Maseru SWAZILAND
SOUTH LESOTHO
AFRICA
Cape Town

Maputo

INDIAN
OCEAN

Tropic of Capricorn

Canberra

40° S

SOUTHERN   OCEAN

Antarctic Circle

ANTARCTICA

80° S

20° W   0°   20° E   40° E   60° E   80° E   100° E   120° E   140° E

KEY

—————— National border

- - - - - Disputed border

⊛ National capital

The World: Physical

Beaufort Sea

Greenland

Baffin Island

Yukon R.

Mackenzie R.

Bering Sea

Hudson Bay

Labrador Sea

Aleutian Islands

ROCKY MOUNTAINS

NORTH AMERICA

CANADIAN SHIELD

Great Lakes

St. Lawrence R.

GREAT PLAINS

Missouri R.

Mississippi R.

APPALACHIAN MTS.

ATLANTIC OCEAN

40° N

Colorado R.

Rio Grande

Gulf of Mexico

West Indies

Tropic of Cancer

20° N.

Hawaiian Islands

Caribbean Sea

MICRONESIA

Equator

0°

Galápagos Islands

Orinoco R.

GUIANA HIGHLANDS

Amazon R.

AMAZON BASIN

SOUTH AMERICA

N

W   E

S

MELANESIA

POLYNESIA

ANDES

BRAZILIAN HIGHLANDS

PACIFIC OCEAN

20° S

Tropic of Capricorn

Tasman Sea

North Island

Rio de la Plata

PAMPAS

40° S

South Island

PATAGONIA

Cape Horn

60° S

Drake Passage

SOUTHERN OCEAN

ANTARCTIC PENINSULA

Weddell Sea

Antarctic Circle

Ross Sea

80° S

ANTARCTICA

180°   160° W   140° W   120° W   100° W   80° W   60° W   40° W   20° W

0 miles   2,000

0 kilometers   2,000

Robinson

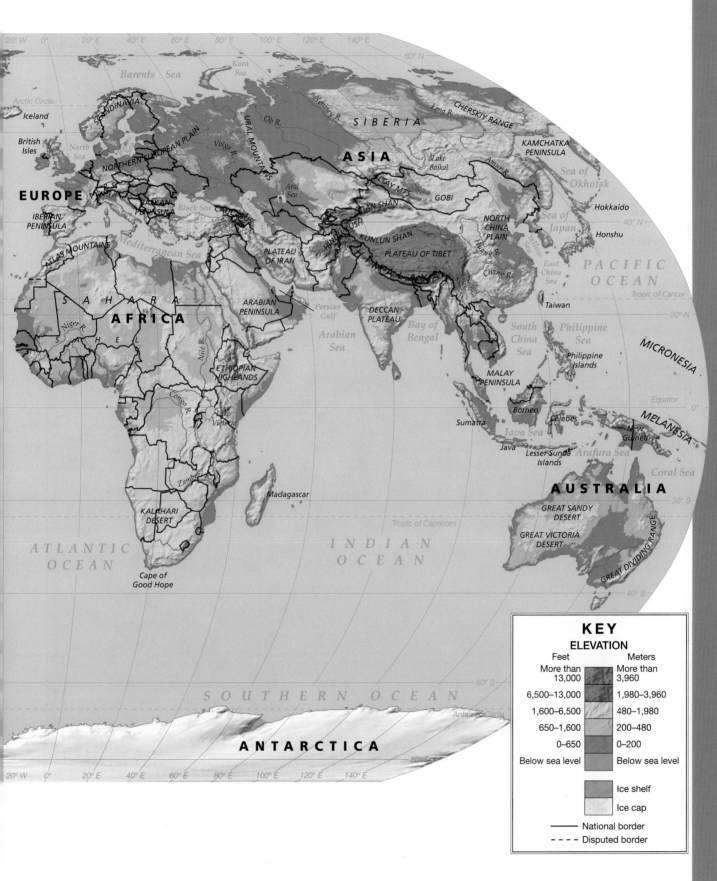

KEY

ELEVATION

Feet		Meters
More than 13,000		More than 3,960
6,500–13,000		1,980–3,960
1,600–6,500		480–1,980
650–1,600		200–480
0–650		0–200
Below sea level		Below sea level
		Ice shelf
		Ice cap
———		National border
– – –		Disputed border

North and South America: Political

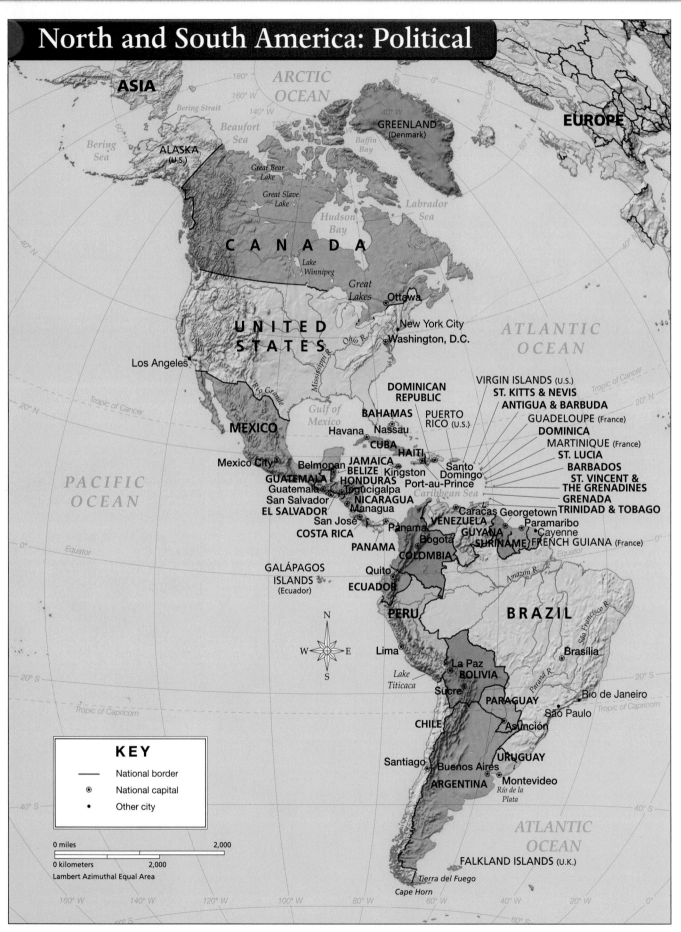

KEY

——	National border
⊛	National capital
•	Other city

0 miles   2,000

0 kilometers   2,000

Lambert Azimuthal Equal Area

North and South America: Physical

ASIA

EUROPE

ARCTIC OCEAN

Bering Strait

Beaufort Sea

Greenland

Bering Sea

Mt. McKinley
20,320 ft
(6,194 m)

Aleutian Islands

Gulf of Alaska

Alaska Range

Mackenzie R.

Great Bear Lake

Great Slave Lake

Baffin Bay

Davis Strait

Baffin Island

Labrador Sea

ROCKY MOUNTAINS

CANADIAN SHIELD

Hudson Bay

Lake Winnipeg

GREAT PLAINS

Great Lakes

Newfoundland

Missouri R.

Colorado R.

Ohio R.

Appalachian Mts.

Mississippi R.

ATLANTIC OCEAN

Tropic of Cancer

Baja California

Río Grande

Sierra Madre Occidental

Sierra Madre Oriental

Gulf of California

Gulf of Mexico

Yucatán Peninsula

Cuba

Greater Antilles

Hispaniola

Lesser Antilles

Caribbean Sea

PACIFIC OCEAN

Isthmus of Panama

Orinoco R.

Guiana Highlands

Galápagos Islands

Equator

AMAZON BASIN

Amazon R.

ANDES

São Francisco R.

Brazilian Highlands

Lake Titicaca

Gran Chaco

Paraguay R.

Paraná R.

Tropic of Capricorn

Aconcagua
22,834 ft
(6,960 m)

Pampas

Río de la Plata

Patagonia

ATLANTIC OCEAN

Falkland Islands

Tierra del Fuego

Cape Horn

KEY

ELEVATION

Feet	Meters
More than 13,000	More than 3,960
6,500–13,000	1,980–3,960
1,600–6,500	480–1,980
650–1,600	200–480
0–650	0–200

Ice cap

National border

0 miles 2,000

0 kilometers 2,000

Lambert Azimuthal Equal Area

N
W E
S

United States: Political

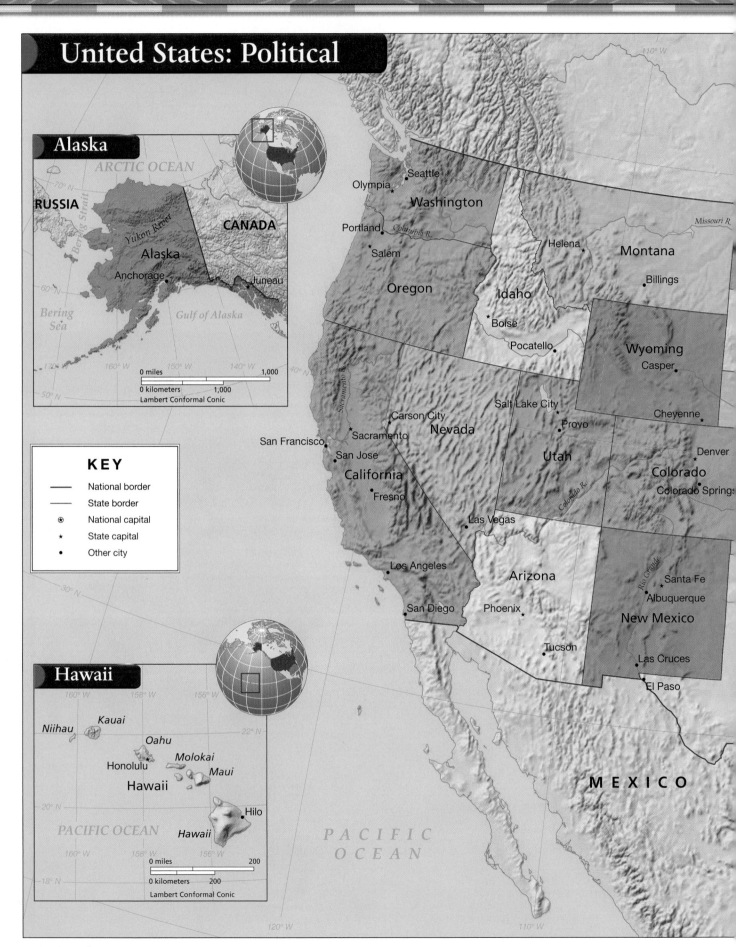

Alaska

ARCTIC OCEAN

RUSSIA

CANADA

Yukon River

Alaska

Anchorage

Juneau

Bering Sea

Gulf of Alaska

0 miles 1,000
0 kilometers 1,000
Lambert Conformal Conic

KEY

——	National border
——	State border
⊛	National capital
★	State capital
•	Other city

Hawaii

Niihau

Kauai

Oahu

Molokai

Honolulu

Maui

Hawaii

Hilo

PACIFIC OCEAN

Hawaii

0 miles 200
0 kilometers 200
Lambert Conformal Conic

Seattle
Olympia
Washington
Portland
Columbia R.
Salem
Helena
Montana
Oregon
Billings
Idaho
Boise
Pocatello
Wyoming
Casper
Salt Lake City
Carson City
Provo
Cheyenne
Sacramento
Nevada
San Francisco
Utah
Denver
San Jose
Colorado
California
Colorado Springs
Fresno
Colorado R.
Las Vegas
Los Angeles
Santa Fe
Arizona
Albuquerque
San Diego
New Mexico
Phoenix
Las Cruces
Tucson
El Paso
Missouri R.
Sacramento R.
Rio Grande

PACIFIC OCEAN

MEXICO

CANADA

North Dakota
Bismarck
Fargo

Minnesota

St. Paul
Minneapolis

South Dakota
Pierre

Sioux Falls

Wisconsin

Milwaukee
Madison

Lake Superior

Michigan

Grand Rapids
Lansing

Lake Huron

Lake Michigan

Detroit

Lake Erie

Lake Ontario

Maine
Augusta

Vermont
Montpelier
Portland

New Hampshire
Concord

Albany

Boston

Massachusetts

Providence

Rhode Island

Hartford

Connecticut

New York City

Nebraska

Omaha

Lincoln

Missouri R.

Iowa
Des Moines

Cedar Rapids

Chicago

Illinois

Springfield

Fort Wayne

Indiana

Indianapolis

Ohio

Cleveland
Pittsburgh

Columbus

Cincinnati

Ohio R.

New York
Buffalo

Pennsylvania
Harrisburg

Philadelphia

New Jersey
Trenton

Delaware
Dover

Baltimore

Annapolis

Washington, D.C.

Maryland

District of Columbia

Richmond

Topeka

Kansas City

Jefferson City

St. Louis

Kansas

Wichita

Arkansas R.

Louisville

Frankfort

Kentucky

Charleston

West Virginia

Virginia

Norfolk

Raleigh

North Carolina

Charlotte

Oklahoma
Tulsa

Oklahoma City

Missouri

Arkansas
Fort Smith
Memphis

Little Rock

Mississippi R.

Nashville

Knoxville

Tennessee

Tennessee R.

South Carolina

Columbia

Charleston

Red R.

Texas

Fort Worth
Dallas

Mississippi

Jackson

Shreveport

Louisiana

Alabama

Birmingham

Montgomery

Atlanta

Georgia

Columbus

Savannah

ATLANTIC OCEAN

Austin

San Antonio

Houston

Baton Rouge

Gulfport

New Orleans

Mobile

Tallahassee

Jacksonville

Florida

Orlando

Tampa

Miami

Gulf of Mexico

N
W E
S

0 miles 250
0 kilometers 250
Lambert Azimuthal Equal Area

Europe: Political

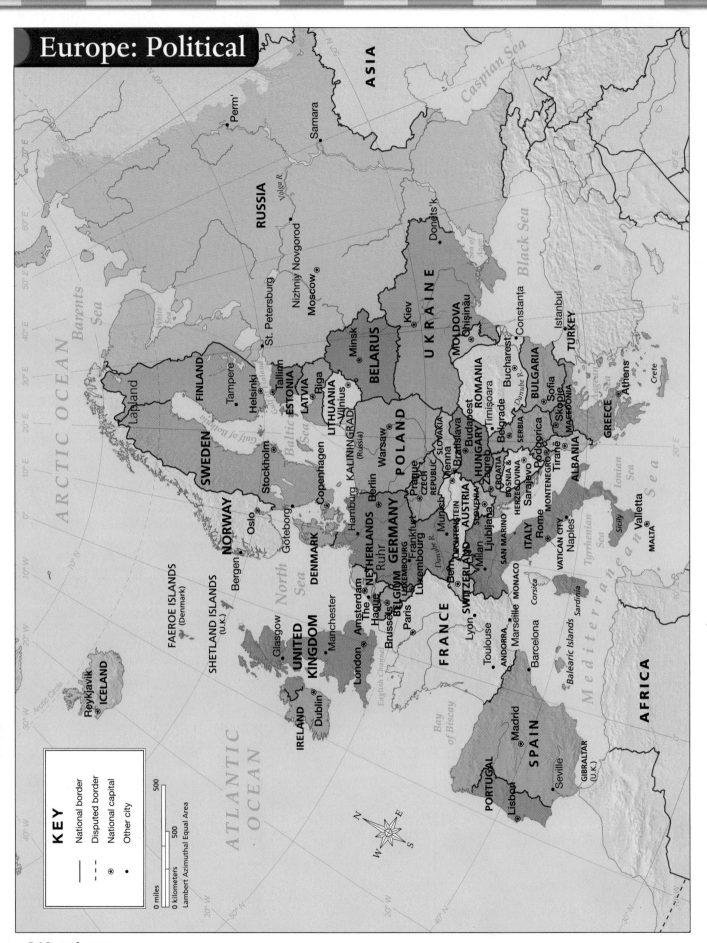

ASIA

Caspian Sea

Perm'

Samara

RUSSIA

Volga R.

Nizhniy Novgorod ⊛

Moscow ⊛

Sea of Azov

St. Petersburg ⊛

Donets'k •

UKRAINE

Kiev ⊛

MOLDOVA

Chişinău ⊛

Black Sea

Constanţa •

Istanbul •

TURKEY

Minsk ⊛

BELARUS

Bucharest ⊛

BULGARIA

Sofia ⊛

Athens ⊛

Crete

FINLAND

Tampere •

Helsinki ⊛

Tallinn ⊛

ESTONIA

LATVIA

Riga ⊛

LITHUANIA

Vilnius ⊛

Warsaw ⊛

POLAND

ROMANIA

Timişoara •

Belgrade ⊛

Danube R.

SERBIA

MACEDONIA

Skopje ⊛

GREECE

Ionian Sea

Aegean Sea

Lapland

SWEDEN

Stockholm ⊛

Göteborg •

Copenhagen ⊛

Hamburg •

KALININGRAD (Russia)

Berlin ⊛

Prague ⊛

CZECH REPUBLIC

SLOVAKIA

Bratislava ⊛

Budapest ⊛

HUNGARY

Vienna ⊛

Zagreb ⊛

CROATIA

SLOVENIA

BOSNIA & HERZEGOVINA

Sarajevo ⊛

MONTENEGRO ⊛

Podgorica

Tiranë ⊛

ALBANIA

NORWAY

Oslo ⊛

Bergen •

North Sea

DENMARK

NETHERLANDS

The Hague ⊛

Amsterdam ⊛

BELGIUM

Brussels ⊛

Ruhr

GERMANY

Frankfurt •

LUXEMBOURG

Luxembourg ⊛

LIECHTENSTEIN

Bern ⊛

SWITZERLAND

Munich •

AUSTRIA

Ljubljana ⊛

Milan •

SAN MARINO

ITALY

Rome ⊛

VATICAN CITY

Naples •

MONACO

Marseille •

Corsica

Sardinia

Tyrrhenian Sea

Sicily

Valletta ⊛

MALTA ⊛

Mediterranean Sea

FAEROE ISLANDS (Denmark)

SHETLAND ISLANDS (U.K.)

Glasgow •

Manchester •

UNITED KINGDOM

London ⊛

English Channel

FRANCE

Paris ⊛

Lyon •

Toulouse •

ANDORRA

Barcelona •

Balearic Islands

Bay of Biscay

Reykjavík ⊛

ICELAND

Arctic Circle

ARCTIC OCEAN

Barents Sea

White Sea

Gulf of Bothnia

Gulf of Finland

Baltic Sea

IRELAND

Dublin ⊛

ATLANTIC OCEAN

SPAIN

Madrid ⊛

Seville •

GIBRALTAR (U.K.)

PORTUGAL

Lisbon ⊛

AFRICA

N E W S

KEY

——	National border
– – –	Disputed border
⊛	National capital
•	Other city

0 miles 500

0 kilometers 500

Lambert Azimuthal Equal Area

Europe: Physical

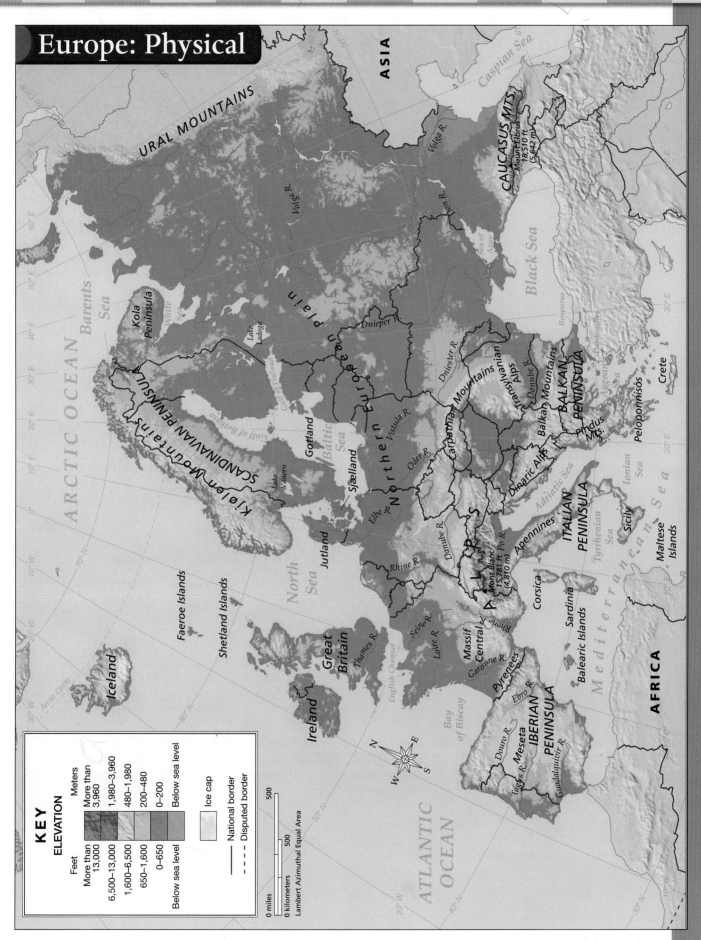

ASIA

URAL MOUNTAINS

Caspian Sea

CAUCASUS MTS.

Mount Elbrus
18,510 ft
(5,642 m)

Volga R.

Volga R.

Don R.

Black Sea

Kola
Peninsula

White Sea

Barents Sea

Lake
Ladoga

Dnieper R.

Dniester R.

Transylvanian
Alps

Danube R.

Bosporus

Balkan Mountains

BALKAN
PENINSULA

ARCTIC OCEAN

Gulf of Finland

Northern European Plain

Vistula R.

Carpathian Mountains

Dardanelles

Pindus Mts.

Crete

SCANDINAVIAN PENINSULA

Gulf of Bothnia

Baltic Sea

Gotland

Oder R.

Dinaric Alps

Aegean Sea

Peloponnisos

Kjølen Mountains

Lake
Vänern

Sjælland

Elbe R.

Danube R.

Adriatic Sea

Ionian Sea

Mediterranean Sea

North Sea

Jutland

Rhine R.

ALPS

Apennines

ITALIAN
PENINSULA

Sicily

Tyrrhenian
Sea

Maltese
Islands

AFRICA

Iceland

Faeroe Islands

Shetland Islands

Ireland

Great
Britain

Thames R.

English Channel

Seine R.

Loire R.

Massif
Central

Garonne R.

Mont Blanc
15,781 ft
(4,810 m)

Rhône R.

Po R.

Corsica

Sardinia

Balearic Islands

Bay
of
Biscay

Pyrenees

Ebro R.

Meseta

IBERIAN
PENINSULA

Arctic Circle

Douro R.

Tagus R.

Guadalquivir R.

ATLANTIC
OCEAN

Arctic Circle

N
E
W
S

KEY

ELEVATION

Feet	Meters
More than 13,000	More than 3,960
6,500–13,000	1,980–3,960
1,600–6,500	480–1,980
650–1,600	200–480
0–650	0–200
Below sea level	Below sea level

Ice cap

—— National border

--- Disputed border

500

0 miles   500
0 kilometers   500
Lambert Azimuthal Equal Area

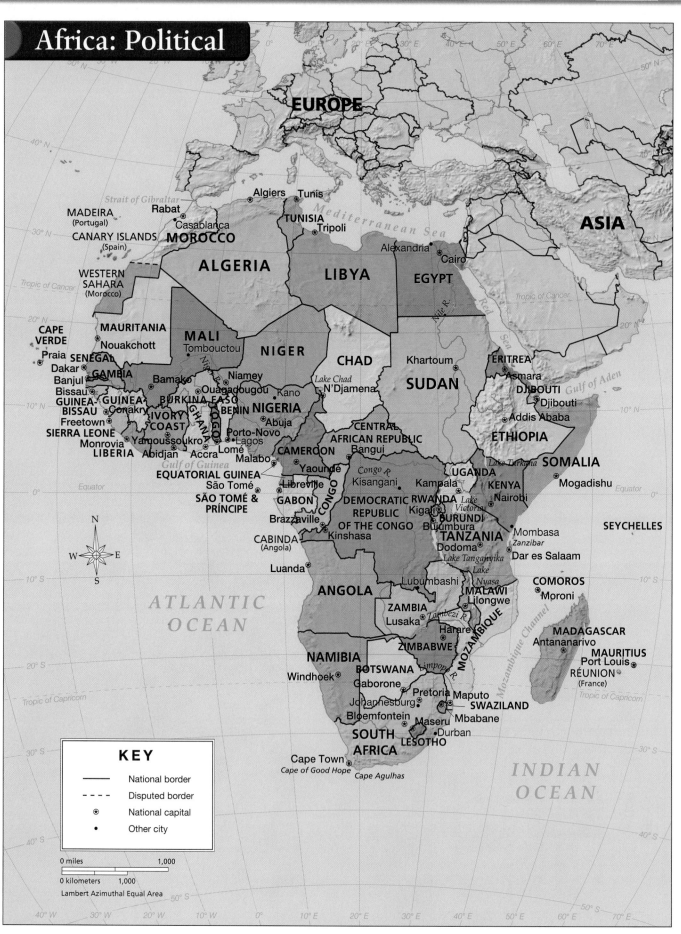

EUROPE

ASIA

Strait of Gibraltar
Algiers · Tunis
MADEIRA
(Portugal)
Rabat
Casablanca
CANARY ISLANDS
(Spain)
MOROCCO
TUNISIA
Tripoli
Mediterranean Sea

WESTERN
SAHARA
(Morocco)
ALGERIA
LIBYA
EGYPT
Alexandria
Cairo
Nile R.
Tropic of Cancer

CAPE
VERDE
MAURITANIA
Nouakchott
MALI
Tombouctou
NIGER
CHAD
Khartoum
ERITREA
Asmara
DJIBOUTI
Gulf of Aden
Praia
Dakar
SENEGAL
GAMBIA
Banjul
Bissau
GUINEA-
BISSAU
GUINEA
Conakry
Bamako
Niamey
Niger R.
Ouagadougou
BURKINA FASO
Kano
N'Djamena
Lake Chad
SUDAN
Addis Ababa
Djibouti
SIERRA LEONE
Freetown
IVORY
COAST
GHANA
TOGO
BENIN
NIGERIA
Abuja
CENTRAL
AFRICAN REPUBLIC
ETHIOPIA
Monrovia
Yamoussoukro
Abidjan
Accra
Lomé
Porto-Novo
Lagos
Malabo
CAMEROON
Bangui
SOMALIA
LIBERIA
Gulf of Guinea
Yaoundé
Lake Turkana
EQUATORIAL GUINEA
São Tomé
Libreville
Kisangani
Congo R.
UGANDA
Kampala
KENYA
Nairobi
Mogadishu
Equator
SÃO TOMÉ &
PRÍNCIPE
GABON
CONGO
DEMOCRATIC
REPUBLIC
OF THE CONGO
RWANDA
Kigali
Lake
Victoria
BURUNDI
Bujumbura
Brazzaville
Kinshasa
TANZANIA
Dodoma
Mombasa
Zanzibar
SEYCHELLES
CABINDA
(Angola)
Lake Tanganyika
Dar es Salaam
Luanda
Lake
Nyasa
COMOROS
Moroni
Lubumbashi
MALAWI
Lilongwe
ATLANTIC
OCEAN
ANGOLA
ZAMBIA
Lusaka
Zambezi R.
MOZAMBIQUE
Harare
MADAGASCAR
Antananarivo
NAMIBIA
BOTSWANA
ZIMBABWE
Limpopo R.
Mozambique Channel
MAURITIUS
Port Louis
RÉUNION
(France)
Windhoek
Gaborone
Pretoria
Maputo
Johannesburg
SWAZILAND
Mbabane
Bloemfontein
Maseru
Durban
SOUTH
AFRICA
LESOTHO
Cape Town
Cape of Good Hope
Cape Agulhas
INDIAN
OCEAN

N
W · E
S

KEY

———	National border
- - -	Disputed border
⊛	National capital
•	Other city

0 miles — 1,000
0 kilometers — 1,000
Lambert Azimuthal Equal Area

Africa: Physical

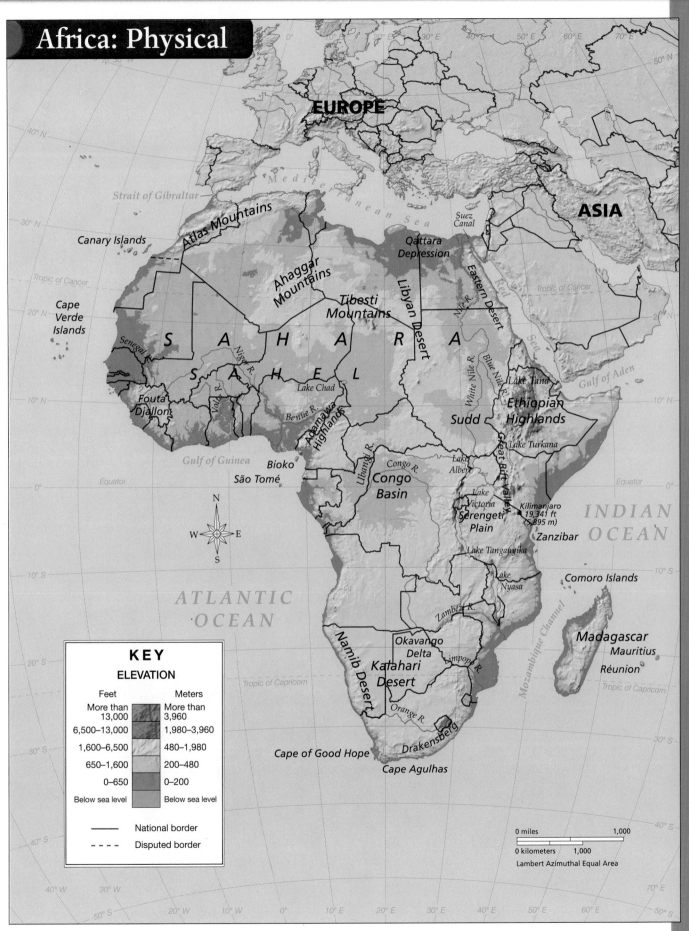

EUROPE

ASIA

Strait of Gibraltar

Mediterranean Sea

Suez Canal

Atlas Mountains

Canary Islands

Qattara Depression

Tropic of Cancer

Cape Verde Islands

S A H A R A

Ahaggar Mountains

Tibesti Mountains

Libyan Desert

Eastern Desert

Nile R.

Red Sea

Tropic of Cancer

Senegal R.

S A H E L

Niger R.

Lake Chad

White Nile R.

Blue Nile R.

Lake Tana

Gulf of Aden

Fouta Djallon

Volta R.

Benue R.

Adamawa Highlands

Ethiopian Highlands

Sudd

Gulf of Guinea

Bioko

São Tomé

Ubangi R.

Congo R.

Congo Basin

Lake Albert

Lake Turkana

Equator

Lake Victoria

Serengeti Plain

Great Rift Valley

Kilimanjaro 19,341 ft (5,895 m)

Zanzibar

INDIAN OCEAN

Equator

Lake Tanganyika

Comoro Islands

ATLANTIC OCEAN

Lake Nyasa

Zambezi R.

Okavango Delta

Namib Desert

Kalahari Desert

Limpopo R.

Mozambique Channel

Madagascar

Mauritius

Réunion

Tropic of Capricorn

Tropic of Capricorn

Orange R.

Drakensberg

Cape of Good Hope

Cape Agulhas

KEY
ELEVATION

Feet	Meters
More than 13,000	More than 3,960
6,500–13,000	1,980–3,960
1,600–6,500	480–1,980
650–1,600	200–480
0–650	0–200
Below sea level	Below sea level

——— National border

- - - - Disputed border

N W E S

0 miles 1,000

0 kilometers 1,000

Lambert Azimuthal Equal Area

Asia: Political

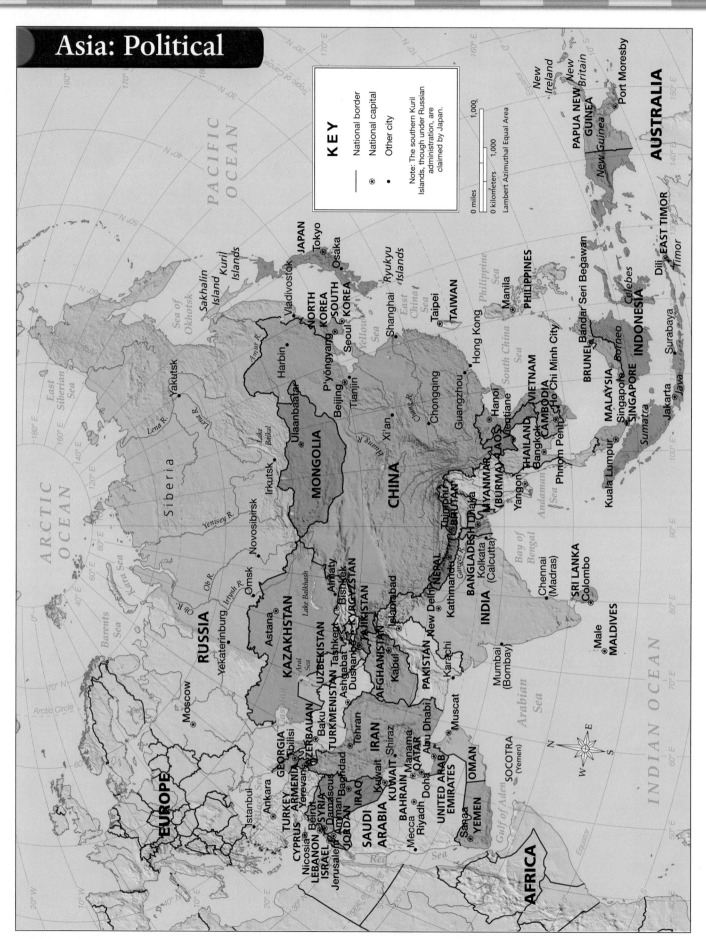

KEY

National border
⊛ National capital
• Other city

Note: The southern Kuril Islands, though under Russian administration, are claimed by Japan.

0 miles   1,000
0 kilometers   1,000
Lambert Azimuthal Equal Area

PACIFIC OCEAN

ARCTIC OCEAN

EUROPE

AFRICA

AUSTRALIA

PAPUA NEW GUINEA
New Guinea
New Ireland
New Britain
Port Moresby

RUSSIA
Moscow ⊛
Yekaterinburg
Siberia
Yakutsk
Novosibirsk
Omsk
Irkutsk
Astana
Vladivostok
Lena R.
Yenisey R.
Ob R.
Irtysh R.
Lake Balkhash
Lake Baikal
Amur R.

Sea of Okhotsk
Sakhalin Island
Kuril Islands

JAPAN
Tokyo
Osaka

East Siberian Sea
Kara Sea
Barents Sea

MONGOLIA
Ulaanbaatar ⊛

Harbin

NORTH KOREA
P'yŏngyang ⊛
SOUTH KOREA
Seoul ⊛

CHINA
Beijing ⊛
Tianjin
Xi'an
Shanghai
Chongqing
Guangzhou
Hong Kong

Ryukyu Islands
TAIWAN
Taipei

Yellow Sea
East China Sea
Philippine Sea
South China Sea

KAZAKHSTAN
Astana
Aral Sea

UZBEKISTAN
Tashkent ⊛
TURKMENISTAN
Ashgabat ⊛
Almaty
Bishkek ⊛
KYRGYZSTAN
Dushanbe ⊛
TAJIKISTAN

AFGHANISTAN
Kabul ⊛
Islamabad ⊛
PAKISTAN
Karachi

NEPAL
Kathmandu ⊛
BHUTAN
Thimphu ⊛
New Delhi ⊛
INDIA
BANGLADESH
Dhaka ⊛
Kolkata (Calcutta)
Ganges R.
Mumbai (Bombay)
Chennai (Madras)

Huang R.
Chang R.

MYANMAR (BURMA)
Yangon
LAOS
Vientiane ⊛
THAILAND
Bangkok ⊛
Hanoi ⊛
VIETNAM
CAMBODIA
Phnom Penh ⊛
Ho Chi Minh City

PHILIPPINES
Manila ⊛

BRUNEI
Bandar Seri Begawan ⊛
MALAYSIA
Kuala Lumpur ⊛
Singapore
SINGAPORE
Borneo
Celebes
INDONESIA
Sumatra
Jakarta ⊛
Surabaya
Java

EAST TIMOR
Dili ⊛
Timor

SRI LANKA
Colombo ⊛
MALDIVES
Male ⊛

Bay of Bengal
Andaman Sea
Arabian Sea
INDIAN OCEAN

TURKEY
Ankara ⊛
Istanbul
GEORGIA
Tbilisi ⊛
ARMENIA
Yerevan ⊛
AZERBAIJAN
Baku ⊛
CYPRUS
Nicosia ⊛
LEBANON
Beirut ⊛
ISRAEL
Jerusalem ⊛
SYRIA
Damascus ⊛
JORDAN
Amman ⊛
IRAQ
Baghdad ⊛
IRAN
Tehran ⊛
Shiraz
KUWAIT
Kuwait ⊛
BAHRAIN
Manama ⊛
QATAR
Doha ⊛
UNITED ARAB EMIRATES
Abu Dhabi ⊛
OMAN
Muscat ⊛
SAUDI ARABIA
Riyadh ⊛
Mecca
YEMEN
Sanaa ⊛
SOCOTRA (Yemen)

Black Sea
Caspian Sea
Red Sea
Gulf of Aden
Tropic of Cancer
Tropic of Capricorn
Arctic Circle
Equator

N
E
S
W

Asia: Physical

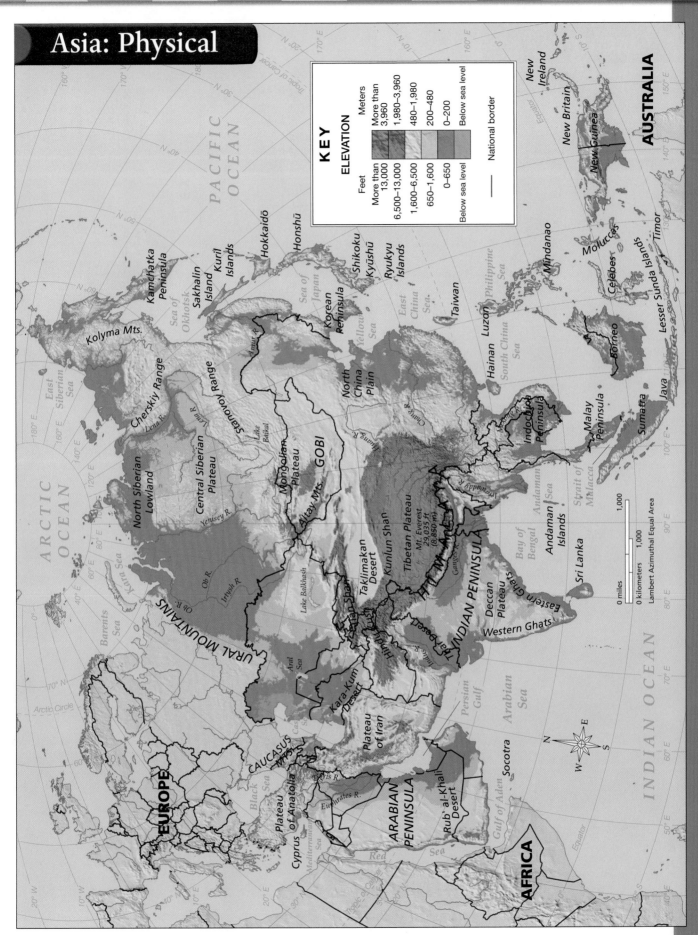

KEY

ELEVATION

Feet	Meters
More than 13,000	More than 3,960
6,500–13,000	1,980–3,960
1,600–6,500	480–1,980
650–1,600	200–480
0–650	0–200
Below sea level	Below sea level

— National border

PACIFIC OCEAN

ARCTIC OCEAN

INDIAN OCEAN

AUSTRALIA

EUROPE

AFRICA

New Ireland
New Britain
New Guinea
Mindanao
Molucces
Celebes
Lesser Sunda Islands
Timor
Borneo
Java
Sumatra
Malay Peninsula
Luzon
Philippine Sea
Hainan
South China Sea
Taiwan
Indochina Peninsula
Andaman Islands
Andaman Sea
Bay of Bengal
Sri Lanka
Eastern Ghats
Western Ghats
Deccan Plateau
INDIAN PENINSULA
Ganges R.
Mt. Everest 29,035 ft (8,850 m)
HIMALAYA
Brahmaputra R.
Mekong R.
Huang R.
Chang R.
Yellow Sea
East China Sea
Ryukyu Islands
Kyūshū
Shikoku
Honshū
Hokkaidō
Kuril Islands
Sakhalin Island
Sea of Japan
Korean Peninsula
North China Plain
Kamchatka Peninsula
Sea of Okhotsk
Kolyma Mts.
Cherskiy Range
East Siberian Sea
Lena R.
Stanovoy Range
Amur R.
Lake Baikal
GOBI
Mongolian Plateau
Altay Mts.
Tibetan Plateau
Kunlun Shan
Taklimakan Desert
Tian Shan
Hindu Kush
Thar Desert
Indus R.
Kara-Kum Desert
Aral Sea
Lake Balkhash
Irtysh R.
Ob R.
Yenisey R.
Central Siberian Plateau
North Siberian Lowland
URAL MOUNTAINS
Kara Sea
Barents Sea
Svalbard
Arctic Circle
Black Sea
Caspian Sea
CAUCASUS MTS.
Cyprus
Plateau of Anatolia
Mediterranean Sea
Tigris R.
Euphrates R.
ARABIAN PENINSULA
Rub' al-Khali Desert
Red Sea
Gulf of Aden
Socotra
Arabian Sea
Persian Gulf
Plateau of Iran

Tropic of Cancer
Equator
Tropic of Capricorn

0 miles 1,000
0 kilometers 1,000
Lambert Azimuthal Equal Area

Oceania

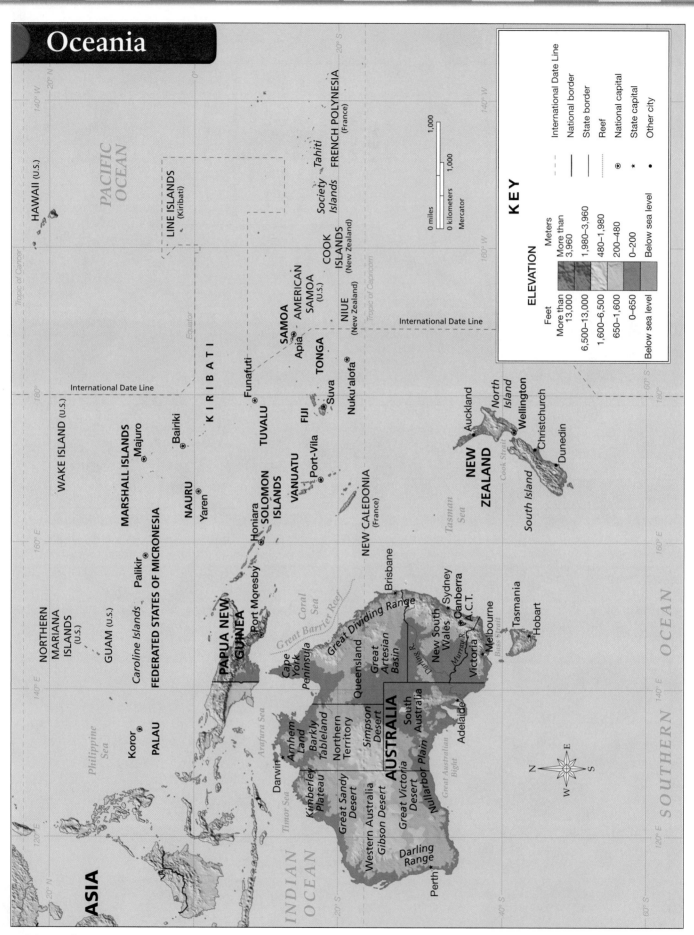

KEY

ELEVATION

Feet	Meters
More than 13,000	More than 3,960
6,500–13,000	1,980–3,960
1,600–6,500	480–1,980
650–1,600	200–480
0–650	0–200
Below sea level	Below sea level

- - - - International Date Line
——— National border
State border
·········· Reef
⊛ National capital
★ State capital
• Other city

HAWAII (U.S.)

PACIFIC OCEAN

LINE ISLANDS (Kiribati)

FRENCH POLYNESIA (France)

Society Islands Tahiti

COOK ISLANDS (New Zealand)

Tropic of Capricorn

SAMOA
AMERICAN SAMOA (U.S.)
Apia
NIUE (New Zealand)
TONGA
Nuku'alofa

International Date Line

Funafuti
TUVALU
FIJI
Suva
VANUATU
Port-Vila

NEW CALEDONIA (France)

KIRIBATI

WAKE ISLAND (U.S.)

MARSHALL ISLANDS
Majuro

NAURU
Yaren

SOLOMON ISLANDS
Honiara

Auckland
North Island
Wellington
Christchurch
Dunedin

NEW ZEALAND

South Island

Cook Strait

Tasman Sea

NORTHERN MARIANA ISLANDS (U.S.)

GUAM (U.S.)

Caroline Islands Palikir
FEDERATED STATES OF MICRONESIA

PAPUA NEW GUINEA
Port Moresby

Coral Sea

Great Barrier Reef

Brisbane

Great Dividing Range

Cape York Peninsula

Queensland

Great Artesian Basin

New South Wales
Sydney
Canberra A.C.T.

Melbourne
Victoria

Tasmania
Hobart

Bass Strait

Philippine Sea

Koror
PALAU

ASIA

Darwin
Arnhem Land

Kimberley Plateau

Barkly Tableland
Northern Territory

AUSTRALIA

Simpson Desert

South Australia

Adelaide

Great Sandy Desert

Western Australia
Gibson Desert

Great Victoria Desert

Nullarbor Plain

Great Australian Bight

Darling Range

Perth

Murray R.
Darling R.

Timor Sea

Arafura Sea

INDIAN OCEAN

SOUTHERN OCEAN

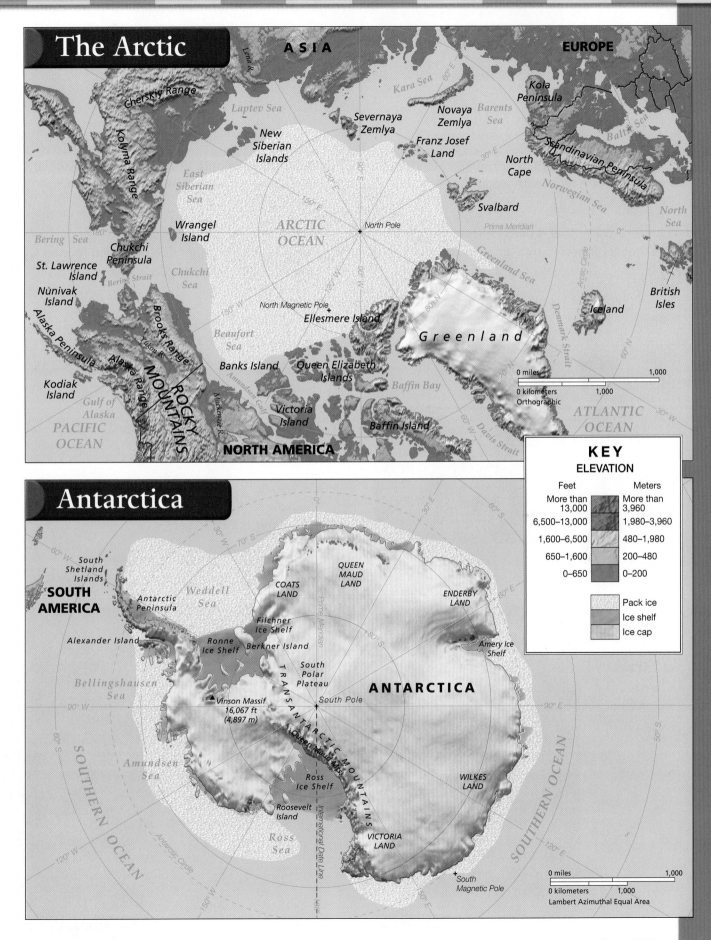

The Arctic

ASIA   EUROPE

Cherskiy Range
Lena R.
Kolyma Range
Laptev Sea
Kara Sea
Severnaya Zemlya
Novaya Zemlya
Barents Sea
Kola Peninsula
Baltic Sea
New Siberian Islands
Franz Josef Land
North Cape
Scandinavian Peninsula
East Siberian Sea
Wrangel Island
ARCTIC OCEAN
North Pole
Svalbard
Norwegian Sea
North Sea
Prime Meridian
Bering Sea
Chukchi Peninsula
Chukchi Sea
Greenland Sea
St. Lawrence Island
Bering Strait
North Magnetic Pole
Ellesmere Island
Arctic Circle
Iceland
British Isles
Nunivak Island
Brooks Range
Beaufort Sea
Greenland
Denmark Strait
Alaska Peninsula
Yukon R.
Alaska Range
ROCKY MOUNTAINS
Banks Island
Queen Elizabeth Islands
Baffin Bay
0 miles 1,000
0 kilometers 1,000
Orthographic
Kodiak Island
Gulf of Alaska
Amundsen Gulf
Mackenzie R.
Victoria Island
Baffin Island
Davis Strait
ATLANTIC OCEAN
PACIFIC OCEAN

NORTH AMERICA

Antarctica

South Shetland Islands
SOUTH AMERICA
Antarctic Peninsula
Weddell Sea
COATS LAND
QUEEN MAUD LAND
ENDERBY LAND
Alexander Island
Filchner Ice Shelf
Ronne Ice Shelf
Berkner Island
Prime Meridian
Amery Ice Shelf
Bellingshausen Sea
South Polar Plateau
ANTARCTICA
Vinson Massif 16,067 ft (4,897 m)
South Pole
TRANSANTARCTIC MOUNTAINS
Queen Maud Mts.
Amundsen Sea
Ross Ice Shelf
WILKES LAND
SOUTHERN OCEAN
Roosevelt Island
International Date Line
VICTORIA LAND
Ross Sea
Antarctic Circle
South Magnetic Pole
0 miles 1,000
0 kilometers 1,000
Lambert Azimuthal Equal Area
SOUTHERN OCEAN

KEY

ELEVATION

Feet		Meters
More than 13,000		More than 3,960
6,500–13,000		1,980–3,960
1,600–6,500		480–1,980
650–1,600		200–480
0–650		0–200

Pack ice
Ice shelf
Ice cap

Glossary of Geographic Terms

basin
an area that is lower than surrounding land areas; some basins are filled with water

bay
a body of water that is partly surrounded by land and that is connected to a larger body of water

butte
a small, high, flat-topped landform with cliff-like sides

▲ **butte**

canyon
a deep, narrow valley with steep sides; often with a stream flowing through it

cataract
a large waterfall or steep rapids

◀ **cataract**

delta
a plain at the mouth of a river, often triangular in shape, formed where sediment is deposited by flowing water

flood plain
a broad plain on either side of a river, formed where sediment settles during floods

glacier
a huge, slow-moving mass of snow and ice

hill
an area that rises above surrounding land and has a rounded top; lower and usually less steep than a mountain

island
an area of land completely surrounded by water

isthmus
a narrow strip of land that connects two larger areas of land

mesa
a high, flat-topped landform with cliff-like sides; larger than a butte

mountain
a landform that rises steeply at least 2,000 feet (610 meters) above surrounding land; usually wide at the bottom and rising to a narrow peak or ridge

▶ **glacier**

◀ **delta**

mountain pass
a gap between mountains

peninsula
an area of land almost completely surrounded by water but connected to the mainland

plain
a large area of flat or gently rolling land

plateau
a large, flat area that rises above the surrounding land; at least one side has a steep slope

river mouth
the point where a river enters a lake or sea

strait
a narrow stretch of water that connects two larger bodies of water

tributary
a river or stream that flows into a larger river

valley
a low stretch of land between mountains or hills; land that is drained by a river

volcano
an opening in Earth's surface through which molten rock, ashes, and gases escape from the interior

▶ **volcano**

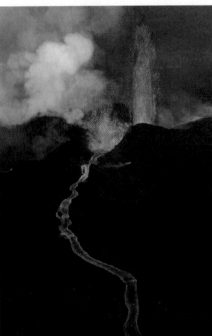

Gazetteer

A

Alpine Mountain System (46° N, 10° E) a range of mountains that extends through south central Europe; Europe's highest mountain system, p. 13

Athens (37°58′ N, 23°43′ E) the capital city of modern Greece; the world's most powerful cultural center in the 400s B.C., p. 39

B

Balkan Peninsula (44° N, 23° E) a region in southeastern Europe also known as the Balkans, p. 183

Berlin (52°31′ N, 13°24′ E) the capital city of Germany; once divided into East Berlin and West Berlin, p. 154

Bosnia and Herzegovina (44° N, 18° E) a country in Eastern Europe, p. 186

C

Central Uplands a region of mountains and plateaus in the center of Southern Europe, p. 13

C

Chernobyl (51°16′ N, 30°14′ E) the city in northern Ukraine where a nuclear power station accident occurred in 1986, p. 194

Czechoslovakia a former Central European country that contained the present-day countries of the Czech Republic and Slovakia, p. 95

D

Danube River (45° N, 30° E) a river that flows 1,770 miles (2,850 kilometers) from Germany to the Black Sea, p. 15

E

Eurasia the world's largest landmass; contains the continents of Europe and Asia, p. 11

Europe (50° N, 28° E) the world's second-smallest continent; a peninsula of the Eurasian landmass bordered by the Arctic Ocean, the Atlantic Ocean, the Mediterranean Sea, and Asia, p. 11

F

France (46° N, 2° E) a country in Western Europe, p. 130

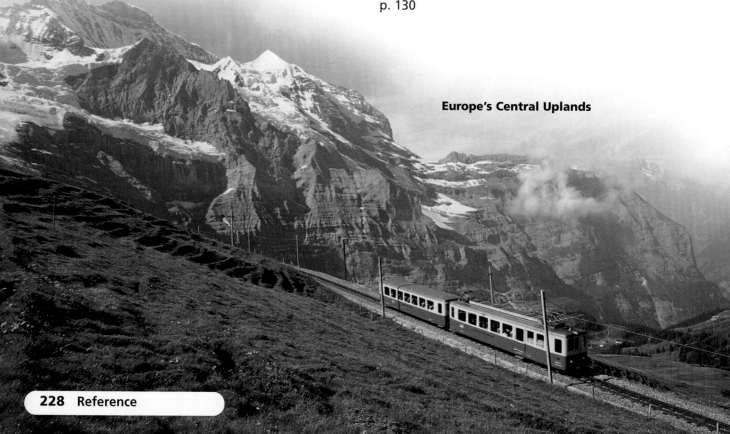

Europe's Central Uplands

G

Germany (51° N, 10° E) a country in Western Europe, p. 154

Gulf Stream a warm ocean current in the North Atlantic, flowing northeastward off the North American coast, p. 18

I

Italy (43° N, 13° E) a country in Southern Europe, p. 145

L

London (51°30′ N, 0°10′ W) the capital city of the United Kingdom, p. 19

M

Macedonia (42° N, 22° E) a country in Eastern Europe, p. 187

Mediterranean Sea (35° N, 20° E) the large sea that separates Europe and Africa, p. 18

Montenegro (43° N, 19° E) a country in Eastern Europe, p. 188

Moscow (55°45′ N, 37°35′ E) the capital city of modern Russia, p. 63

Tearing down Germany's Berlin Wall

N

Netherlands, The (52° N, 6° E) a country in Northern Europe, p. 10

North Atlantic Current a warm ocean current in the North Atlantic, flowing northeastward toward Europe, p. 18

North European Plain plain extending from Russia to France; contains Europe and Russia's most productive farmland and largest cities, p. 13

North Sea (56° N, 3° E) an arm of the Atlantic Ocean located between Great Britain and the European mainland, p. 26

Northwestern Highlands a mountainous, forested region in northern Europe, p. 13

A North Sea oil rig

Polish folk dancers

P

Paris (48°52′ N, 2°20′ E) the capital city of France, p. 130

Poland (52° N, 19° E) a country in Eastern Europe, p. 174

R

Rhine River (52° N, 6° E) a river that flows about 865 miles (1,392 kilometers) from Switzerland to the Netherlands, p. 15

Rome (41°54′ N, 12°29′ E) the capital of modern Italy; one of the world's greatest ancient civilizations and empires, p. 41

Ruhr (51° N, 7° E) an industrial region in Germany; also the name of a river there, p. 28

Russia (60° N, 80° E) a country in northern Eurasia, p. 198

S

St. Petersburg (59°55′ N, 30°15′ E) a city and important cultural center in Russia, p. 105

Sarajevo (43°52′ N, 18°25′ E) the capital city of Bosnia and Herzegovina, p. 181

Scandinavia a historical region of northern Europe that includes Norway, Finland, Sweden, Denmark, and Iceland, p. 23

Serbia (44° N, 21° E) a country in Eastern Europe, p. 183

Siberia (65° N, 110° E) a resource-rich region of northeastern Russia; contains the West Siberian Plain, the Central Siberian Plateau, and the East Siberian Uplands, p. 14

Silesia (51° N, 17° E) a coal-rich region where Poland, the Czech Republic, and Germany meet, p. 29

Slovenia (46° N, 15° E) a country in Eastern Europe, p. 185

Soviet Union a former communist country that included present-day Russia and several other Eastern European countries, p. 67

Sweden (62° N, 15° E) a country in Northern Europe, p. 138

U

Ukraine (49° N, 32° E) a country in Eastern Europe, p. 189

United Kingdom (54° N, 2° E) a nation in Northern Europe that includes Great Britain and Northern Ireland, p. 122

Ural Mountains (60° N, 60° E) a mountain range in northern Eurasia that forms the border between Europe and Asia, p. 11

V

Vatican City (41°54′ N, 12°27′ W) a nation-state completely surrounded by Rome, Italy; the seat of the Roman Catholic Church, p. 145

Volga River (46° N, 48° E) Europe's longest river; it flows 2,291 miles (3,687 kilometers) through western Russia to the Caspian Sea, p. 15

Y

Yugoslavia a former Eastern European country that contained the present-day countries of Serbia, Montenegro, Bosnia and Herzegovina, Croatia, Slovenia, and Macedonia, p. 95

Vatican City

Glossary

A

alliance (uh LY uns) *n.* an agreement between countries to protect and defend each other, p. 58

B

basilica (buh SIL ih kuh) *n.* a Roman Catholic church that has a special, high status because of its age or history, p. 146

C

capitalism (KAP ut ul iz um) *n.* an economic system in which businesses are privately owned, p. 177

chernozem (CHEHR nuh zem) *n.* rich, black soil, productive for farming, p. 191

city-state (SIH tee stayt) *n.* a city with its own government that was both a city and an independent state, p. 39

civil war (sih vul wawr) *n.* a war between groups of people within the same nation, p. 181

collective (kuh LEK tiv) *n.* a huge government-controlled farm, p. 192

colony (KAHL uh nee) *n.* a territory ruled by another nation, p. 50

communism (KAHM yoo niz um) *n.* a political system in which the central government owns farms, factories, and offices, p. 66

constitution

constitution (kahn stuh TOO shun) *n.* a set of laws that describes how a government works, p. 126

constitutional monarchy (kahn stuh TOO shuh nul MAHN ur kee) *n.* a government in which a monarch is the head of state but has limited powers, p. 127

D

democracy (dih MAHK ruh see) *n.* a kind of government in which citizens govern themselves, p. 39

dialect (DY uh lekt) *n.* a version of a language found only in a certain region, p. 93

E

economic sanctions (ek uh NAHM ik SANGK shunz) *n.* actions to limit trade with nations that have violated international laws, p. 188

embargo (em BAHR goh) *n.* a ban on trade, p. 185

entrepreneur (ahn truh pruh NOOR) *n.* a person who develops original ideas in order to start new businesses, p. 178

ethnic group (ETH nik groop) *n.* a group of people who share the same ancestors, culture, language, or religion, p. 93

euro (YER oh) *n.* the official currency of the European Union, p. 71

Prices for fruit in Spain are shown here in euros and pesetas.

F

feudalism (FYOOD ul iz um) *n.* a system in which land was owned by kinds of lords but held by vassals in return for their loyalty, p. 43

foreign minister (FAWR in MIN is tur) *n.* a government official who is in a charge of a nation's foreign affairs, p. 73

fossil fuel (FAHS ul FYOO ul) *n.* a source of energy that forms from ancient plant and animal remains, p. 28

H

heritage (HEHR uh tij) *n.* the customs and practices passed from one generation to the next, p. 101

Holocaust (HAHL uh kawst) *n.* the mass murder of six million Jews, p. 157

hydroelectric power (hy droh ee LEK trick POW ur) *n.* the power generated by water-driven turbines, p. 28

I

immigrant (IM uh grunt) *n.* a person who moves to one country from another, p. 88

imperialism (im PIHR ee ul iz um) *n.* the pursuit of economic and political control over foreign territories, p. 57

Industrial Revolution (in DUS tree ul rev uh LOO shun) *n.* the life-changing period in the 1800s when products began to be made by machines in factories, p. 53

inflation (in FLAY shun) *n.* an increase in the general level of prices, p. 200

investor (in VES tur) *n.* someone who spends money on improving a business in the hope of making more money if the business succeeds, p. 199

L

land reform (land ree FAWRM) *n.* the process of dividing large properties into smaller ones, p. 150

loess (LOH es) *n.* a type of rich, dustlike soil, p. 27

M

manufacturing (man yoo FAK chur ing) *n.* the process of turning raw materials into finished products, p. 149

Middle Ages (MID ul AY juz) *n.* the time between ancient and modern times, about A.D. 500–1500, p. 38

migration (my GRAY shun) *n.* movement from place to place, p. 91

monarch (MAHN urk) *n.* the ruler of a kingdom or empire, such as a king or queen, p. 48

N

national debt (NASH uh nul det) *n.* the amount of money a government owes, p. 142

nationalism (NASH uh nul iz um) *n.* pride in one's country, p. 58

navigable (NAV ih guh bul) *adj.* wide and deep enough for ships to travel through, p. 15

Alessandro Volta demonstrates his battery.

P

Parliament (PAHR luh munt) *n.* the lawmaking body of the United Kingdom, p. 126

peninsula (puh NIN suh luh) *n.* a land area nearly surrounded by water, p. 12

permafrost (PUR muh frawst) *n.* a permanently frozen layer of ground below the top layer of soil, p. 23

philosophy (fil LAHS uh fee) *n.* a system of ideas and beliefs, p. 131

plateau (pla TOH) *n.* a large raised area of mostly level land bordered on one or more sides by steep slopes or cliffs, p. 13

population density (pahp yuh LAY shun DEN suh tee) *n.* the average number of people living in a square mile or square kilometer, p. 11

propaganda (praph uh GAN duh) *n.* the spread of ideas designed to support a cause, p. 104

R

rain shadow (rayn SHAD oh) *n.* the area on the dry, sheltered side of a mountain, which receives little rainfall, p. 19

Renaissance (REN uh sahns) *n.* a period of European history that was characterized by the rebirth of interest in learning and art, p. 46

representative (rep ruh ZEN tuh tiv) *n.* a person who represents, or stands for, a group of people, p. 126

reunification (ree yoo nih fih KAY shun) *n.* the process of becoming unified again, p. 159

revolution (rev uh LOO shun) *n.* a far-reaching change, p. 50

revolutionary (rev uh LOO shuh neh ree) *adj.* ideas that relate to or cause the overthrow of a government, or other great change, p. 66

A rainy day in St. Petersburg, Russia

S

secede (sih SEED) *v.* to leave a group, especially a political group or a nation, p. 185

shrine (shryn) *n.* a holy place, p. 175

single market (SIN gul MAHR ket) *n.* system in which goods, services, and capital move freely with no barriers; used to describe the European Union, p. 72

standard of living (STAN durd uv LIV ing) *n.* the level of comfort in terms of the goods and services that people have, p. 159

steppe (step) *n.* the grassland of fertile soil suitable for farming in Russia, p. 22

T

textile (TEKS tyl) *n.* a cloth product, p. 54

tributary (TRIB yoo tehr ee) *n.* a river or stream that flows into a larger river, p. 15

tsar (zahr) *n.* a Russian emperor, p. 64

tundra (TUN druh) *n.* a cold, dry region covered with snow for more than half the year, p. 23

U

urbanization (ur bun ih ZAY shun) *n.* the movement of populations toward cities, p. 85

W

welfare state (WEL fair stayt) *n.* a country in which many services and benefits are paid for by the government, p. 139

westernization (wes tur nuh ZAY shun) *n.* the adoption of Western culture, p. 62

A Polish Eastern Orthodox church

Index

The *m, g,* or *p* following some page numbers refers to maps (*m*), charts, diagrams, tables, timelines, or graphs (*g*), or pictures (*p*).

population of, 153*g*
religion in, 150
trade of, 147, 147*g*
workforce in, 153*g*
in World War II, 58
**Ivan IV, Tsar of Russia
(Ivan the Terrible),** 64

J

Japan, 58, 220*m*
Jesus of Nazareth, 42, 42*p*
Jews, 42
in Nazi Germany, 155, 157, 157*p*
in Poland, 175
John, King of England, 125
John Paul II, Pope, 175, 175*p*

K

Kandinsky, Wassily, 104, 104*p*
Kenya, M17*p*, 218*m*
key, M8, M9
Kiev, Ukraine, 173, 189, 195,
195*p*
knights, 43
Kosovo, 186, 188
Kraków, Poland, 179*p*
Kremlin, 3*p*
Kublai Khan, 45, 45*p*, 60

L

labor force, in Western Europe,
85*g*
land reform, 150, 233
land use, M16–M17
in France, 134*g*
landforms, M1, 12–14, 12*m*, 13*p*,
14*p*
of Russia, 201
landowners, 65
languages, M1
of Balkan Peninsula, 182, 182*g*,
182*m*, 183
dialect, 93

of Eastern Europe, 92*m*
in European Union, 72
of France, 131, 135
maps of, M13*m*
of Poland, 177
of Russia, 101*m*, 102
Slavic, 93, 177
of Ukraine, 193
of Western Europe, 86*m*
language arts, 108
Latin America, M15*m*
latitude, M4
Latvia, 3*m*, 7*m*, 216*m*
data about, 169
Lavoisier, Antoine Laurent, 50*p*
laws, Roman, 41
Leeuwenhoek, Anton van, 51
Lenin, Vladimir Ulyanov, 66,
66*p*, 67
Leningrad, 105. *See also*
St. Petersburg
Liechtenstein, 3*m*, 6*m*, 216*m*
data about, 116
life expectancy, 178*g*, 200
Lisbon, Portugal, 119
Liszt, Franz, 97
literature
of France, 131
Pearl in the Egg, 78–81
projects, 208
of Russia, 104, 104*p*, 105, 105*p*
Travels of Marco Polo, 45
Lithuania, 3*m*, 7*m*, 218*m*
data about, 169
Ljubljana, Slovenia, 173
location, M1
locator globe, M8
Locorotondo, Italy, 149, 150
loess, 27, 233
London, England, M9, 19, 20*p*,
87, 121, 229
longitude, M5
lords, 43
Louis XIV, King of France, 49,
49*p*
Louisiana, M5, 217*m*
Louvre Museum, 132

Luxembourg, 3*m*, 6*m*, 218*m*
data about, 117
in European Coal and Steel
Community, 70
Luxembourg-Ville, 117
L'viv, Ukraine, 189

M

Maastricht Treaty, 71
Macedonia, 3*m*, 6*m*, 40, 40*m*,
184, 187, 229
culture of, 182, 182*g*, 182*m*
data about, 170
Madrid, Spain, 87, 119
Magna Carta, 125
Magyars, 93
Malta, 3*m*, 6*m*
data about, 117
manorialism, 43
manufacturing, 149, 149*p*, 233
map skills, 111*m*
analyze information, 21*m*, 37*m*,
101*m*
apply information, 22*m*, 57*m*,
94*m*
compare and contrast, 37*m*, 123*m*
contrast, 9*m*
draw conclusions, 27*m*
human-environment interaction,
27*m*
identify, 9*m*, 12*m*, 18*m*, 57*m*,
71*m*, 83*m*, 92*m*, 94*m*, 123*m*
identify point of view, 155*m*
infer, 18*m*, 40*m*, 86*m*
locate, 27*m*, 63*m*, 86*m*, 101*m*,
155*m*
location, 9*m*, 22*m*, 63*m*, 155*m*
movement, 40*m*, 57*m*, 71*m*, 83*m*
note, 30*m*
place, 18*m*, 30*m*, 37*m*, 86*m*,
101*m*
predict, 12*m*, 30*m*, 83*m*
regions, 12*m*, 21*m*, 92*m*, 94*m*,
123*m*
transfer information, 63*m*, 71*m*,
92*m*
use the map key, 21*m*
use a scale, 22*m*, 40*m*

religion
in ancient Rome, 42, 42*p*
in Balkan Peninsula, 182, 182*g*, 182*m*, 183
ethnic groups and, 93, 93*p*
in Italy, 150
in Middle Ages, 44, 44*p*
in Poland, 94, 175, 175*p*, 233*p*
in Russia, 100, 100*p*, 101, 102, 203
in Soviet Union, 100
See also individual religions

Renaissance, 234
art, 46–47, 46*p*, 47*p*
in Europe, 46–49, 46*p*, 47*p*, 48*p*, 49*p*

representative, 126, 234

research papers, RW4–RW5

reunification, 159–160, 160*p*, 234

revolution, 50–51, 234

revolutionary, 66, 234

Revolutionary War, 50, 50*p*

Reykjavik, Iceland, 115

Rhine River, 15, 15*p*, 230

Rhone River, 36*p*

rice farming, M17*p*

Riga, Latvia, 169

Risorgimento, 148

river mouth, 227

rivers, 15–16, 15*p*, 16*p*

roads, Roman, 41

Robinson maps, M7

Roma people, 92*p*, 93, 182*g*, 183

Roman Catholic Church, 94, 121, 145, 145*p*, 146, 146*p*, 148, 150
in Middle Ages, 43, 44, 44*p*
in Poland, 175, 175*p*

Roman Empire, 41, 42–43, 61, 123, 148

Romania, 3*m*, 7*m*, 216*m*
culture of, 182, 182*g*, 182*m*
data about, 171
ethnic groups in, 93

Romanov, Michael, 64

Rome, 116, 230
ancient, 41–43, 41*p*, 42*p*
decline of, 42–43

rotation, M2

Rousseau, Jean-Jacques, 131

Ruhr River, 27*m*, 28, 230

Runnymede, 125

rushlight, 78

Russia, 3*m*, 5*p*, 6, 7*m*, 7*p*, 91, 165*m*, 218*m*, 222*m*, 230, 232*p*
art of, 104, 104*p*, 105, 105*p*, 200, 200*p*
capitalism in, 199–202
Catherine the Great in, 62, 62*p*
climate regions of, 9*m*, 20, 20*p*
communism in, 198
culture of, 100–104, 201, 201*g*, 201*m*, 202–203
economy of, 199–202, 204
education in, 106, 106*p*
ethnic groups of, 101–102, 101*m*, 102*p*, 203, 203*p*
geography of, 11, 11*p*
government of, 65
history of, 62–69, 63*m*
landforms of, 12–14, 12*m*, 13*p*, 14*p*
languages of, 101*m*, 102
life expectancy in, 200
literature of, 104, 104*p*, 105, 105*p*
location of, 2, 2*m*
mountains of, 4, 4*m*
music of, 104, 104*p*, 105, 105*p*
Muslims in, 203, 203*p*
natural resources of, 30–32, 30*m*, 31*g*, 202, 204
population of, 5, 5*m*, 11–12, 203
Regional Overview, 2–7
religion in, 100, 100*p*, 101, 102, 203
Russian Revolution in, 66
size of, 2, 2*m*, 11, 201*g*, 203
Time of Troubles, 64
transportation in, 32
vegetation of, 21–23, 22*m*, 23*p*
waterways of, 15–16, 16*p*
in World War I, 58, 66
See also Soviet Union; Russian Federation

Russian Federation, 69
data about, 171
education in, 106, 106*p*
government of, 102

Russian Orthodox Church, 44, 101, 102

Russian Revolution, 66

S

St. Basil's Cathedral, 100*p*

St. Peter's Cathedral, 46*p*, 145*p*, 146, 146*p*

St. Petersburg, Russia, 14, 24*p*, 64, 65, 105, 230, 234*p*

same-shape maps, M6

Sami people, 5

San Marino, 3*m*, 6*m*, 119

Sarajevo, 167, 181, 181*p*, 186, 230

scale bar, M8

Scandinavia, 23, 230

Scandinavian Peninsula, 217*m*

Schuman, Robert, 70, 70*p*

Schumann, Conrad, 154

science, 143, 143*p*
in Age of Revolution, 51, 51*g*
Einstein and, 159, 159*p*
nuclear power, 194, 194*p*
pollution, 206
in the Renaissance, 47

scientific method, 51, 51*g*

Scientific Revolution, 51

Scotland, 28*p*, 123, 123*m*, 125, 231*p*
government in, 127, 127*p*

secede, 185, 235

semiarid climate, 20

Serbia, 3*m*, 6*m*, 184, 186, 188, 218*m*, 230
culture of, 182, 182*g*, 182*m*
data about, 172

serfs, 43, 43*p*, 65, 78

shrines, 175, 175*p*, 235, 235*p*

Siberia, 2, 14, 14*p*, 21, 22*m*, 201–203, 222*m*, 230
climate in, 17, 20*p*
life in, 203, 203*p*
natural resources of, 30*m*, 32, 202

Silesia, 29, 230

single market, 72, 235

Sistine Chapel, 146

Skopje, Macedonia, 170

Slave Coast, M15

Slavic cultures, 63, 92–93

Slovakia, 3*m*, 6*m*, 95, 168, 218*m*
data about, 172

Acknowledgments

Cover Design

Pronk&Associates

Staff Credits

The people who made up *World Studies* team—representing design services, editorial, editorial services, educational technology, marketing, market research, photo research and art development, production services, project office, publishing processes, and rights & permissions—are listed below. Bold type denotes core team members.

Greg Abrom, Ernie Albanese, Rob Aleman, Susan Andariese, **Rachel Avenia-Prol,** Leann Davis Alspaugh, Penny Baker, Barbara Bertell, **Peter Brooks,** Rui Camarinha, John Carle, **Lisa Del Gatto,** Paul Delsignore, Kathy Dempsey, Anne Drowns, Deborah Dukeshire, Marlies Dwyer, **Frederick Fellows,** Paula C. Foye, Lara Fox, Julia Gecha, **Mary Hanisco,** Salena Hastings, Lance Hatch, Kerri Hoar, **Beth Hyslip,** Katharine Ingram, Nancy Jones, John Kingston, Deborah Levheim, Constance J. McCarty **Kathleen Mercandetti,** Art Mkrtchyan, Ken Myett, **Mark O'Malley,** Jen Paley, Ray Parenteau, **Gabriela Pérez Fiato,** Linda Punskovsky, Kirsten Richert, **Lynn Robbins,** Nancy Rogier, Bruce Rolff, Robin Samper, Mildred Schulte, Siri Schwartzman, **Malti Sharma,** Lisa Smith-Ruvalcaba, Roberta Warshaw, Sarah Yezzi

Additional Credits

Jonathan Ambar, Tom Benfatti, Lisa D. Ferrari, Paul Foster, Florrie Gadson, Phil Gagler, Ella Hanna, Jeffrey LaFountain, Karen Mancinelli, Michael McLaughlin, Lesley Pierson, Debi Taffet

The DK Designs team who contributed to *World Studies* were as follows: Hilary Bird, Samantha Borland, Marian Broderick, Richard Czapnik, Nigel Duffield, Heather Dunleavy, Cynthia Frazer, James A. Hall, Lucy Heaver, Rose Horridge, Paul Jackson, Heather Jones, Ian Midson, Marie Ortu, Marie Osborn, Leyla Ostovar, Ralph Pitchford, Ilana Sallick, Pamela Shiels, Andrew Szudek, Amber Tokeley.

Maps

Maps and globes were created by **DK Cartography.** The team consisted of Tony Chambers, Damien Demaj, Julia Lunn, Ed Merritt, David Roberts, Ann Stephenson, Gail Townsley, Iorwerth Watkins.

Illustrations

Kenneth Batelman: **39, 85;** DK Images: **56;** Trevor Johnston: **51;** Chris Orr/DK Images: **103;** Jen Paley: **10, 17, 19, 24, 26, 31, 38, 45, 48, 53, 55, 62, 70, 84, 91, 99, 100, 109, 122, 124, 130, 131, 134, 138, 140, 142, 145, 147, 153, 154, 156, 174, 176, 178, 181, 182, 189, 190, 198, 201, 207**

Photos

Cover Photos

tl, Ed Pritchard/Getty Images Inc. **tm,** Jerry Kobalenko/Getty Images Inc. **tr,** Angelo Cavalli/Getty Images Inc. **b,** Mary Liz Austin/Terry Donnelly

Title Page

Mary Liz Austin/Terry Donnelly

Table of Contents

iv, Alain Le Garsmeur/Getty Images, Inc.; **v t,** Giraudon/Art Resource, NY; **v m,** Thomas Dannenberg/Masterfile Corporation; **v b,** Rykoff Collection/Corbis; **vi,** Shaun Egan/Getty Images, Inc.; **vii,** Bettmann/Corbis; **xi,** Laski Diffusion/East News/Liaison/Getty Images Inc.

Learning With Technology

xiii, Discovery Channel School

Reading and Writing Handbook

RW, Michael Newman/PhotoEdit; **RW1,** Walter Hodges/Getty Images, Inc.; **RW2,** Digital Vision/Getty Images, Inc.; **RW3,** Will Hart/PhotoEdit; **RW5,** Jose Luis Pelaez, Inc./Corbis

MapMaster Skills Handbook

M, James Hall/DK Images; **M1,** Mertin Harvey/Gallo Images/Corbis; **M2-3 m,** NASA; **M2-3,** (globes) Planetary Visions: **M5 br,** Barnabas Kindersley/DK Images; **M6 tr,** Mike Dunning/DK Images; **M10 b,** Bernard and Catherine Desjeux/Corbis; **M11,** Hutchinson Library; **M12 b,** Pa Photos; **M13 r,** Panos Pictures; **M14 l,** Macduff Everton/Corbis; **M14 t,** MSCF/NASA; **M15 b,** Ariadne Van Zandbergen/Lonely Planet Images; **M16 l,** Bill Stormont/Corbis; **M16 b,** Pablo Corral/Corbis; **M17 t,** Stone Les/Sygma/Corbis; **M17 b,** W. Perry Conway/Corbis

Guiding Questions

1, Wally McNamee/Corbis

Regional Overview

2, ABC Press-Hofstee/Sygma/Corbis; **3,** Royalty-Free/Corbis; **4,** Roger Antrobus/Corbis; **5 t,** Anders Ryman/Corbis; **5 b,** DK Images; **6 t,** DK Images; **6 b,** Raymond Gehman/Corbis; **7 t,** Jose Fuste Raga/Corbis; **7 b,** Uwe Schmid/Corbis

Chapter One

8–9, Derek Croucher/Corbis; **10,** Wolfgang Kaehler/Corbis; **11 t,** The Fringe/Index Stock Imagery, Inc.; **11b,** Konrad Wothe/Minden Pictures; **13 t,** Discovery Channel School; **13 b,** Ray Juno/Corbis; **14,** Natalie Fobes/Getty Images, Inc.; **15,** Zefa Visual Media-Germany/Index Stock Imagery, Inc.; **16,** Gregor Schmid/Corbis; **17 t,** Angela Maynard/Life File/Getty Images, Inc.; **17 b,** Dean Conger/Corbis; **18,** William Manning/Corbis; **20 t,** Dean Conger/Corbis; **20 b,** Mary Rhodes/Animals Animals/Earth Scenes; **23,** Wolfgang Kaehler/Corbis; **24,** Bob Krist/Corbis; **26,** Arnulf Husmo/Getty Images, Inc.; **27,** Paul Thompson; Eye Ubiquitous/Corbis; **28,** Dr. Eric Chalker/Index Stock Imagery, Inc.; **29 t,** Ed Kashi/Corbis; **29 b,** Chris Niedenthal//Time Life Pictures/Getty Images Inc.; **30,** Dave G. Houser/Corbis; **31 l,** Breck P. Kent/Animals Animals/Earth Scenes; **31 m,** Mark Schneider/Visuals Unlimited; **31 r,** Michael St. Maur Sheil/Corbis; **32,** Sovfoto/Eastfoto; **33 t,** Mary Rhodes/Animals Animals/Earth Scenes; **33 b,** Ed Kashi/Corbis

Chapter Two

36–37, John Elk III/Lonely Planet Images; **38,** AFP Photo/John Mottern/Corbis; **40,** Scala/Art Resource, NY; **41 t,** ML Sinibaldi/Corbis; **41 b,** Alinari/Art Resource, NY; **42 l,** McRae Books, Srl; **42 r,** Erich Lessing/Art Resource, NY; **43 t,** HIP/Scala/Art Resource, NY; **43 b,** R. G. Ojeda/ Réunion des Musées/Art Resource, NY; **44 t,** Adam Woolfitt/Corbis; **44 b,** Owen Franken/Corbis; **45,** Bettmann/Corbis; **46 t,** John Heseltine/Corbis; **46 b,** Bridgeman Art Library; **47 tl,** Musee du Louvre/Philippe Sebert/Dorling Kindersley; **47 tr,** The Granger Collection, New York; **47 bl,** Bettmann/Corbis; **47 br,** James L. Amos/Corbis; **48,** Historical Picture Archive/Corbis; **49 t,** Archivo Iconografico, S.A./Corbis; **49 b,** Art Resource; **50 l,** The Granger Collection; **50 r,** Picture History; **52 t,** Bettmann/Corbis; **52 b,** Sheila Terry/Photo Researchers, Inc.; **53,** Corbis; **54 l,** Dorling Kindersley Media Library; **54 r,** The Granger Collection, New York; **55 l,** Art Resource, NY; **55 m,** Bettmann/Corbis; **55 r,** Scala/Art Resource, NY; **56 t,** Science & Society Picture Library; **58 t,** The Granger Collection, NY; **58 b,** Museum of the City of New York; **59,** AP/Wide World Photos; **60,** Giraudon/Art Resource, NY; **61 t,** Roger Wood/Corbis; **61 b,** Christi Graham and Nick Nichols/Dorling Kindersley; **62,** Archivo Iconografico, S.A./Corbis; **64 t,** Discovery Channel School; **64 b,** Christie's Images/Corbis; **65,** Bettmann/Corbis; **66 t,** Hulton-Deutsch Collection/Corbis; **66 b,** Bettmann/Corbis; **67 t,** Yevgeny Khaldei/Getty Images, Inc.; **67 b,** U.S. Army; **68 t,** Corbis; **68 b,** PhotoDisc/Getty Images, Inc.; **69,** AFP/Corbis; **70 t,** Time Life Pictures/Getty Images, Inc.; **70 b,** Culver Pictures, Inc.; **72 t,** Thomas Dannenberg/Masterfile Corporation; **72 b,** AP/Wide World Photos; **73,** M. Taner/Masterfile Corporation; **74,** AP/Wide World Photos/Lawrence Jackson; **75,** Thomas Dannenberg/Masterfile Corporation

Literature

79, Giraudon/Art Resource, NY; **80,** Scala/Art Resource, NY

Chapter Three

82–83, Holton Collection/SuperStock, Inc.; **84,** Georgina Bowater/Corbis; **86,** Powerstock/Index Stock Imagery, Inc.; **87 t,** Howard Davies/Corbis; **87 b,** Terry Why/Index Stock Imagery, Inc.; **88 t,** SuperStock International; **88 b,** Sion Touhig/Getty Images, Inc.; **89 t,** Discovery Channel School; **89 bl,** Sean Gallup/Getty Images, Inc.; **89 br,** Julio Etchart/The Image Works; **90,** H. Mollenhauer/Masterfile Corporation; **91,** Courtesy of University of Texas at Austin; **92,** Chin Allana/Corbis Sygma; **93 l,** AP Photo/Boris Grdanoski; **93 r,** Taner/Masterfile Corporation; **95 t,** Reuters NewMedia Inc./Corbis; **95 b,** Peter Turnle/Corbis; **96,** Anthony Cassidy/Getty Images, Inc.; **97,** Archivo Iconografico, S.A./Corbis; **98,** David Turnley/Corbis; **99,** Richard Haynes; **100,** David Sutherland/Getty Images, Inc.; **101 l,** A. Kuznetsov/Trip Photographic; **101 r,** Dean Conger/Corbis; **102,** James Hill/Getty Images, Inc.; **103 t,** Bettmann/Corbis; **103 b,** RIA, Novosti; **104 t,** Laski Diffusion/East News/Liaison/Getty Images Inc.; **104 bl,** Topham/The Image Works; **104 bm,** Bettmann/Corbis; **104 br,** Swim Ink/Corbis; **105 l,** Scala/Art Resource, NY; **105 m,** Liaison/Getty Images, Inc.; **105 r,** Archivo Iconografico, S.A./Corbis; **106,** Gideon Mendel/Corbis; **107 t,** Sion Touhig/Getty Images, Inc.; **107 b,** Laski Diffusion/East News/Liaison/Getty Images Inc.

Chapter Four

110–111, Simeone Huber/Getty Images, Inc.; **112 t,** Discovery Channel School; **112 b,** Ric Ergenbright/Corbis; **113,** Willy Thiria/Corbis; **114,** Staffan Widstrand/Corbis; **117,** Swim Ink/Corbis; **118,** Staffan Widstrand/Corbis; **120,** Chris Trotman/Corbis; **122,** TravelPix/Getty Images, Inc.; **123,** Robert Estall/Corbis; **125,** Bridgeman Art Library; **126 t,** Royal Collection Enterprises Ltd.; **126 b,** AP Photo/John Stillwell, Pool; **127 t,** The British Library/Topham-HIP/Image Works; **127 m,** AP/Wide World Photos/Donald McLeod-POOL; **127 b,** Peter Macdiarmid/Reuters NewMedia/Corbis; **128 t,** Topham/The Image Works; **128 b,** Discovery Channel School; **128 m,** Rykoff Collection/Corbis; **129,** Annie Griffiths Belt/Corbis; **130,** Nogues Alain/Corbis Sygma; **131 t,** Stapleton Collection/Corbis; **131 tm,** Elisabeth Louise Vigee-Lebrun/Galleria degli Uffizi, Florence, Italy/Bridgeman Art Library; **131 bm,** National Gallery Collection; by kind permission of the Trustees of the National Gallery, London/Corbis; **131 b,** Christie's Images/Corbis; **132,** K. Yamashita/Mon Tresor/Panoramic Images; **133 t,** Snark/Art Resource, NY; **133 b,** Discovery Channel School; **135 l,** Philippe Desmazes/AFP/Getty Images, Inc.; **135 r,** Stuart Cohen/The Image Works; **136,** EPA/Alfred France Out/AP/Wide World Photos; **137,** C.Garroni Parisi/Das Fotoarchiv/Peter Arnold, Inc.; **138,** Björn Andrén Bilder; **139 t,** Steve Raymer/Corbis; **139 b,** Blaine Harrington; **141 t,** Discovery Channel School; **141 b,** AP/Wide World Photos/Toni Sica; **143,** SuperStock, Inc.; **144,** Macduff Everton/Corbis; **145,** John Miller/Robert Harding World Imagery; **146,** Owen Franken/Corbis; **148 t,** Discovery Channel School; **148 b,** Hulton Archive Photos/Getty Images Inc.; **149 t,** Allsport UK/Getty Images, Inc.; **149 b,** Mimmo Jodice/Corbis; **150,** Shaun Egan/Getty Images, Inc.; **151,** Burstein Collection/Corbis; **152,** Stephen Studd/Getty Images, Inc.; **154,** AP/Wide World Photos; **155,** Hulton-Deutsch Collection/Corbis; **156,** Collection of Stuart S. Corning, Jr. Photo © Rob Huntley /Lightstream; **157 t,** Sovfoto/Eastfoto; **157 b,** Bettmann/Corbis; **158,** David Brauchli/Corbis; **159 t,** Bettmann/Corbis; **159 b,** Discovery Channel School; **160,** Ken Straiton/Corbis; **161,** Burstein Collection/Corbis

Chapter Five

164–165, Jonathan Blair/Corbis; **166,** Discovery Channel School; **168,** Niall Benvie/Corbis; **171 t,** Topham Picturepoint/Image Works; **171 b,** Dave King/Dorling Kindersley; **172,** Tim Thompson/Corbis; **174,** Hideo Haga/The Image Works; **175 t,** AP/Wide World Photos/Rudi Blaha; **175 b,** Raymond Gehman/Corbis; **177 t,** Discovery Channel School; **177 b,** Peter Turnley/Corbis; **179 t,** Raymond Gehman/Corbis; **179 b,** Hicks/Premium/Panoramic Images; **180,** Raymond Gehman/Corbis; **181 t,** David Cannon/Allsport/Getty Images, Inc.; **181 b,** AP/Wide World Photos/Rikard Larma; **183 t,** Jonathan Blair/Corbis; **183 b,** Jim McDonald/Corbis; **185,** Jules Frazier/Getty Images, Inc.; **186 t,** Discovery Channel School; **186 b,** Ron Haviv/VII Photo; **187,** AP/Wide World Photos/EPA/Georgi Licovski; **188,** Janez Skok/Corbis; **189,** Novosti/Sovfoto; **191 t,** Mary Evans Picture Library; **191 m,** TASS/Sovfoto; **191 b,** Robert Capa/Magnum Photo Library; **192–193 b,** TASS/Sovfoto; **193 t,** Ed Kashi/Corbis; **194 t,** Discovery Channel School; **194 b,** Yann Arthus-Bertrand/Corbis; **195,** Sean Sprague/Peter Arnold, Inc.; **196,** Raymond Gehman/Corbis; **197,** Paul Almasy/Corbis; **198,** Peter Turnley/Corbis; **199 t,** Discovery Channel School; **199 m,** TASS/Sovfoto; **199 b,** Demetrio Carrasco/Getty Images, Inc.; **200,** TASS/Sovfoto; **202,** Alain Le Garsmeur/Getty Images, Inc.; **203 t,** B&C Alexander/AgPix; **203 b,** Reuters NewMedia Inc./Corbis; **204;** Marc Garanger/Corbis; **205,** Hideo Haga/The Image Works

Projects

208 t, Andy Crawford/Dorling Kindersley; **208 b,** Wally McNamee/Corbis

Reference

209, Paul A. Souders/Corbis

Glossary of Geographic Terms

226 t, A. & L. Sinibaldi/Getty Images, Inc.; **226 b,** John Beatty/Getty Images, Inc.; **226–227 b,** Spencer Swanger/Tom Stack & Associates; **227 t,** Hans Strand/Getty Images, Inc.; **227 m,** Paul Chesley/Getty Images, Inc.

Gazetteer

228, Ray Juno/Corbis; **229 t,** David Brauchli/Corbis; **229 b,** Arnulf Husmo/Getty Images, Inc.; **230,** Hideo Haga/The Image Works; **231,** John Miller/Robert Harding World Imagery

Glossary

232, AP/Wide World Photos; **233 t,** The Fringe/Index Stock Imagery, Inc.; **233 b,** Scala/Art Resource, NY; **234,** Bob Krist/Corbis; **235,** Raymond Gehman/Corbis

Text

78, Excerpt from *Pearl in the Egg: A Tale of the Thirteenth Century* by Dorothy van Woerkom. Copyright © 1980 by Dorothy van Woerkom.

Note: Every effort has been made to locate the copyright owner of material used in this textbook. Omissions brought to our attention will be corrected in subsequent editions.